STAND BY ME

Also by Jim Downs:

Sick from Freedom: African-American Illness and Suffering
    During the Civil War and Reconstruction
Why We Write: The Politics and Practice of Writing for Social Change
Taking Back the Academy: History of Activism, History as Activism

STAND BY ME

The Forgotten History of Gay Liberation

JIM DOWNS

BASIC BOOKS
A Member of the Perseus Books Group
New York

Books published by Basic Books are available at special discounts for
bulk purchases in the United States by corporations, institutions, and
other organizations. For more information, please contact the Special Markets Department at the Perseus Books Group, 2300 Chestnut
Street, Suite 200, Philadelphia, PA 19103, or call (800) 810-4145, ext.
5000, or e-mail special.markets@perseusbooks.com.

Designed by Jack Lenzo

Library of Congress Cataloging-in-Publication Data

Names: Downs, Jim, 1973– author.
Title: Stand by me : the forgotten history of gay liberation / Jim
Downs.
Description: New York : Basic Books, [2016] | Includes bibliographical
  references and index.
Identifiers: LCCN 2015040030| ISBN 9780465032709 (hardcover) |
ISBN 9780465098552 (ebook)
Subjects: LCSH: Gay liberation movement—United States—History. |
  Gays—United States—History—20th century. | Gays—Political
  activity—United States—History—20th century. | Gay rights—United
  States—History—20th century.
Classification: LCC HQ76.8.U5 D69 2016 | DDC 306.76/6—dc23
LC record available at http://lccn.loc.gov/2015040030

10 9 8 7 6 5 4 3 2 1

For all those who stood by me

IN PROVINCETOWN, 1995
Bill Coyman
Jaimie Fauth
Jennifer Gannon
Jen Manion
Scott Paro

IN REHOBOTH BEACH, 1996–2001
John Bantivoglio
Dave Bornmann
Ross Buntrock
Joe Figini
Bobby Jasak
David McFadden
Rob O'Connor
Douglas Warren Schantz
Jared Silverman
Ryan Walker

IN NEW YORK CITY, 2007–2014
Christi Helsel Botello
Shay Gipson
Geoff Lewis
Mike Montone
Christopher Stadler

CONTENTS

INTRODUCTION

This is what I remember.

There were boxes from floor to ceiling, overflowing with magazines, playbills, and photographs. Newspapers and books were stacked everywhere. I made my way to the back of the room, where I found a shelf made of egg crates and plastic bags containing more mysterious papers. I had been told that Tommi Avicolli, a gay activist from Philadelphia, donated a portion of the materials before he moved to San Francisco. My assignment was to go through his boxes and identify the contents.

I found that I became easily distracted. I would open a box and quickly find myself raptly reading a dusty newspaper, staring at the photos of men from the 1970s, some shirtless and muscular, others with long hair and pensive affects. I studied their faces and became mesmerized by their bodies. I don't remember what intrigued me more: that I was uncovering an unknown past, or that I was finding part of myself in the dust.

This was in the 1990s. I was in college, an English major. My best friend, who was a history major, encouraged me to come with her to the William Way Lesbian, Gay, Bisexual and Transgender Community Center in Philadelphia, located on a narrow cobblestone side street that resembled a back alley. She studied the past and understood the connections between the boxes in the center's archive and the lives that we ourselves were making twenty blocks away at the

University of Pennsylvania. Unlike our university library, which remained open until midnight, seven days a week, the gay library and archive at the William Way Community Center could afford to stay open for only a few hours a week.

My friend took careful notes on yellow legal pads about the contents of the boxes she unpacked. I remember her standing amid the debris of the past, in command of the history that rose up to her waist. I remember hoping, as I sat on egg crates, that she would not see me reading instead of writing, memorizing the images instead of making sense of them.

"This was part of the politics of gay history," my friend told me as we walked back to campus that day, past the gay bars and coffee shops. She explained that gay people had to collect their own history and tell their own stories because they couldn't rely on straight people to record their past. She reminded me that gay people were barely mentioned in the courses that we were taking.

She was politically fierce and intellectually formidable, but even while listening to her most compelling arguments, my mind would return to the photos—to the images of the shirtless guys who appeared in ads in the old newspapers. She would sense me drifting. "That's why we are volunteering," she would remind me. "So that gay history will not be forgotten."

Eventually I not only absorbed that message but became inspired by it. She and I and other friends of ours and gay people across the country had a responsibility to document the past and to tell our own history.

A newly minted history PhD, I was in line at the Tribeca Film Festival in New York City for the opening screening of a documentary, *Gay Sex in the 70s.* It was 2005, and gay liberation was over thirty years old, but in the city where it began gay culture was still surprisingly limited. There were the occasional gay documentaries and films that played at the independent movie houses. There were a handful of cable television series that portrayed gay characters and had gay-themed story lines. Most of the representations of gay life appeared in the gay neighborhoods—on the covers of magazines in the coffee shops, on calendars showcased in card and gift storefronts, and on weekly events newsletters stacked at the entrances of gay bars.

That night the theater was packed, and some people even had to be turned away. *Gay Sex in the 70s* charted the rise of gay liberation. Men who had lived through the era were interviewed and recounted having had sex all the time. One man told how he worked from home but spent most of his day at a nearby cruising spot having sex with anonymous men. Another explained how easy and available sex was: "All you had to do was walk down the street." Others told stories about sex in abandoned trucks along the Hudson River piers in the middle of the night, in the shrubs near the beach, at parties in vacation homes. Interspersed with the interviews were clips of crowded bathhouses, of discos that catered to well-endowed men, of semi-naked men groping each other. "Life was a pornographic film," one of the interviewees explained. In the film's narrative, gay liberation was the liberation of gay men's sexual urges.[1]

Toward the end of the film, the tone began to darken and the disco music stopped. The talking heads on-screen now wore worried expressions. No one uttered the phrase "free love." And then someone said it: AIDS. The outbreak of HIV, a virus that seemed to only infect gay men, would put an end to the rampant sexual activity that defined the 1970s. As depicted in the film, unrestrained sex had led, more or less inevitably, to the illness and death that accompanied the spread of HIV.

The film ended. The audience applauded. The director told the audience during the question-and-answer session afterward that he decided to make the film after having a conversation with a young gay couple who had no knowledge of the sexual history of the seventies. He saw his film as a chance to correct what he perceived as widespread ignorance of an important time.

I wanted to ask him a question, but I could not put what I was feeling into words. Something about the film did not sit right with me. There were a few more comments and questions from the audience, all of them couched in a congratulatory spirit about the importance of the film and a nostalgic feeling for the days when gay men could have sex without worrying about HIV.

Finally I asked my question, but it came out muddled. I said something about how the film effectively blamed gay people for AIDS. The director gave a quick, pat answer and moved on.

A few weeks later, the film was shown at the Philadelphia Gay and Lesbian Film Festival. I went with my college friend, the woman I had volunteered with at the William Way Community Center archive. After seeing the film a second time, I finally found the right words for my frustration: "The narrative arc of the 1970s is too simplistic," I told her. The film mentioned a political uprising, Stonewall, when gay people rose up in protest against a police raid, signaling the start of gay liberation. Then it detailed an orgy that spanned the decade before abruptly turning to the arrival of HIV and the end of the good times. The film had flattened the history of the 1970s in order to rationalize the spread of HIV.[2]

I remembered the piles of newspapers and magazines, the boxes of poetry stacked in the corners. The history I remembered from that room in the William Way Community Center was different from the history offered by the documentary. Sure, there had been photos of sexy shirtless guys, ads about bathhouses, and articles about gay men having group sex at outdoor parks, but these images told only a small sliver of the experience of gay people in the 1970s. Sex was only part of what had mattered to gay men as they began to make gay liberation meaningful in their lives.

As an undergraduate, I had worried about straight people not telling gay history. Ten years later, I now started worrying about gay people themselves putting forth a narrative about the 1970s that was more invested in explaining the origins of the AIDS epidemic than in actually documenting the past.

I decided that I would try to intervene. I began to return to the William Way Community Center archive every Wednesday night from 6:00 to 9:00 PM, the only time it was open. The archivist remembered me and gave me full access to the collections. No longer scattered around in knee-high stacks, the materials had been organized and filed in protective boxes. Each Wednesday night I would take a newspaper out of one of the white boxes and start reading and taking notes. I had encountered many of the documents during my first visit as an undergraduate, but now I read them more purposefully.

After a few months of research, I wrote a short article for the *Gay and Lesbian Review* that I hoped would help reframe the conversation about gay liberation that *Gay Sex in the 70s* had prompted. I had found compelling evidence in the gay newspapers in the archive that gay people had founded their own churches, led political campaigns for equality, and, most importantly, theorized, explored, and investigated the meaning of sex. They were doing more than just engaging in sex—they were using the gay press as a forum in which they could explore its meaning and implications.

The article was published, and I figured my work was done. Those hours spent in the archive, however, had made me sensitive whenever I heard someone talk about the 1970s. The documentary was merely an expression of the dominant narrative that had been embraced by both the gay community and the broader American public as a way to explain (and rationalize) HIV. I started to notice this explanation not only in history books and films but also in my everyday interactions with friends and colleagues. Talking about bathhouses as cesspools for HIV, gay friends were often advancing the problematic formulation that promiscuity causes HIV.

Where did this idea come from? More broadly, why have we latched on to a narrative of the 1970s as a period of unlettered sex in order to rationalize the spread of an epidemic?

One reason why HIV transmission was linked to promiscuity was the fact that, in the early 1980s, some gay men and physicians began to argue that being repeatedly infected with sexually transmitted infections weakened the immune system and paved the way for HIV transmission. Dr. Joseph Sonnabend reached this conclusion when he realized that many of his gay male patients who had become infected with HIV had a long medical history of sexually transmitted infections. He likened HIV transmission to "pushing a wheel down an incline. When it achieves sufficient momentum, it will take off on its own. It's promiscuity that provides the push."[3]

The explanation that promiscuity leads to the spread of HIV not only was medically and scientifically significant but also had a profound, uninterrogated effect on how the history of the 1970s was narrated: the nuanced social history of the 1970s got pushed aside in favor of a narrative that emphasized sex.

I remembered the conversations I had with my friend as an undergraduate as we walked back to campus from the William Way Center—that all history is political, that people in the present often construct a particular past in the service of a particular ideological agenda. I went back to the archive and took more notes. I wanted to document the forgotten episodes that constituted gay liberation. I wanted to tell the stories that surprised me of how gay people built churches, founded newspapers, established bookstores, and rethought the meaning of gay identity. I wanted to show how the 1970s was more than a night at a bathhouse.

What follows is the result. This book tells the history of gay people that I found in archives in Philadelphia, Los Angeles, New Orleans, and New York over the course of ten years—a history that has often been overshadowed by the narrative that attempted to rationalize the spread of HIV. Downplayed, marginalized, and erased by that narrative, the history of gay liberation began in the 1970s, when the term "gay liberation" encompassed for some a social movement, for others an end to oppression, and for most if not all gay people a major turning point in how they defined culture and community.[4]

The conventional narrative of the decade often fails to capture the nuanced ways in which many gay men in the 1970s thought about sex. There were debates in newspapers about the meaning of gay sex and its impact on gay culture, but the outbreak of HIV/AIDS extinguished those conversations. An image of gay men as hypersexual began to be promoted in order to rationalize the spread of the virus, and in the process gay men were turned into the leading protagonists in the 1970s. Lesbians, lesbian-feminists, transgender people, and queer people all participated in the making of gay liberation, but their contributions have often been overlooked due to the ways that promiscuity defined the decade. My focus here is to correct the hypersexual caricature of gay men in the 1970s by exploring and recounting the everyday ways in which gay men sustained an identity and culture. What happened when they got home from the bars? What did they read? What did they think about? How did they frame their sexuality? How did they develop a vocabulary to speak about what it meant to be gay? How did they understand their identity as a way to create a distinct culture? How did they find their place in the world?[5]

At the outset of my research, I came across headlines about a fire in New Orleans that killed thirty-two people on June 24, 1973. I looked for references to the fire in the mainstream press and found only a few scattered articles about it—one in the *New York Times,* a handful in local newspapers in New Orleans, and a few televised news broadcasts. The papers reported that the fire exploded on the second floor of a bar on the edge of the French Quarter. It was a bar that the mainstream reporters described as a place that "homosexuals frequented." The news stories recounted jokes that locals made about the fire. Few called it a tragedy, and none called it what it was: the largest massacre of gay people in American history.

The gay press was more useful. *The Advocate,* which originated in Los Angeles, served in the 1970s as the national gay newspaper. It published a few stories about the fire, highlighting the experiences of the victims and the demands by leaders in the gay community for a thorough investigation by the local police and fire departments. *The Advocate* mentioned that the men and women in the bar that evening were Metropolitan Community Church members who gathered on Sunday evenings to hold services.

I came across a photograph of one of the victims of the fire. As he had attempted to squeeze his body through a narrow window on the second floor, the flames reached his lower body, and shortly after, an air conditioner from the third floor fell on his head and torso. His lifeless body was stuck in the window throughout the night. The local press took a photograph of him, but never mentioned his name or his affiliation with the church. His name was William Larson, and he was the minister who had led the congregation earlier that night in prayer and song. His story and those of other men and women who perished that fateful evening are recounted in chapter 1.

The story of the fire led me to investigate the history of gay churches in the seventies, and chapter 2 chronicles what I found out. Much of what I came across at first had to do with gay people's aversion to organized religion, especially Christianity, which many gay men and women saw as the foundation of gay oppression. But as I read through more of the gay newspapers, a different story came into view. I came across groups like the Gay Catholics, saw references to synagogues for gay Jews, and read articles about spirituality. Above all, there were countless articles about the Metropolitan Community Church (MCC), which was founded by and for gay people in 1968. Gay newspapers printed announcements about the openings throughout the country of MCC churches, which clustered not in the major urban hubs on the coasts but in the middle of Texas, Arizona, and Ohio. There was news about social events and prayer groups and feature articles on MCC leaders.

Many of the gay people who turned to the new religious organizations were searching for not just a place to worship but for a community and culture in which to seek refuge. In the early 1970s, few institutions outside of these new churches could offer such refuge. As one writer for *Gay Sunshine,* a newspaper based in San Francisco, explained to readers: "I'm sure you've heard the phrase time and again; 'you're just animals all you think about is sex.' . . . One of the most effective tactics that straights use on us is our own belief that we are sexual entities; that we can easily be kept in 'our place.' Our place being the three Big B's—the Bars, Beaches, and the Baths. These are to keep us happy, controlled and patrolled."[6]

With the start of gay liberation, gay religious organizations grew exponentially not just because gay people feared being locked into the "three Big B's" but also because some gay men simply did not like those places. Meanwhile, countless other gay men and women were devoting their time, energy, and often their own money to creating other alternative spaces for gay people to congregate. Among the most influential was Craig Rodwell, founder of the Oscar Wilde Memorial Bookshop in New York City. With money he earned from working as a bartender on Fire Island for the summer, Rodwell rented a storefront and opened the bookstore, the first of its kind in the country. He refused to sell erotica or any magazine that included pornography, instead stocking his shelves with books by and about gay people and their history. The bookstore became a cultural hub where gay people met during the day to drink coffee and discuss books and gathered in the evenings for readings, political meetings, and other events. Rodwell, the impresario behind the annual gay pride marches in New York City, would eventually expand his vision to all of Christopher Street, but his first goal was to build a literary community that would allow gay people to engage with, and take pride in, the best expressions of their culture. He accomplished this goal with the Oscar Wilde Memorial Bookshop, which attracted international tourists and whose success led to the founding of similar bookstores throughout the country. Drawing on Rodwell's correspondence, his personal papers, and the records of his store, I tell the history of the Oscar Wilde Memorial Bookshop in chapter 3.

One of the most significant and powerful books of the many that lined the shelves at the Oscar Wilde Memorial Bookshop was *Gay American History,* an anthology of documents revealing the presence of gay people in the United States from the colonial period into the late twentieth century. The book's 1976 publication turned its author, Jonathan Ned Katz, into a celebrity within the gay community. Katz gave readings at bookstores across the country, and the gay press followed him as he spoke in front of readers in community centers and other gay venues. The book had also appeared in an earlier version as a play that would be read widely and performed in gay theaters throughout the 1970s.[7]

In chapter 4, I describe the political, social, and cultural forces that led Katz to see the need for gay people to seek out and understand their past and eventually to write *Gay American History.* He began his career as a historian of black history, inspired by the rise of the American civil rights and black freedom struggles. The emergence of the gay liberation movement had a similar effect on him. Katz studied gay history with various political and literary groups that I attempt to capture in telling his story. In their search for the origins and causes of gay oppression, Katz and his cohort drew on Marxist theories about power to critique the ways in which heterosexual society defined homosexuality.

As I uncovered details about Katz's life, the Oscar Wilde Memorial Bookshop, and the gay religious movement, I saw that the very sources I was relying on—the gay newspapers—had their own unique history, one that challenged the conventional narrative of the seventies. Founded mostly if not exclusively by gay activists who volunteered their time, resources, and money, the gay newspapers that proliferated in the 1970s helped promote a sense of culture and community among gay people in the United States and even throughout the world.[8]

Chapter 5 tells the history of gay newspapers, with a particular emphasis on *The Body Politic,* founded in Toronto by Canadians and American expatriates. One of the most important gay newspapers in the 1970s, *The Body Politic* catered to an intellectual and political audience that promoted gay liberation. Even more prominent in the early 1970s was *The Advocate;* the leading national gay newspaper, it cultivated a sense of community among gay people and would be the mouthpiece for the gay liberation movement. By 1976, however, *The Advocate* had become less invested in reporting on the progress of gay liberationist organizational efforts and more interested in covering celebrities' lives. Some critical journalists in the 1970s suggested that *The Advocate*'s transformation into an apolitical publication implicitly encouraged "a return to the closet." *The Body Politic,* on the other hand, continued to act as a forum throughout the 1970s to connect gay people and promote gay identity as a political identity. *The Body Politic* followed the plight and politics of gay people across the world, ran features on important moments in gay history, and reported on contentious debates about sex.[9]

As more and more gay people moved to cities after Stonewall, *The Body Politic* and other papers launched advice columns that combined mother wit with tips on living alone. A column in *Arizona Gay News* called "Happiness Is" reminded readers to "get filters for your heaters" and offered guidelines for entertaining guests during the holidays (make "orange butter rum cake").[10] As these tidbits suggest, the gay newspapers of the 1970s, like mainstream newspapers, published a good deal of ephemera: stories about gay businesses, fund-raisers, art, and so on.

One topic of increasing concern among gay journalists as the decade wore on was the growing population, and predicament, of gay prisoners. The advancement of the gay liberation movement had enabled many radical and progressive gay activists to draw attention to the historic problem surrounding the incarceration of gay people. The major gay newspapers first reported on the issue, but soon some writers had banded together to found newspapers devoted exclusively to it, such as *Join Hands*. In chapter 6, I examine how gay newspaper staffs along with gay religious groups responded to the crisis of gay incarceration. Both groups worked assiduously to provide gay prisoners with legal assistance and spiritual and psychological counseling. Both newspapers and religious groups also wanted to help gay prisoners cultivate a sense of gay identity and an awareness of gay culture. To that end, the newspapers began to publish poems by gay people in prison and offered them opportunities to write articles about their experiences. They sent prisoners books, newspapers, and magazines about gay liberation, and gay religious groups worked with prison ministries to create prayer groups and religious services for prisoners. By the end of the decade, the gay activist Stephen Donaldson had begun a highly charged political campaign to draw attention to sexual abuse and rape among men in prisons.

Around the same time, the progress and promise of the years after Stonewall began to diminish. Gay people witnessed the closing rather than the opening of opportunities. The excitement that had led to the explosion of religious groups, newspapers, and political activism dissipated in favor of a homogenized gay identity that privileged whiteness, muscularity, and masculinity.

In the early part of the decade, virtually every leading gay intellectual, activist, or group, from Craig Rodwell and Jonathan Ned Katz to newspaper staffs and activist associations, credited the influence of both the black civil rights movement and the women's movement on the gay liberation movement.[11] The early gay liberation movement was thus relatively diverse, and many gay people understood the links between their oppression and the struggles of ethnic and racial groups. In fact, the journalists who criticized *The Advocate* for no longer functioning as a political outlet for the movement also lashed out at *The Advocate* for refusing to acknowledge gay people's participation in political marches for racial, ethnic, and gender equality.[12]

Nevertheless, by the end of the decade the "macho clone" had begun to define gay culture and identity.[13] Wearing blue jeans, black boots, aviator sunglasses, and often no shirt, this type surfaced within the gay community and soon defined gay identity as white, masculine, and muscular. Many gay men strived to look and dress like the clone, who soon proliferated in bars and on city streets. The popularity of this image erased women and people of color from the gay community.[14]

In chapter 7, we witness the macho clone emerging and splintering the gay community. Although the macho clone served as a sex symbol, his rise was not just about sex, but also about creating the kind of masculine identity often thought to be the province of heterosexual men. Before Stonewall, doctors, therapists, and others in power defined gay men as effeminate, as aberrant, or even as a third sex. The intellectual work of Jonathan Ned Katz and other gay thinkers during the 1970s shattered this definition and in the process showed that ideology, not biology, shapes gender roles. One indirect result of this insight was the adoption by many gay men of the persona of the macho clone in order to perform a version of masculinity that they had previously believed was beyond them. Anyone who catches a glimpse of the macho clone might intuitively blame him, in part, for the conventional narrative of the decade that emphasized sex, but an understanding of the social, cultural, and political forces that led to the development of the macho clone undermines this assumption.

In his classic novel about gay men in the 1970s, *Faggots,* the activist and historian Larry Kramer indicted gay culture for its emphasis on sex, its celebration of the clone, and the inability of gay men to forge meaningful relationships. Yet in making this critique, Kramer unwittingly reified the conventional narrative, giving it great power. Craig Rodwell, for instance, refused to sell *Faggots* in his bookstore because he did not agree with the book's message and its representation of gay culture. By not showing gay life as it was—by not showing that it was not defined exclusively by sex—Kramer perpetuated the reigning mythology about the decade.[15]

Without a doubt, sex mattered in the seventies. It motivated gay men in ways that historians cannot document. For some, sex represented a radical political act; for others, it was pure enjoyment. But in the end, sex is only a piece of the story. One fact omitted from the conventional narrative, for instance, is that many gay men condemned the mere mentioning of the word "sex" in gay newspapers.[16] That narrative also fails to mention that Kramer may have been the best-known critic of gay sex in the 1970s, but he was not the only one. Many gay people articulated sophisticated, incisive critiques of sex and worked hard to create alternative cultures.[17] Yet these critiques and alternative cultures have been erased. Consequently, unfettered sex became the leading headline of the decade rather than part of a much richer and broader collection of stories. The San Francisco newspaper *Gay Sunshine,* for example, published an article in March 1972, six years before the publication of *Faggots,* that included the following:

> I think so many gay people try to get rid of their loneliness and get caught up in the bar syndrome. On the surface they may appear to get rid of the loneliness. They're laughing with people, joking perhaps, but deep down it's still there. For many people, of course, there are no alternatives and so they ask "why do you criticize the bars?" Maybe gay lib has criticized the bars too much. We've got to provide alternatives. There are so few alternatives, even in San Francisco. There are a few gay dances, gay rap, Gay Sunshine, a few small community centers—Emmaus House, MCC for some people. Isn't this a function of Gay Sunshine—to promote this kind of thing, to have articles on alternatives that people can get involved in?[18]

In the following chapters, I try to capture the stories of gay men who have been largely silent in the historical record and forgotten in the public memory. While this book does not seek to document the entire LGBTQ community, it does record the settings and periods when gay men stood alongside others in the LGBTQ community. I have mostly attempted to tell the stories of gay men who stood together not as lovers but as friends, fellow believers, and colleagues to create a sense of community among a population of people who felt alienated from mainstream society. For them, being gay meant being part of a culture that had its own history and religion, its own literature and bookstores, even its own language and body type. It is notable, moreover, that gay people in the 1970s did not devote all— or even most—of their energies to convincing heterosexual people to accept them or to creating political movements for equality. For example, long before the legal recognition of gay marriage in 2015, gay people in the 1970s got married in their own churches. They did not look to the government for recognition of their unions but instead stood by each other in the communities that they had built and in which they professed their vows. In the wake of the victory for gay marriage, it is more important than ever to remember that gay life in America has not always been front-page news; neither has it always been defined by the fight for equality.[19]

In fact, the stories in this book reveal that many gay people sought community and their own culture over legal rights and political recognition. They wanted to stand together as a community rather than stand in front of city hall petitioning for rights. This is another part of the conventional narrative that I hope this book overturns: the idea of gay people as consistently engaged in a political debate with the state. During the 1970s, gay people did not expend all of their efforts on trying to have their plight recognized by government, whether at the local, state, or federal level. In fact, many gay activists critiqued democracy and capitalism; they believed that some aspects of US society were fundamentally flawed and did not aspire to be embraced by it. Many gay people turned away from the mainstream to devote enormous energy, time, and effort to creating their own culture—newspapers, churches, bookstores—and by extension their own history and identity. That is not to say that some groups of gay people were not politically committed to changing laws and gaining legal recognition, but only to point out that for many gay people in the 1970s, and even later, gay liberation and its promises had meanings other than political recognition. Many gay men did not see their sexuality at odds with their political visions, but the problem is that they have often only been remembered for their sexual proclivities and not for their cultural contributions.

Unlike other minorities, many gay people often grew up in families that had no understanding of homosexuality and harbored prejudices against it. As a consequence, they often could not depend on their families and communities to support them and had to invent new families and communities that could offer some haven from oppression.[20] Where did they find refuge?

At a service of the MCC. In the pages of *The Body Politic*. At the Oscar Wilde Memorial Bookshop. At the theater staging *Gay American History*. Gay people in 1970s America found one another and together created a lexicon, an idiom, newspapers, prayer groups, churches, beauty contests in bars, bookstores of their own—a culture and a history that said their name. That culture, now largely forgotten, sustained them as they stood together as a community inspired by the promise of liberation.

1 THE LARGEST MASSACRE OF GAY PEOPLE IN AMERICAN HISTORY

There was a lot of noise coming from the French Quarter in New Orleans on the Sunday evening of June 24, 1973: the music of jazz pianos and trumpets from the clubs, the streetcars squealing on aluminum rails, tourists loudly parading out of bars on Bourbon Street, catcalling to the working women in high heels. There was also the piercing sound of sirens as they tore down the narrow pathways of the Quarter. Just months before, a band of armed robbers had stormed into the local Holiday Inn, shot at guests, set fire to the hotel, and then engaged in a shoot-out with police that left three policemen and four assailants dead. Afterwards, security guards at hotels warned tourists to avoid walking the streets alone. Since cabs, not daring to stand idle, had begun to demand that customers call in advance, the soundtrack of the city that night also included cabs honking for the attention of their customers.[1]

But there was another sound in New Orleans on that "hot and clear" June night, a sound that was uncommon even in a city known for the diversity of its people and cultures.[2] It was a church song, a spiritual of sorts, part inspirational, part pop, and it was being sung in harmony by a large group of people who had gathered on the second floor of a bar on the edge of the French Quarter that had been considered lewd. These people were not lascivious or lewd, but this was how the local and national press would later describe them. In fact, this was how they had always been described, even though they had come together in a place of worship, two even sitting with their mother by their side.

Most of the churches in the French Quarter and the surrounding area closed by 7:00 PM.[3] The churches in which gay people had been raised refused to allow openly gay people to worship and pray together. So these residents of New Orleans had formed their own congregation and every Sunday night sixty or more of them worshiped in the Up Stairs Lounge around a white baby grand piano.

Sandwiched between Jimani's Bar on the first floor and a flophouse on the third floor, the Up Stairs Lounge was located on the second floor of a building at the intersection of Chartres and Iberville Streets. The owner tried to attract customers to the Lounge by covering up the grittier parts of the building. He hung a canopy bearing the bar's name over the door on the first floor, carpeted the thirteen steps that led up to the entrance, and hung drapes over the utility meters and plumbing.[4] Inside the Lounge were three rooms. The owner decorated the walls in the main room, where the bar was located, with red wallpaper and covered the floors with red carpet. He hung posters on the wall, mostly of shirtless, hunky men, including a semi-nude one of Burt Reynolds. But he also posted important information about upcoming events, community announcements, and newspaper clippings. The other two rooms were a meeting room in the front, with many tables and chairs, and a room in the back with painted black windows. This was where the bar's "beer busts" were held.[5]

Earlier that afternoon, over 120 patrons had crowded into the Up Stairs Lounge to celebrate the fourth anniversary of the Stonewall uprising, the night in 1969 when drag queens, gay men, lesbians, and transgender people rioted against a police raid of a bar in Greenwich Village in New York City. The revelers at the Lounge beer bust that afternoon danced to disco and pop music and remembered the news that they had first heard bits and pieces of four years earlier—news of the beginning of gay liberation. In fact, the very presence of the Lounge in that part of the Quarter represented the shift brought about by gay liberation. Before the Up Stairs Lounge was established, the corner of Iberville and Chartres had been the province of hustlers and those prowling to pay for sex. The opening of the Lounge changed the complexion and the culture of that part of the Quarter. More than just a hangout for sex, the Lounge hosted cultural events for the community, including theater productions, Easter bonnet contests, and Halloween drag shows.[6]

For the people gathered in the Up Stairs Lounge on June 24, 1973, liberation had not just given them the opportunity to gather in a bar, drink $1 drafts, and dance to Cher's hit song "Half-Breed." It had offered them a chance to radically transform each dimension of their lives, especially their faith. By 7:30 PM, when the beer bust ended, those who were part of the religious congregation had moved to the middle room.

There they gathered around the piano and listened to Rev. William Larson, the leader of their congregation, as he said a few words. Then David Gary sat down at the piano. His main gig was at the Marriott Hotel lounge across the street, but on Sunday nights he led the congregation in song. The room began to sing "United We Stand," a song that had been made popular earlier that decade by the British pop group the Brotherhood of Man. With lyrics that evoked the American civil rights movement, the congregation stood side by side and sang: "For united we stand, divided we fall, and if our backs should ever be against the wall, we'll be together, you and I." These words foreshadowed what was about to come.

Around 7:50 PM, an individual or possibly a group stopped at the entrance to the stairwell on Iberville Street. They doused the drapes and the meters in the stairwell with lighter fluid, as well as the steps leading to the second floor, where the worshipers were talking of God, praying for salvation, and trusting in the lyrics of a British pop band.[7]

The main door to the Up Stairs Lounge was always locked when services were in session. When members of the congregation arrived by taxi, they had to ring the doorbell to be allowed in. There was even a secret hatch—modeled after those on the doors to Prohibition-era speakeasies—through which the bartenders could get a glimpse of anyone who rang the bell. That night, when the bell rang, the bartender, Buddy Rasmussen, realized that he had not called for a cab to pick up any of the patrons. Buddy yelled to one of the regulars to tell the cabbie to leave. When he opened the steel door, all hell broke loose. Flames exploded into the room, and within seconds the staircase was on fire. The congregation was trapped in a barricaded bar on the edge of the Quarter.[8] (Metal bars and boards had been installed over the windows in an effort to protect them.)

In a city known for its sounds, we cannot hear the screams of fear and confusion as fire incinerated the second floor. We cannot hear the sounds of flames burning the clothes off bodies, or of a roomful of people choking on smoke. We cannot hear the cries for help as many of the congregants realized that they were trapped.

Dean Morris was sitting at a table in the main room with Reverend Larson, Frank Dean, and a few others. Sometime between 7:30 and 8:00 PM, Morris heard a "pop" that he assumed was a "bottle bursting near the front door entrance." The sound was familiar. As a former military man, he thought it could have been a Molotov cocktail. The next thing he saw was "a flame that filled the entire floor and extended in a rectangular shape from the door about eight feet on the inside." Frank Dean, who also had been in the military, noticed a "gust of black smoke" as a "huge flame appeared to sear across the floor." He thought it looked like a "flame shot from a flamethrower."[9] The flames quickly spread to the ceiling as people in the fire at the entrance began shouting and running.[10]

Rusty Quinton, who worked part-time at the Lounge, heard someone yell "Fire!" He saw the flames and ran to a corner window in the front of the bar, which faced Chartres Street. He lifted the window up, crawled out, and slid down to the street on a pipe attached to the side of the building. He ran to a nearby bar and asked those inside to call the fire department. He then ran back to the Lounge, where he saw people trying to squeeze through the bars covering the windows. Others stood behind the bars, afraid. A small crowd of locals assembled in the street and yelled to those at the windows to jump, promising to catch them. But many refused to jump.[11] Black smoke was filling the room, and then the power went out. The flames, quickly catching hold of the velvet drapes and designer tablecloths, had soon consumed the entire front bar. To those still inside, the windows appeared to be the only escape. Unable to remove the bars or even bend them, a few of the leaner men miraculously managed to wiggle their bodies through the bars and jump two stories, breaking bones or bruising themselves on landing.[12]

Francis Dufresne managed to get through the bars, despite being on fire, and pushed his way out of the window. He fell onto the sidewalk, unconscious.[13] Another jumper fell sixteen feet, and "his head landed on concrete." Yet another, Michael Wayne Scarborough, later recalled, "When somebody opened the door and that fire jumped out, I just run over there and started breaking glass." He didn't see the exit light illuminating a door near the dance floor. "Without thinking that I could have got on the dance floor and got a table or something and just knocked the hell out of that playboard and jumped out through there." Instead, Scarborough ran in the opposite direction. "Well, I just went through the building and broke the glass and just wiggled through the bar." He jumped two stories, but survived.[14]

Reverend Larson made his way to a window, but was unable to wedge his body between the bars. He went to another window, one that had an air conditioning unit in it. He pulled the air conditioner out and tried to escape through the narrow space, but got stuck. His head and his right arm were out of the building, but he could not lift the window any further. Pushing to get out, his green shirt becoming soaked with sweat, Larson broke wooden casements and the glass windowpanes with his bare hands, to no avail. He was still stuck. As flames caught his lower body, he screamed, "Oh God, no!"[15] An air conditioner from the third floor then fell onto his head and killed him.

Across the street at the Marriott Hotel, tourists watched from their rooms as the men in the bar struggled to escape. According to some observers, everyone recognized Reverend Larson's green shirt and saw him lodged in the window. His face, some said, was "covered with grime and perspiration" before he was struck by the falling debris. Within a few seconds, he was on fire. According to a witness, "His face burst into a ball of flames. His hair flashed into a gray ash, his skin burned, and he was gone."[16]

When the commotion started, Richard Cross, whom everyone in the bar jokingly called "Mother Cross," remembered seeing flames near the front door. Telling the friends he was with, "Don't panic," he followed some others he saw running toward the area behind the stage. When he got to the back room, he "laid on his stomach so that he could look for legs or feet of other people so that he could help lead them out or help to lead them to the floor."[17] He could not see anyone through the dark smoke.

As soon as the fire broke out, Buddy Rasmussen, the bartender, began yelling for people to follow him through an unknown back door behind the makeshift cabaret stage. Telling everyone to remain calm, he took the "lock off the back door, moved a stool and some costumes. He then opened the door and started pulling the people through." The smoke was getting darker, and some of the people, who had been drinking beer for hours, had been burned. Buddy started slapping and grabbing them in order to get them through the archway behind the stage to the fire door. He then "directed them across the roof into what appeared to be a safe area."[18]

Buddy managed to lead a small group of twenty people through the smoke and fire, out the door, and onto the roof of the bar.[19] Once outside, they ran across the rooftop until they found a safe way down to street level.[20] In the midst of the chaos, George Mitchell realized that his partner, L. Horace Broussard, was not among this small group of survivors. He scanned the faces, screamed Horace's name, and ran back into the fire. His body was later found next to Broussard's.[21]

Richard Cross also tried to go back to the bar to save a loved one or a friend. He had escaped with the others, but then ran back to the theater area, "attempting to re-enter the bar." Preventing him from doing so was Buddy, who "grabbed him and brought him away from the door and made him leave the exit." Buddy then called into the bar area for any others. When no one responded, he left. Once he got down to the street, he ran to the corner of Chartres and Iberville Streets, a few feet from the side entrance of the Up Stairs Lounge. No fire truck had arrived. Buddy noticed several burned congregants lying on the ground. Crossing Chartres Street to get a better view of the Lounge, he saw three other congregants burning alive. He later told police that he recognized two of them, Hilly Lawson and Adam Roland Fontennot. After this sight, "he just started to wander around and give comfort to the people he knew."[22]

Katherine Kirsch lived nearby; she and her husband were home watching television when she decided to go out to buy cigarettes. Outside she saw fire coming from the stairwell of the Up Stairs Lounge. Kirsch ran into the Mid-ship Bar and told the barmaid to contact the fire department, which logged the call at 7:56 PM and dispatched "two pumps, a hook and a ladder, and a District Chief" to the scene.[23]

On the first floor below the Up Stairs Lounge was Jimani's Bar, where a little more than a dozen customers were drinking when the fire broke out upstairs. Francis Holehen, the bartender, told police that just before 8:00 PM, he heard a "pounding noise coming from the second floor." He then noticed a strange smell. A customer in the bar "walked to the front door . . . and yelled that the building was on fire."[24] Holehen and the Jimani's customers escaped from the bar safely.

By this point, there were many people in the street, both survivors and onlookers. Traffic on Iberville Street started to get backed up. Near the intersection with Chartres Street, a motorist named Harold Bartholomew heard a man yelling, "I am telling you, you better get out of here." Bartholomew was in his car with his three children; they had just left a theater a few blocks away. He pulled his car closer to the side of the building so that it was "almost parallel with the burning doorway." Bartholomew saw two men jump out of a second-floor window onto Chartres Street. He looked up and saw a few others standing on the fire escape, their clothes on fire. Within minutes, the "windows started exploding" and showered his car with "glass and debris." He sped "one block downtown" to Conti Street, where he parked his car and "consoled his children."[25]

The fire department eventually arrived, but too late to save anyone. Thirty-two people died. According to the *New York Times,* three hours after the fire was extinguished, rescue workers struggled to remove the bodies. A reporter at the scene "saw at least 20 bodies, all melted together, jammed against front windows." A University of New Orleans student reported, "I saw bloodstains on the sidewalk and a man sitting in the gutter with his skin burned off, crying he was in such pain."[26]

Among the thirty-two people who died were two men, Eddie Hosea Warren and James Curtis Warren, who died with their mother, Mrs. Willie Inez Warren. She had joined her sons as a member of the congregation. One of her sons tried to protect her from the fire and the suffocating smoke. His body was found on top of her, near the piano.[27]

Over forty years later, two of the bodies have still not been identified. A third victim was not identified until June 2015. This is not surprising. Even though many of the men in the bar earlier that afternoon were celebrating the anniversary of the start of gay liberation, it was no safer to be openly gay in New Orleans than it was in most other places in the country. In fact, a number of the men were protecting themselves by using fake IDs to get into the bar. A number of the dead could only be identified through their dental records, which had been kept by Dr. Perry Lane Waters, a Jefferson Parish dentist who was also a member of the MCC congregation and perished in the fire.[28]

This is how the fire department recorded the positions of the bodies in the aftermath of the fire:

1. The corner bar of Iberville side—male
2. The entrance to restroom—male
3. Ditto—male

4. The restroom under basin—male
5. The restroom alongside toilet—male
6. In front of the stage on Chartres side—male
7. Between rear piano and wall—male
8. Ditto—female
9. Under front of piano—male
10. On stage in window—male
11. _____—male
12. _____—male
13. The corner of the building (Iberville and Chartres)
14.
15.
16.
17.
18.
19.
20.
21.
22.
23.
24.
25.
26.
27.

No names. Just blank lines. A vertical arrow to represent that persons 14 through 27 died in the same place as person 13 in the corner of the building. Burned, unidentified bodies, registered as anonymous. The bodies of sons, of friends, of lovers. This is part of the forgotten history of gay liberation: unidentified gay bodies shipped to a morgue.

The police report offered a few more details.

Detectives [Charles] Schlosser and [Sam] Gebbia observed the charred body of what appeared to be a human male in a crouched position leaning against the lake side of the bar. Near this body was a window which leads to the fire escape. Upon checking a small hallway located in front of the restroom, Detectives Schlosser and Gebbia observed the burned bodies of two white male subjects; one lying on top of the other. The door to the rest room was partially opened. Inside the restroom, Detectives Schlosser and Gebbia [observed] two more bodies of white males, one lying on the floor, head facing a lake direction, feet facing a river direction. This subject was partially under the wash basin. The second subject was observed sitting inside the stall by the toilet, facing Iberville Street wall.[29]

After the fire, the police were generally less invested in documenting the identities of the survivors than in trying to find the culprit.[30] Detectives Schlosser and Gebbia claimed that "it was impossible to interview the majority of the victims because of the seriousness of their injuries, and because of the doctors and nurses treating them."[31] When they searched the scene for evidence of an arsonist, their investigation proved equally inconclusive.

By 9:50 PM, the coroner-investigator and his staff arrived along with rescue workers to begin removing the bodies. Before they took them away, the coroner's staff and the rescue workers moved the bodies from the bathroom, the hallway, and the doorway entrance to the center of the bar and took photographs of them. Since so many had perished, the bodies could not be sent to the local morgue but instead had to be "conveyed to Charity Hospital," where the coroner would begin the process of trying to identify them.[32]

Kenneth Harrington was among the victims. He went to the Up Stairs Lounge that night with a friend. He did not like to go out much, preferring to spend Sunday nights at friends' houses or home alone with his cats. His partner, Frank Landry, had died a few years earlier of kidney failure; they had been together for seventeen years. Kenneth and Frank were religious, and according to some of their friends, their faith was one reason why they had been drawn to each other. They met in New York City when Frank was visiting from New Orleans and Kenneth was working as an usher in the Paramount Theater. They fell in love, and Kenneth moved to New Orleans to live with Frank. They built a life together there. Frank worked as a hair-stylist near the French Quarter, and Kenneth got a job with the US Department of Agriculture. They developed a community of friends, hosted dinner parties, and had Frank's mother move in with them when his father died.

It is unclear where Kenneth was when the fire broke out. He didn't slip through the bars covering the front windows or through the back door when Buddy Rasmussen was leading others to safety. Over 35 percent of his body was burned. According to the coroner's report, he probably died of carbon monoxide inhalation. The rescue workers found him near the entrance of the men's room wearing white jeans with a black belt that had a yellow metal buckle.[33] He had on sandals, but the detectives who searched his body for identifying markers could not determine what color they were. They did determine, however, that he was wearing a "black and white flowered shirt" and had a "white metal cigarette lighter in the front pocket." The detectives recorded that Kenneth wore a "yellow metal ring with several white stones on his ring finger of the left hand." The ring that Frank probably put on Kenneth's finger as a symbol of their union remained on his hand until the moment he took his last breath.[34]

Kenneth was not the only married gay man in the Up Stairs Lounge who died in the fire. The detectives noted that another man found next to him, under the basin in the men's room, had no identification (unlike Kenneth) and wore "a white metal wedding band on the ring finger of the left hand. He wore blue pants with gray stripes, blue button-up shirt, black boots and purple socks." Another two victims, identified by the police and fire reports as "victim 19" and "victim 26," were also found with yellow metal wedding bands.[35] It is unclear whether they were married to men or women or whether they wore rings to avoid suspicion.

Other victims bore little trace of their identities or their lives on their bodies. The official reports documented that a few wore watches; one or two had keys and cigarette lighters in their pants or shirt pockets. Some had money, but often no more than a few dollars and a couple of coins. Some of the men even appeared to be nude—their bodies had been burned so badly that their clothing had melted off them.[36]

By Thursday, June 28, 1974, four days after the fire, Detectives Schlosser and Gebbia had a list of people who survivors had said were at the Up Stairs Lounge the night of the fire. The detectives went first to the home of Reginald Adams, called Reggie by his friends, at 1017 Conti Street in the French Quarter, a few blocks away from the Lounge. They knocked on a gated door that led to the entrance of the house. Adams's home stood in the shadow of Our Lady of Guadalupe Church, the oldest church building in New Orleans. A man named Richard Soleto greeted the officers at the door. He told them that he was Adams's roommate and that he had been at the Up Stairs Lounge the night of the fire. He had left the bar ten or fifteen minutes before the fire started to go home to retrieve a hat he had borrowed from another friend who was at the Lounge that night. When he returned, the bar was on fire.

When the detectives asked him where Adams was, Soleto told them that he died in the fire. The detectives asked him for more identifying information about Adams. Soleto replied that Adams was a "negro male," twenty-six years old, and "born and raised in Houston, Texas." The detectives took down information about Soleto, noting that he was white, that he was twenty-one years old, and that both he and Adams were homosexuals. They did not know that Adams was Soleto's boyfriend. Like many of the survivors of the fire (and many gay men both before and even after Stonewall), Soleto avoided questions from the police about the details of his romantic life by using the terms "roommate" and "friend" to describe Adams.[37]

Even though he told police that Adams had died in the fire, Soleto refused to believe that he was gone. He later fell into a state of denial. He continued to lay out Adams's clothes each morning and set a place for him at dinner. His mother moved in with him to help him cope. Soleto was hopeful in part because the coroner's report did not at first list Adams as dead. But it turned out that the reason for the omission was that Adams's body had been burned too badly to be identified; only his dental records could confirm his death. Soleto was utterly devastated when he was told, and for two weeks after the fire, his life was a blur.[38]

He continued to live in the French Quarter and eventually moved in with a woman named Marcy Marcell, who also lost a number of friends in the fire. Years later, Richard Soleto began living as a woman and changed his name to Regina Adams.[39]

According to one account that surfaced decades later, on the day after the fire an employee at Jimani's Bar returned to the scene to retrieve the cash box and the money register. When he left Jimani's, which was on the first floor, the facade of the building rattled. Objects fell to the ground, including Reverend Larson's limbs and body.[40] The fire department hadn't removed Reverend Larson's body from the window frame.

A photographer from the *New Orleans Times-Picayune* captured the image of Reverend Larson's body trapped in the window. The paper's front page also had a photograph of a man's foot in a black leather boot and black sock jutting out from the building and a head shot of the survivor Rusty Quinton, weeping as he looked up at the remains of the ruined building. Still other photos showed victims on stretchers as rescue workers and civilians helped carry them into ambulances.[41]

The headline on the front page of the *Times-Picayune* read, "29 Killed in Quarter Blaze." Another headline read, "Scene of French Quarter Fire Is Called Dante's 'Inferno,' Hitler's Incinerators." The *Times-Picayune* reported on the death toll and the conditions of the victims, attempted to piece together how the fire unfolded, and interviewed a few survivors. New Orleans Fire Department superintendent William McCrossen told the paper that the death toll made the Up Stairs Lounge fire "one of the worst fires in the history of New Orleans."[42] The newspaper also speculated about who started the fire. Witnesses told reporters that they saw a "man being ejected from the Up Stairs Lounge shortly before the fire broke out." A security guard at the Marriott Hotel claimed that he heard a man say that he wanted to burn the building down. The police and fire department investigation would corroborate these details and rule the fire an arson, but ultimately fail to identify a culprit; their investigation would be declared inconclusive.[43]

The Advocate, a leading national gay newspaper, ran the headline "Holocaust in New Orleans," and the gay people who both survived and witnessed the fire understood it as a direct assault on their community.[44] On the night of the fire, a man who refused to give his name to a CBS news reporter stated, "I am saying what was done was done intentionally."[45]

The gay press reported not only on the fire but on the mainstream press's coverage of it. Gay reporters criticized their fellow journalists for not acknowledging the existence of the "gay community" in New Orleans. They claimed that by not having done stories on gay people, mainstream journalists did not have the skills and experience to accurately report on the fire. For example, the gay press took offense to the mainstream press's reference to the Up Stairs Lounge as "a queer bar"; in the seventies, the term "queer" was often used derogatorily. Even the references to the Up Stairs Lounge as just a "bar" were problematic, since they signaled that many mainstream journalists did not understand that bars served many functions in the gay community. The Up Stairs Lounge was not just a "homosexual hangout" that was "frequented" even by "thieves," as the mainstream press put it, but a place that also served as a community center, a theater, and, of course, a place of worship.[46]

Unlike the uncomprehending descriptions of the victims in the mainstream press, *The Advocate* described them, accurately, as members of the New Orleans chapter of the Metropolitan Community Church, a church founded specifically for gay people in Los Angeles in 1968. *The Advocate* noted that about "a third of the membership in New Orleans were missing or dead." In its coverage of the story, it continually referred to both the victims and the survivors by name and by their affiliation with the MCC. *The Advocate* also reported on the responses of national leaders of the MCC in Los Angeles to the fire. Unlike the mainstream press, *The Advocate* made it clear in its coverage of the fire that the arsonists attacked a gay religious community and the victims were people of faith.

The Advocate also recorded some of the bigoted reactions in the immediate wake of the fire. One person in the French Quarter commented, "I hope they burned their dress[es] off." Others reportedly asked, "What major tragedy happened in New Orleans on June 24?" To which the answer was, "That only thirty faggots died—not more!"[47] An offensive joke that became popular throughout the city and was promulgated by New Orleans radio hosts ridiculed the victims of the fire by asking: "What will they bury the ashes of queers in? Fruit jars."[48]

The gay community took the question of burial much more seriously. The coroner's office had identified twenty-nine of the thirty-two who died and made burial arrangements with family and friends, but three victims remained unidentified. What would happen to their remains? The police had no family or friends to contact. Compounding the issue was that many at the bar knew each other by first name only—and some did not even know that.[49]

For some gay people in the seventies, gay liberation was not about "coming out" to family and friends but about starting over or reinventing oneself. The unidentified men who died in the bar may have been doing just that—trying to start over, to begin a new life in New Orleans, to cut their ties with their families and past experiences. It's also possible that their family had cut ties with them. According to some accounts, some families of the identified victims "refused to claim the bodies of their children for burial."[50] One source claimed that Reverend Larson's mother did not allow his body to be shipped home once she discovered in the newspaper reports that he was gay. She said that if he was cremated, she did not want the ashes.[51] As for the unidentified victims, city officials had no choice but to bury them anonymously in Potter's Field, the paupers' cemetery where poor and unknown people had historically been buried.

The question of anonymity trails the story of the fire at the Up Stairs Lounge in other ways too. Some of those who survived faded in and out of the news coverage. It's likely that, after jumping out of the burning building and landing on the street, some fled the scene altogether. They may have made their way down the street, away from the fire trucks and the rescue workers, away from the tourists spilling out of the Marriott Hotel, away from the motorists parking their cars on the side streets and the locals turning off their TVs to run down the street to see the commotion. These survivors would have walked by everyone who was there because they did not want to be seen. They did not want to give their names to the police or explain anything to the press. They did not want to document where they were or what they were doing. So they left.[52]

While some fled, others saw the fire as a chance to advance the cause of gay liberation. Among those was the Reverend Troy Perry, the founder of the Metropolitan Community Church. As soon as he learned about the fire, Perry hurried from the church's headquarters in Los Angeles to New Orleans, where he told the mainstream press that the people in the Up Stairs Lounge were part of a congregation and part of a larger religious organization that stretched from Los Angeles to Atlanta. They were spiritually minded people, he said, who were driven by their faith and who had turned a Sunday afternoon beer bust into a chance to gather as a religious community.

One of Perry's goals in coming to New Orleans was to organize a memorial for the dead. Since many of the churches in the city would not permit the New Orleans MCC to use their buildings as a worship site, Perry struggled to find a place to hold the service. Eventually, St. Mark's United Methodist Church allowed Perry to host the memorial, on Sunday, July 1, 1973. Some of the mourners, however, including some members of the MCC congregation, feared that their identity would be exposed if they attended the memorial. The notion of a public memorial was problematic to those who had liked the clandestine location and blackened windows of the Up Stairs Lounge. But Perry in his ministry emphasized the need for gay people to openly embrace their spirituality and their sexual identity. Further, given the ways in which he believed that the press slighted gay people, he wanted an open and public memorial because he feared that the deaths of the victims of the fire would be forgotten if the service was private. He also believed that the goals of gay liberation would be advanced if the public learned about the violence and oppression that gay people experienced.[53]

On the day of the memorial, survivors, congregants, family members, and friends filed into St. Mark's Church under a sign that read, METHODIST CHURCH OF THE VIEUX CARRÉ, connoting the church's historic origins in the "old square" known as the French Quarter. Reverend Perry addressed the terrible violence of the fire and the many deaths that it caused, but he called on his audience to turn to scripture, to remember their relationship to the Lord, and to continue to fight fearlessly for acceptance. Then, in a tribute to those who perished, the audience sang "United We Stand," repeating it again and again.[54]

As they sang, Perry was told that TV cameras had arrived. Despite his desire to be out and open, he recognized that some of the mourners wanted to remain concealed. When the singing ended, signaling the end of the services, he told his audience that they could use the rear door to exit so that no one would see them leave. But everyone, according to Perry, refused this offer. All of the mourners left through the front door and faced the cameras and the reporters. As Perry later recalled, "In a city where people were really frightened, nobody left by the back door . . . they walked out with their heads held high."[55]

After the memorial, Perry joined others in the gay community to help raise funds for the victims. Gay groups as far away as San Francisco, South Dakota, and Boston hosted blood drives, raised money, and offered support for those still in the hospital.[56] The Kalos Society–Gay Liberation Front in Hartford, Connecticut, donated sixty-two pints of blood.[57] The *Gay Community Newsletter* in Boston explained to its readers the dire need to send aid: "Problems arising from this tragedy include the refusal on the part of some of the gay people's families to pay funeral expenses, inability of the victims to pay hospital costs, and the adjustment of a number of families of supposedly 'straight' people killed in the fire."[58] The *Gay Community Newsletter* described the fire as "the greatest act of genocide against us since the witch burnings in Salem."[59] The paper urged readers to write to their local mainstream press and police departments, as well as Congress, to demand an investigation, arguing that "letting this slip by would not only be in ignorance of the people killed and injured, but would also convince other erratics that it's easy to get away with. We must unite and defend ourselves against the senseless hostility of others who feel our existence a threat."[60]

Reverend Perry made similar demands of both the police and fire departments in New Orleans. Years later he recalled, "The events in the following days helped to pull the community together and strengthened the resolve of the national gay equality movement. We called press conferences. We demanded investigations and apologies from the police department. With one voice we called for assistance from both the mayor and governor. Out of this terrible, terrible tragedy grew a sense of empowerment for gays, lesbians, bisexuals and transgendered persons."[61]

Despite Perry's efforts and the work of other activists in New Orleans, neither the police nor the fire department ever convicted anyone of the crime. In August, a few months after the fire, Raymond Wellender told police in Sacramento, California, where he had been arrested for grand theft and assault, that he set the fire at the Up Stairs Lounge. Detective Gebbia flew from New Orleans to Sacramento to question Wellender, who told him that he poured a bucket of gasoline on the first floor of the bar in order to avenge a friend who had not been paid $200 for sex by a patron of the Lounge.[62] Despite the confession, Gebbia was not persuaded by the story, since the fire had very likely been started in the stairwell leading up to the Lounge, not on the first floor. A few weeks later, when Wellender was brought to New Orleans by authorities, he recanted his confession. By then, there were other reasons to doubt him. For one, most hustlers charged $5 to $10, not $200. John Volz, a First Associate District attorney in New Orleans who investigated the case, told the press, "He's not the man . . . he didn't do it."[63]

In the midst of this, Bill Rushton, managing editor of the *Vieux Carré Courier* in New Orleans, wrote an editorial in *The Advocate* offering a bit of context for readers hoping to better understand the fire. He doubted, he wrote, that homophobic heterosexuals started the fire and suggested that an alienated member of the gay community might have done it. He explained that changing social dynamics in New Orleans were causing some gay men to feel ostracized, possibly to the point of violence. To Rushton, the social geography of the French Quarter was shifting as a result of gay liberation. New figures had arrived on the scene: the "beautiful people in bowties who sipped Bloody Marys during Sunday brunches frequented the restaurants and bars on Bourbon Street; the middle class gay men who migrated to New Orleans from small Southern towns who worked as decorators and hairdressers, and who can't make it here and can't go home, repasting buffet spreads like you'll only find elsewhere on Southern Baptist picnics." On Iberville Street, Rushton observed, hustlers and johns had prowled the block until the establishment of the Up Stairs Lounge, which brought Sunday night worship services, community events, and plays to the area. The result was despair and isolation among gay men who felt left out of this new kind of community. In Rushton's view, this was itself a tragedy. He ended his article with a poignant question: "Get yourself a grudge against a place like the Up Stairs in the middle of a place like Iberville Street and where are you supposed to turn? The society that jokes about burying the remains of your victims in 'fruit jars' isn't about to hear your pleas for help."[64]

Many in the gay community in the Quarter agreed with Rushton, at least about the possible identity of the arsonist, and in fact they suspected one man in particular. His name was Roger Nunez. Before the fire, Michael Scarborough told the bartender that a man, allegedly Nunez, was cruising for sex in the bathroom. The bartender went into the bathroom and told the man to leave, which might have aggravated him. The police believed that Nunez was a likely suspect, but failed to locate him to question him. They had no address or other identifying information to go by. A year after the fire, he allegedly confessed that he started the fire, and then committed suicide. None of this information about Nunez was ever confirmed.[65]

No definitive identification of the person or persons who set the fire was ever made. Based on Nunez's alleged confession, it is tempting to decide that he was the arsonist. But in the broader context of the violence committed against gay people in the 1970s, this is not the only possibility. Gay people being attacked by homophobic individuals remains one of the most underreported themes of gay liberation. There are seemingly endless reports in the gay press from that decade of gay men, lesbians, and transgender people being beaten up outside of bars, assaulted on their way home, or found murdered. Five months before the Up Stairs Lounge fire, *The Advocate* reported on two separate murders in one month.[66] About a month after the fire, the paper published a story about a gay man who had been poisoned and then mutilated.[67] Two weeks later, *The Advocate* ran a story about the death of possibly forty gay people in a string of murders in Texas.[68]

In the mid- to late 1970s, stories of the "trash bag murders" filled the pages of both gay and mainstream newspapers, reporting on rumors of a serial killer who targeted gay bar patrons and hitchhikers.[69] In 1977, for example, *The Body Politic,* a leading gay newspaper published in Toronto but widely distributed throughout the United States, Europe, and other parts of the world, ran the following headlines, among others:

> February 1, 1977: "Thugs Terrorize Park"
> February 1, 1977: "Police Continue Bar Raids"
> February 1 1977: "One Dead in Fire—Montreal"
> March 1, 1977: "Three Murders Still Unsolved"
> June 1, 1977: "Gay Groups Aid Fire Victims"
> September 1, 1977: "A 27-Year-Old Shot and Wounded After Leaving Bar, Miami"
> September 1, 1977: "'All Faggots Should be Castrated'"
> September 1, 1977: "In San Fran a 33-Year-Old Man Was Savagely Beaten to Death Outside of His Home"

In this context, it is not difficult to imagine that the fire was a homophobic attack or that the intention behind the attack was not only to terrorize but to kill.

The fire was also emblematic of the homophobic violence trailing the expanding gay religious community. About a month after the fire, *The Advocate* ran a photograph showing a gay priest raising a gun in his right hand. The caption read, "San Francisco's fiery Rev. Broshears brandishes a shotgun after announcing formation of a 'Lavender Patrol' to combat teenage attacks on homosexuals." As this photo suggests, the MCC in New Orleans was not the only church or congregation targeted in the 1970s.[70]

Arson was a preferred method. Arsonists set fire to gay churches in Los Angeles, Santa Monica, Nashville, and San Francisco in 1973 and 1974.[71] Six months before the fire at the Up Stairs Lounge, on January 27, 1973, a fire broke out at the "Mother Church" of the MCC in Los Angeles. The blaze began on a Friday night after a gay Jewish group met for services. The congregation had just changed its name from Metropolitan Community Temple to Beth Chayim Chadash ("House of New Life"). Its members were at a nearby restaurant when the fire started; upon hearing the news, they ran back to the building, hoping to save the congregation's Torah. This particular Torah had come from Czechoslovakia and had been hidden from the Nazis during World War II.[72] The fire damaged the Torah as well as the congregation's original cross, sacred vessels, and main altar.[73] The building suffered significant structural damage. Reverend Perry was in Denver when the fire broke out; he flew back to Los Angeles the next morning. According to a reporter from *The Advocate*, "at the sight of the ruined building, Perry broke down and sobbed. For several minutes, he could hardly speak."[74]

A month after the Up Stairs Lounge fire in New Orleans, on July 27, 1973, arsonists set fire to an MCC church in San Francisco. No one was hurt, but the fire caused over $100,000 of damage to the building, which the MCC had rented from the San Francisco Presbytery of the United Presbyterian Church. For the third time in a year, Rev. Perry faced another attack on the MCC, another attempt to intimidate and harm the rapidly growing community of people who defined themselves as both openly gay and religious. He told a reporter for *The Advocate* that the fires were certainly frightening to MCC members, "but again, we've crossed a bridge, and we've burned the bridge behind us a long time ago, and we've made up our minds that we're going to go forward and we won't be intimidated by anybody or anything else, including the burning of buildings."[75]

Perry was not the only minister to show his resolve—and he was not the only one who had to. Six months later, on January 15, 1974, arsonists set fire to the MCC church in Santa Monica, California. The day before, minister Bonnie Daniel had received a phone call in a "woman's voice" telling her, "We don't want queers getting married in our church." The next day fire struck a chapel in Santa Monica rented by the West Bay MCC. Reverend Daniel told *The Advocate,* "The congregation isn't going to let the setback stomp us down. We've already had a meeting over it, and most of our people have promised to stay with us. But some of them are really scared, you know."[76]

Throughout the country, MCC congregants faced not only attacks by arsonists but also raids by their supposed protectors, the police. In Indianapolis in October 1973, a vice squad raided a meeting of a fledgling religious congregation who had gathered in a parishioner's home for services and a communion dinner. After the dinner, about ten of the fifty-three members stayed for a discussion hosted by Rev. Bo McDaniel, the church's pastor. Five men dressed in "hippie clothes" entered the house unannounced and began to circulate among them. Within minutes, one of the men identified himself as Officer Roy Schaefer and told the church members that they were under arrest for "frequenting a dive." Recalling the experience to an *Advocate* reporter a few weeks later, McDaniel explained how she intervened. "I said, 'Just a minute here,' and identified myself as a minister in MCC—I gave him some official papers. . . . I said, 'If you want to arrest someone in this church, start with me.'" According to McDaniel, the officers then "began to ease off" and no arrests were made.[77]

Afterwards, McDaniel called for a police investigation and also solicited the help of the FBI to ensure that such intrusions would not happen again. Like Perry, who saw hope for the gay liberation movement in the ashes of the Up Stairs Lounge, McDaniel believed that "the raid may be a blessing in the long run—something that will solidify the gay community, something that will help us walk with pride, knowing we are children of God and that we have a right to live on God's earth." Indeed, this was one immediate effect, though in an unexpected way. Despite the media's promise to McDaniel that they would not publish the names of any of the parishioners present at the raid, a local radio station identified Dennis Murray, who had not been out to his family, coworkers, or friends, on a news broadcast covering the story. He told an *Advocate* reporter that, with the help of McDaniel, he was "bearing up under my sudden role as a so-called gay activist." McDaniel later commented that after the raid many people began "to show courage some of us may have never known."[78]

With the exception of a few newspaper reports in both the gay and mainstream press, the story of the Up Stairs Lounge fire disappeared from the historical record. In New Orleans, stories of the fire were passed along from one generation to the next in conversations at bars, in churches, and on the street. A few sentences or pages about the fire appeared in some gay history books, but the victims and the circumstances of the massacre faded from view.[79]

In the late 1980s, Johnny Townsend, a graduate student in English with (in his own words) "no training in history," began the herculean task of interviewing the survivors of the fire and anyone else who knew those who had died. By his own admission, Townsend did not provide documentation about the interviews in the resulting book, which he had begun, as he stated in the foreword, because "I simply wanted the story to be recorded and told before too many people were lost to AIDS and age." Townsend initially did not plan to publish his findings as a book but instead intended to donate his research to gay history repositories: a local archive in New Orleans and the ONE National Gay & Lesbian Archives at the USC Libraries in Los Angeles. A decade later, however, around 1990, he self-published the anthology of interviews as *Let the Faggots Burn: The Upstairs Lounge Fire*. Then, in 2008, drawing on Townsend's interviews, archival research, and local lore, artist Skylar Fein assembled a breathtaking installation in New Orleans, "Remember the Upstairs Lounge," which re-created the Up Stairs Lounge using surviving artifacts and other artistic materials. The exhibit later appeared in New York City, in 2010.[80]

Although Townsend did manage to capture large chunks of the history of the fire "before too many people were lost to AIDS and age," the response to the outbreak of the epidemic unwittingly over-shadowed the history of those who perished in the fire. The massive, chilling mortality that ripped through the gay community caused by HIV/AIDS diverted the nation's attention away from an arson attack on a New Orleans bar converted into a church to a virus that was mysteriously infecting the gay population across the country in the early 1980s. Even before the onset of the epidemic, the Up Stairs Lounge fire seemed to have been lost in the turmoil of the 1960s and 1970s, which included the 1963 bombing in Birmingham, Alabama, of the Sixteenth Street Baptist Church by white supremacists that left four young black girls dead and the shootings of unarmed college students at Kent State by the Ohio National Guard in 1970. Unlike the antiwar and civil rights movements, gay liberation had not yet gained the power or momentum to broadcast "the horror upstairs."

Based on the little we know about the Up Stairs Lounge massa-cre, those who died defied the stereotypes of gay people in the sev-enties. The victims were neither constantly on the prowl for sex nor dancing at all-night discos, nor marching in loud protests down city streets. Some had just moved to the city for love, and others had lived and worked in the French Quarter for most of their adult lives. Some were married; others were veterans of the armed forces; two were brothers who had come to the service that night with their mother. At 7:45 PM, after the needle had run off the vinyl record, the beer bust had ended, and the front door had been locked, they stood together as a congregation. Rocking back and forth as they sang, they embraced each other, believing in the hope of a revolution that had transformed a bar into a church and a people into a movement.

The victims and survivors of the Up Stairs Lounge fire remind us of the spiritual impulses, cultural beliefs, and intimate desires that bring people together as a community—as well as of the vio-lence and horror that stalked gay liberation in the 1970s. Like them, the religious movement they made has often been ignored, forgotten, or even purposely erased from the historical record and from public memory.

2 THE GAY RELIGIOUS MOVEMENT

They went to Atlanta in August 1973, the same weekend UFOs were being reported in the city and the Ku Klux Klan was holding a meeting. Six hundred gay people crowded into a room, holding hands and embracing, only two months after the fire at the Up Stairs Lounge. They were attending the annual conference of the Metropolitan Community Church Fellowship. Founded in 1968 by Rev. Troy Perry, by 1973 the MCC had established scores of churches in major US cities and begun making inroads throughout the country. As Perry later explained, "We have founded hundreds of churches and offered devotion within the boundaries of many nations, always praising the Almighty, believing our Creator helps those who help themselves, carrying our inspirational message to gay people that God loves you."[1]

In Atlanta, in keeping with the spirit of Rev. Martin Luther King's hometown, the gay religious congregation sang "United We Stand" and "We Shall Overcome." Over the course of the five-day conference held over Labor Day weekend, delegates discussed and debated a range of issues, from the clergy's voting procedures to requests by women parishioners that everyone in the MCC stop referring to God as "He." Congregants also celebrated coming together as

a faith-based community and held a number of social events, including comedy skits, drag shows, and poetry readings. During one of
the church services, they stood and applauded Perry's mother, Mrs.
Edith Perry, who was attending the conference.[2]

It was all a homecoming—of sorts. In 1946, Rev. George
Augustine Hyde, along with John Augustine Kazantks, a bishop in
the Orthodox Church of Greece, founded the first gay church, the
Eucharistic Catholic Church in Atlanta. Kazantks had been a bishop
in Greece but was excommunicated from the church for defending
priests accused of being "sodomites" and for later identifying himself to the church as having "a same gender affectional and sexual
orientation." He later moved to Atlanta, where he met Hyde, who
had attended seminary but was kicked out before his ordainment for
having sexual relations with another man.[3]

Hyde was working as a high school teacher in Atlanta when he
met Kazantks. They decided to create an independent Catholic congregation for gay people because the priest at Sacred Heart Roman
Catholic Church in Atlanta had asked gay parishoners to acknowledge their homosexuality as a sin in order to gain absolution in the
confessional, but they refused to do so. The priest then denied them
communion during mass, which caused a controversy within the
church community. Some straight parishioners sympathized with
the gay people and fought against the restriction, with no success.

Hyde and Kazantks named their congregation the Eucharistic
Catholic Church to emphasize gay people's access to the sacrament
of communion. Their first meeting took place in a hotel room, where
they used two tables as an altar and Kazantks officially ordained
Hyde as a priest. The gathering included about a dozen men and
women, gay and straight. A local gay bar paid for the hotel room. In
less than a year, they had raised enough money to rent a home that
served as both a chapel and a residence for the clergy; it later became
known as "the Radical Gay Christians."[4]

For the rest of the decade and into the 1950s, gay people could
read about Hyde and Kazantks's gay parish in articles that circulated
through a clandestine network of underground newspapers. Robert
Clement, who in 1970 founded the Church of the Beloved Disciple,

the first gay church in New York City, recalled: "So we had nothing to work with except in knowing that in the near past, in the forties or fifties, there had been a parish in Atlanta. That's good to know when you have nothing, when there was no way to know how to create anything." Yet even as Hyde and Kazantks's Eucharistic Catholic Church offered its members hope, they would be attacked for their involvement with the church.[5]

Despite these attacks, Clement and other would-be founders of gay congregations, including Perry, would press on, aided by the fact that earlier activists had started a debate about the place of homosexuality in religion. Throughout the 1950s and 1960s, various gay rights activists led local campaigns against church restrictions on homosexuality. They made little headway, but did succeed in drawing attention to the issue from both church and gay political organizations. Jack Nichols, for example, a gay activist, who in 1961 cofounded a branch of the Mattachine Society, a gay rights group in Washington, DC, founded another organization, the Washington Area Council on Religion and the Homosexual, in 1965; he was a key activist in creating a dialogue between churches and gay rights groups before the 1970s.[6]

Gay liberation quickly transformed the few scattered gay religious organizations into a national movement, and prayer groups, congregations, and churches began cropping up across the country. Clement remembered:

> I didn't know how soon they exploded, but we exploded with Stonewall. I mean, it was paint on the walls, whatever you want to call it. We exploded, and that parish was there for the full formal work one year later, to let the world know. Because I had to put together a context of what it was about, what it meant, and how accepting we were of our brothers and sisters, that something existed. Because at that time, they had nowhere to go. There was no such thing as an open affirming parish of any sort.[7]

The still-new MCC witnessed tremendous growth, establishing numerous churches across the country, not only in major urban centers but also in small towns in the South and rural communities in the Midwest. Although often not formally supported, gay Roman Catholics founded a group called Dignity, while gay Episcopalians founded one called Integrity. Gay Jews founded synagogues, and gay Quakers and Unitarians founded congregations as well. In 1971 the *New York Times* reported on the proliferation of gay religious groups across various faiths, noting that "hundreds of homosexuals have banded together to form an estimated 12 to 15 predominately homosexual congregations in major American cities and many who have chosen to stay within mainline churches have escalated their demands."[8]

In the standard narrative of gay liberation, gay people before Stonewall struggled to embrace their sexual orientation because many believed that homosexuality was a sin. Then, when they started to come out of the closet, they rejected religion or were shunned by their religious communities.

But as suggested by the history and prehistory of the MCC and these other gay offshoots of mainstream religions and denominations, many gay people actually turned toward religious organizations in the 1970s, not away from them. Gay churches and other gay religious communities actually became a refuge that supported, embraced, and helped to galvanize the gay liberation movement throughout the decade. Religion, which had been (and remains) a tool with which to attack homosexuality, helped many gay people in the 1970s learn how to accept their sexuality and feel comfortable in mainstream society.

The gay religious movement also transformed the ways in which dozens of religions and denominations, from Episcopalians to Unitarians to Jews, understood their faith and mission in society. Most importantly, the religious movement provided gay men with a social outlet beyond the bar and bathhouse culture of the seventies. When a young gay man wrote to an advice columnist in 1973 for suggestions on where to meet other guys his own age, the columnist suggested that he attend a meeting of the MCC Heritage Mission and provided the dates and location of the weekly Sunday services.[9]

The gay religious movement expanded in numbers and ambition through the seventies. Early in the decade, gay people organized social groups, held prayer meetings, and defined themselves as a distinct cohort within both gay and religious communities. By the mid-1970s, as religious gay people began to gain more recognition from traditional religious orders, their demands increased. They called for the ordination of gay men and women and for their access to the same services and sacraments enjoyed by others in the congregation. The enormous controversy within religious communities prompted by these requests eventually made headlines in national newspapers. In fact, according to some observers, that controversy was the reason gay churches became the targets of arson and vandalism.

By the late 1970s, the gay religious movement had attracted a great deal of public attention, spurring debates beyond religious institutions. No longer were gay religious issues merely a concern of gay people and their congregations. In fact, the rise of the gay religious movement probably provided some of the fodder for the right wing's attack on homosexuality and its campaigns in support of "family values." The history of the gay religious movement shows that early conservative activists, like Anita Bryant, did not simply disapprove of homosexuality but were also responding to the demands of gay religious activists for full membership in the church, recognition of their marriages, and acknowledgment of their families. Indeed, as discussed later in this chapter, the campaign for gay marriage began in the churches, not in the courts.

The gay religious movement also represented a forgotten kind of gay political activism. Rather than marching in the streets and storming city halls, gay religious activists took a quieter, more somber approach. Gay religious leaders encouraged their congregations to openly and publicly embrace their sexual orientation and to see their sexual orientation not as antithetical to their faith but as central to it. Underscoring their leaders' lesson that congregants should be open and honest about their sexual orientation was the fact that, unlike the bar scene, church and religious meetings took place in open settings during daylight hours. As Perry announced in 1972, "The Lord is my Shepherd and he knows that I'm gay." Reverend

Perry often told dubious gay congregants, "Don't be afraid anymore," a call that he later would use as MCC's slogan.[10]

The stakes were much higher for members of Dignity, Integrity, and other religious groups, since those groups had sprouted from mainstream denominations and so they remained congregants within these denominations. Coming out meant telling priests, rabbis, and their families about their sexuality and then educating them about their faith and sexual orientation not being at odds with but rather equally constitutive of their identity. At the University Episcopal Center in Minneapolis, a gay man whom we only know as "Frank" recognized the importance of organizing a local chapter of Integrity but was petrified at the idea of attending a meeting. "Walking into that meeting took all the guts I could muster," Frank explained. "I never had seen myself as a leader. I had minimal self-confidence, yet knew that if I could succeed in organizing an INTEGRITY chapter, I might be able to help spare many other gay men some of the agony that I and others had suffered."[11]

Some gay religious groups wanted to be able to congregate in synagogues and churches—even if that meant being relegated to a basement, as one Washington, DC, Episcopalian prayer group was.

On July 19, 1970, in New York City, Father Robert Clement held the first mass for the Church of the Beloved Disciple at the Episcopal Church of the Holy Apostles, which permitted him to use its building. Later he would remember his anxiety in the hours leading up to that first service at 2:00 PM on a Sunday afternoon. Not only was Clement concerned that no one would even show up, but he also feared for the safety of the gay men and women who would be openly congregating in the middle of the day in a public location. He got in touch with a few of his friends from the "Levi and Leather community"—muscular men who sported leather jackets and blue jeans and who agreed to guard the entrance to the church to ward off any potential trouble. Two of them sat on motorcycles on the street while others stood at the door.[12]

Father Clement sat in the sacristy, peeking through the door to observe the people filing in. At 1:45 PM there were only one or two congregants, and Clement worried that maybe the fliers he and his partner had distributed had not had the intended effect. He reassured himself that even if only a few people showed up, it would still be a "lovely service." At 2:00 PM, he decided to go ahead and begin the service and walked from the sacristy into the main church, where he couldn't believe what he saw. "It wasn't just that every seat in the church was filled, the aisles were packed. That church, which would hold maybe six hundred plus in a squeeze, had over eight hundred people in it. They say six hundred. We know, with the squeeze. And we don't know how many people were turned away that day who couldn't get in. It was just phenomenal."[13]

Many of the people in the gay religious movement didn't just fight to be allowed to worship in traditional settings. They also wanted to be able to perform other rituals—marriage above all. Although legally prohibited, gay marriage developed as a popular ritual and tradition in the 1970s and became, in churches and synagogues across the country, the symbol of their new culture for many gay Americans. In New York City, Father Clement married his partner, John Noble, at the Church of the Beloved Disciple in 1971 and then led his congregation to city hall in a protest to demand legal recognition. Meanwhile, Rev. Troy Perry often officiated marriages and insisted, at least in the early 1970s, that couples stay together for at least six months before coming to him. The wedding bands recovered from some of the victims in the Up Stairs Lounge fire in New Orleans in 1973 evinced the rituals, traditions, and symbolic importance of marriage for the gay community.[14]

Gay religious groups offered their members more than just regular services and weddings. Especially early in the decade, their focus was often on other activities, such as volunteering, and social events, including dances and conferences. In those parts of the country outside of the major urban centers where there were few gay bars, religious communities became particularly important. Gay people of faith were looking for one another in the 1970s and looking to develop a shared sense of community and spirituality.[15]

This is not to say that gay religious groups were not serious about their faith. The main function of Father Clement's church was no different from that of the mainstream Catholic church: to offer communion and the other sacraments (such as the sacrament of marriage). The major difference was that the Church of the Beloved Disciple's congregants were gay people who had been shunned, some even excommunicated. Some of the gay Catholic churches still identified as Catholic but defined themselves as independent, citing a common practice among some Catholics in the early twentieth century who had disagreed with the Roman Catholic Church. These independent gay Catholic churches traced their heritage to Catholic traditions that began in the nineteenth century and followed liturgical practices that dated to the sixth-century Gothic mass. Father Clement departed from his medieval predecessors in one respect: he was often spotted wearing a clerical collar and a lavender shirt. He also offered an original reading on the relationship between Jesus and his "Beloved Disciple" John, claiming that it had homoerotic undertones (hence the name of his church).[16]

The unifying theme of the various strands of the gay religious movement was the belief that religion could and should offer shelter to gay people of faith, emboldening them to openly embrace both their sexuality and spirituality. As recalled by Patrick McMullan, a gay man who arrived in New York City in 1970 and became a member of the Church of the Beloved Disciple: "Self-loathing was rampant in the gay 1970s, reflected in sex and substance addiction. Gay men and lesbians were as polarized from each other as pre-Stonewall straights and gays. A polar opposite message came from The Church of The Beloved Disciple. . . . No matter how the 'outside' world tries to compartmentalize us, 'gays' are firmly entrenched in virtually every facet of our society, and not exclusively relegated to Fire Island Pines." Rev. Troy Perry claimed that gay men in particular became involved in the church because they no longer felt that the "only public places they could meet are 'gay' bars." As he put it, "In bars the emphasis is too much on sex. Homosexuals want to meet in low pressure, congenial settings as much as heterosexuals do." Unlike the bar and bathhouse culture of the seventies that created divisions and hierarchies among men based on their body type and social demeanor, gay religious communities fostered a sense of community, which also brought gay men and lesbians together.[17]

The gay religious community did not represent an escape from sex. In fact, it became a forum in which gay people could reflect on the role of sex in their lives. The quarterly and monthly publications of gay religious organizations examined the impact of sex and intimacy, of love and relationships, in the broader gay culture on the lives of people of faith. Many gay religious men engaged in serious, thoughtful discussions about the meaning of promiscuity. Writing from Gainesville, Florida, a member of Dignity explained in a letter in the group's newsletter that he and his friends "can't seem to really define promiscuity and, if we feel that we are promiscuous, we can't seem to understand why." He further theorized that promiscuity existed among gay people because "society almost seems to force us to be preoccupied with sex by setting us in a separate category *because of* our sexual orientation." He ended the letter by stating that he would continue to work hard to pursue a career, develop his spirituality, cultivate relationships with both gays and straights, and find a place to live "not just because there is a lot of gay life there." The gay religious press facilitated the underground discourse among gay men who imagined a world not centered on "gay life"; to read these publications now is to uncover a forgotten portrait of gay men who did not just engage in sex but thought about its meaning.[18]

Newsletters were not only a means of conducting frank debates but also, more simply, a way for gay religious communities to reach followers—and would-be followers—across the nation. A member of Dignity in Scottsbluff, Nebraska, wrote in a newsletter, "Certainly life would seem far less comfortless without your efforts and direction in DIGNITY. I surely would not want to 'get along' without it! . . . DIGNITY—in its own essence—and as the wonderful publication it is, is an indispensable part of my daily living." The gay religious movement also depended on both the gay press and its own publications to forge ties among people of faith. As a member of the New York–New Jersey chapter of Dignity recounted in a 1972 newsletter, a three-line ad for Dignity in *The Advocate* had resulted in a meeting in New York City of a dozen men who "I doubt . . . could really appreciate the full import of what they were about to undertake."[19]

Gay religious networks arose that enabled gay people of faith to interact with gay religious communities from different denominations. In November 1973, members of Dignity met with Reverend Perry "to cement the shared goals and fellowships already existing between local DIGNITY chapters and MCC churches." At the meeting, leaders agreed that "bringing Christ to the Gay Community" was the most important part of their missions. One of the most important ways in which gay groups worked together was by sharing church buildings and other spaces. Before the arson at the MCC church in Los Angeles in January 1973, a fledgling gay Jewish organization had been renting space in the church for its Friday night service.[20]

When a gay branch of a mainstream religion was created, others were frequently inspired to create a gay branch in their own denominations. Modeling themselves on Dignity, gay Episcopalians in San Francisco in 1972 set out to establish the "Faithful Stewards" by placing an ad in Dignity's newsletter. In Seattle, the founding of an MCC church in 1972 quickly led to the establishment of five other religious groups of various denominations. Year later, the leaders of six religious organizations in the city recognized their common bond and came together for a joint meeting. The *Seattle Gay News* reported: "While the purpose of the meeting was to present [the] activity and purpose of each organization, many in attendance saw the possibility exceeding this. . . . Several comments from the floor suggested the possibility of a united coalition or council among gay religious leadership to promote common concerns and strengthen the movement."[21]

Though it made some inroads into mainstream religious culture, on the whole the gay religious movement struggled for validation and acceptance. Religious doctrine and ideology proved to be challenging obstacles. Nick Benton, a member of the Pacific School of Religion in Berkeley, California, who set out to chart the rise of the gay religious movement, explained to readers of *Christianity Today* that "religion was one of the main causes of homosexual oppression." Indeed, opponents of homosexuality often condemned gay people by invoking certain biblical passages suggesting that homosexuality promotes immorality. Gay religious people contested these kinds of readings. Ruth Sudul, a Seventh-Day Adventist, argued in 1970 that the Bible's teachings against homosexuality actually refer to "promiscuity and lust, not homosexuality per se."[22]

By debating references to homosexuality in the Bible and making requests of religious leaders, gay people gave mainstream religious organizations no choice but to respond. Many religious organizations, however, simply denied the existence of a gay population in their congregations. Jefferson Keith, a Quaker living in Holyoke, Massachusetts, in 1974, attempted to place an announcement about an upcoming event for gay people in the monthly newspaper of the Religious Society of Friends, but Quaker officials refused to publish it. Although Quakers historically had held strongly liberal political views, they considered an endorsement of a homosexual gathering as a "contradiction" to the "disciplines and standards" of their faith.[23]

Nevertheless, in the early seventies some churches did begin to reconsider policies of this kind. Local denominations began to accept homosexuality despite resistance from the broader national institutions. In Illinois in 1974—the same year Keith approached the New England Quakers—a group of Quakers concerned about the condition of gay people in their congregation formed an ad hoc committee to discuss the "Friends position on homosexuality." Often working alone, gay people met one on one with local religious leaders and members of congregations to plead their case. Unlike the "zaps" of gay political organizations in the 1970s—public protests often aimed at homophobic politicians—gay religious people worked more quietly, usually behind closed doors, and used their personal connections to a religious institution to advance their cause. Gay religious activists also mobilized support by attending meetings of national religious organizations. At an Episcopalian convention in 1976, national members passed a resolution that protected the rights of gay people and declared that they are indeed "children of God and have a full and equal claim with all other persons upon the love, acceptance, and pastoral concern and care of the Church."[24]

When gay people appeared on the steps of churches or at national conventions, many religious leaders did not close their doors and turn their backs. Some who understood gay people's struggles listened and were sympathetic to their cause. Some even viewed gay people as Christ-like figures. In a letter to Dignity, a priest in Louisiana explained his rejection of the theory that gay people were "sick." "I see gays," he wrote, "as truly experiencing the suffering and humiliation that Christ had to go through to show the world what true loving is all about. . . . Perhaps a few enlightened theologians can bring forth new enlightenment to Gay Catholics everywhere."[25]

In 1972 an enlightened Catholic theologian did emerge. The *US Catholic,* the official weekly of the Roman Catholic Church in the United States, approached Father Henry Fehren to write "A Christian Response to Homosexuals." Fehren jumped at the opportunity, since he had felt for many years that "something should be said on the Christian and homosexuality which is more Christian and human and sensible than much of what the church has said in the past." He added that "the Church has forced on homosexuals an uncalled for sense of shame."[26]

In his article, Father Fehren provided a rich and comprehensive analysis of homosexuality. He examined everything from the actual meaning of the term "homosexual" to medical literature on the topic and recounted historical and cultural anecdotes that ranged from Dutch catechisms to John Stuart Mill's reflections on man and society. In an effort to debunk Catholic teachings on sexuality, Fehren criticized the church's stance that "all directly voluntary sexual pleasure is mortally sinful outside of marriage." He also poked fun at the notion that "touching someone's back," for example, "is a venial sin." He then urged his readers to consider the plight of gay people. "In general, homosexual life appears far from an idyllic life. From what homosexuals say and write, many are plagued by loneliness. . . . Many have found faith a great help," he explained. "Since the loneliness of homosexuals is intensified when they feel themselves subtly isolated from heterosexual society, it would help if they were genuinely accepted as persons, not as freaks."[27]

For many gay men, Fehren's article proved inspiring. Weeks after it appeared his essay was republished in Dignity's newsletter.

Within days, responses began to fill the editorial section, applauding Fehren's frank description of gay Catholics and congratulating the newsletter for publishing his article. A subscriber from Oil City, Pennsylvania, wrote: "I read and re-read this month's issue of Dignity, . . . I am so very happy and excited over the contents. It has given me more courage and incentive to be myself. It is so great to be an individual, a human again. . . . Father Fehren's article . . . is unique and very interesting. I found it quite positive and healthy."[28]

Fehren used his ministry to advance the cause of gay liberation, and others would do the same. At the fourth-anniversary mass for gay people in Chicago in 1974, Rev. Mario DeCicco, a Franciscan priest, explained how religious ministry could help gay people by "attempting to involve gays as part of the whole church while breaking down the stereotypes of a 'straight' society that looks on gays as only 'limp-wristed fags' and 'screaming queens.'" Another priest added, "The ministry is not an attempt to 'redeem' the gays from the so-called 'sickness and sin' of homosexuality, but to treat them as 'normal, healthy, loving people.'"[29]

Of the many religious institutions in the United States, the Quakers, despite initial resistance, proved to be one of the most supportive and politically sensitive to the cause of gay religious people. Building on a long-standing tradition of helping other oppressed minority groups, many Quakers vowed not only to support gay members within their congregations but also to advance the larger aims of gay liberation. In 1973 the Baltimore yearly meeting of the Religious Society of Friends pledged to put "new energy into the struggle to end the oppression, often unconscious, that is imposed on people because of their sex or their sexual orientation." On the discussion topic of "Gay Civil Rights," the Quakers stated that "the myths about bisexuality and homosexuality, myths that perpetuate deep rooted discrimination, need to be dispelled through educational efforts, perhaps undertaken by the monthly meetings." In 1975 the Pennsylvania yearly meeting, at the behest of gay Quakers, supported the larger gay movement by donating money to various gay political organizations, including the Gay Activist Alliance.[30]

Even though many Quaker churches embraced the gay religious movement as the decade wore on, other religious orders remained unwilling to alter their stance on homosexuality. This led gay religious activists to alter their strategies. By the mid-1970s, some gay religious activists were taking extreme measures to get the attention of mainstream religious organizations, while others began to frame their cause in the language of civil rights.

For instance, in September 1974, Brian McNaught, a reporter for a Detroit archdiocesan newspaper, went on a twenty-seven-day hunger strike in order to get the Detroit Catholic Church to address the struggles of gay Catholics. McNaught's iron-jawed activism worked: two bishops promised "to give attention to the problems of homosexuals." McNaught called the bishops' promise "a major victory for gay people."[31]

The gay religious movement also borrowed the rhetoric and strategies employed by the women's liberation movement and black freedom struggle to make a sympathetic case to religious institutions. The success of using terms like "civil rights" and "discrimination" to frame gay people's plight was reflected in the 1975 conclusion of the National Council of Churches, in its investigation of the treatment of homosexuals in its member denominations, that "there has been discrimination against gays." The Council "urged its 31 member denominations to work to ensure the enactment of legislation that . . . would guarantee the civil rights of all persons without regard to their affectional or sexual orientation."[32]

Calling on the rhetoric of civil rights was part of the gay religious movement's effort to gain access to all aspects of religious institutions—not just acceptance of gay members but also ordination of gay ministers. Although some congregations had ordained openly gay ministers, such as a group in San Francisco that did so in 1972, it was not until the gay religious movement gained momentum in the mid-1970s that ordination became one of its major goals. Across the nation, gay religious men and women fought either to be anointed as ministers or, in some cases, to retain their posts after publicly disclosing their sexual orientation. The geographic sweep of ordination requests reveals the reach of gay liberation, which emboldened religious people across the Great Plains, the South, and the major urban centers to pursue the highest ranks within their religious institutions.[33]

Resistance was strong. In San Antonio, Texas, Methodist leaders suspended a clergyman who was a "self-described homosexual." Wearing a pink lapel button with the word GAY on it, the suspended minister, Gene Legget, continued to spread his ministry and his outreach work. He operated a covenant home for people in need whom he claimed the church did not reach, including gay people. Nevertheless, the church remained opposed to his ordination. In Madison, Wisconsin, Methodist leaders denied Steven Webster's ordination, stating that they "did not believe at this time that homosexuality is compatible with being a clergyman of the Christian Faith." Similarly, at its national meeting in 1976 in Louisville, the National Executive Council of the Episcopal Church deferred making a decision on whether to allow homosexuals to pursue ordination. According to the *Chicago Tribune*, the question had come up in the first place owing to the recent ordination of Rev. Ellen Marie Barrett in New York, an out lesbian.[34]

Barrett's ordination not only signaled a victory for the gay religious movement but also marked an achievement for the women's movement of the seventies. Much of the campaign surrounding the ordination of gay people followed in the wake of earlier campaigns launched by heterosexual women. As a result, in the mid-1970s the women's movement and the gay religious movement protested side by side for change in church policy. In newspapers and journals covering church reform, women's and gay issues often made the headlines, just as in meetings and conference sessions on church reform the question of women and homosexuality often topped the list as the most pressing and explosive issues. In religious institutions across the country, the question of the ordination of heterosexual women and gay people sparked heated debates and splintered organizations. For instance, in a suburban community in New Jersey in 1977, members of an Episcopal congregation broke ties with the national church based on the leadership's decision to ordain heterosexual women and discuss the issue of homosexuality. One member of the church explained to a reporter for the *Wall Street Journal* that she left the church because "this liberation is just another way of destroying civilization."[35]

The push for ordination not only encountered resistance but also elicited a backlash against gay people. In 1977, the singer, actress, and Southern Baptist Anita Bryant launched her campaign against gay rights and equality when she opposed an ordinance in Dade County, Miami, to prohibit discrimination on the basis of sexual orientation. Bryant received a great deal of publicity when she argued that homosexuality was a sin and that homosexuals recruited child molesters. Her campaign emerged after the start of the gay religious movement in the early seventies and after the debates in many religious communities about homosexuality in the mid-1970s. Bryant's antigay activism may have been triggered by the Miami ordinance, but it unfolded against the backdrop of the gay religious movement, which was at its height.[36]

Bryant's political campaign against a city ordinance morphed into a national crusade when she mobilized Southern Christian fundamentalists against gay people. Many Christians had already been debating and arguing against homosexuality within their churches, among their congregations, and at their national conventions in the early to mid-1970s, but they did not have a mainstream political outlet until Bryant emerged as their conduit. She provided them with the stage to broadcast their opposition to gay people's fight to gain access to churches and ordination. Religious revivals invited Bryant to deliver scathing critiques of homosexuality; these events mobilized the religious right against gay liberation, broadly defined. Many religious fundamentalists began going door to door petitioning against gay people. The Southern Christian right's hostile campaign against homosexuality on the national stage obscured the origins of that campaign in the churches, where gay people had been advocating for their rights throughout the 1970s.[37]

Bryant's response and much of the religious fundamentalists' vilification of homosexuality can be traced to the gay religious movement of the seventies. The religious right's claim that it was protecting the sanctity of the family derived not from an original ideological platform of its own but rather in response to the gay religious movement's efforts to gain recognition.[38]

If the history of the gay religious movement was partially obscured by the virulent response to it, it was also obscured by the events of the decade and the chroniclers who narrated the history of gay liberation. In general, the accounts of gay writers, historians, and scholars have emphasized the sweaty political struggles in the streets in the 1970s rather than the radical push by gay people of faith to be able to recite prayers in churches. Compounding this problem, many of the early chroniclers of gay liberation came from the political left and considered religion patriarchal, hierarchical, and the root of gay oppression. In a forum published in 1974 in *The Body Politic* on religion in the gay community, a lesbian writer acknowledged how the church had been patriarchal and homophobic toward many "women-identified women."[39]

In the seventies, many gay people turned to the gay press as a way to indict religious doctrines that vilified gay people. That another segment within gay culture wanted to use the pages of the same newspapers to announce the times and places of church services or the meetings of prayer groups points to a major tension within the gay community at the time. Having more than just a difference of opinion, these segments of the gay community had different definitions of liberation. For gay people of faith, joining a community of people with similar beliefs and the same sexual orientation represented the fulfillment of gay liberation. Others found fulfillment in revolting against organized religion.

Over the decade, the tension surrounding gay people's embrace of traditional religion did not subside. An article in 1978 reminded gay readers that the churches believed that homosexuality was "an abomination" and that "homosexuals deserved to be killed."[40] Many gay people were skeptical about their contemporaries' involvement in religion, which they perceived as an innately oppressive institution that restricted gay rights. When an MCC church opened in Toronto, an editorialist argued that "Christian belief and gay liberation are contradictory." Although the writer acknowledged the MCC's popular mantra that "gay is good," he nevertheless contended that "MCC stands with one foot in gay liberation and the other in Christian faith," which he claimed made both the MCC and its members "conflicted." Robert Wolfe, a pastor of an MCC church, responded to such claims by arguing that "the essential teaching of Jesus of Nazareth . . . is a message of liberation." He further claimed that Christ's message and the message of gay liberation "are one [and] the same." Both, he explained, "affirm life and [the] community of love in a positive, confident way."[41]

In 1976 the publication of *The Church and the Homosexual* by John McNeil, a Jesuit priest and theologian, illuminated these internal debates within the gay community. In his examination of the Catholic Church's attitudes toward homosexuality, McNeil argued that the Bible does not condemn homosexuality. In the gay press, many reviewers claimed that the book was a "positive contribution to gay liberation." They celebrated the fact that a member of the Catholic Church had written a sympathetic account of homosexuality. Yet the positive reviews irked a journalist at *The Body Politic*; in his scathing review of the book reviews, he pointed to a number of contradictions, nuances, and ironies in McNeil's argument that undermined gay liberation.[42]

Gay critics of the religious movement targeted the ways in which the church had oppressed gay people and demonized their culture. The tenor of their critique was often harsh, hostile, and condescending. Some newspapers asked if Jesus was a "cocksucker," while others claimed he was gay. Other papers blatantly dismissed religion as a credible set of practices and beliefs.[43] These indictments, however rigorous, witty, or offensive, failed to consider the nuances of the gay experience, particularly how faith and a sense of spirituality offered many people guidance, solace, and strength. Gay religious advocates never stopped responding to the vitriol spewed against them with quotations from the Bible and messages about God's love for all people. Growing up in a particular faith tradition often led to internal struggles for gay people, but to recognize that they found a community of people who shared their beliefs and intimate desires is to tell a different story about gay liberation, one in which gay people did not strip themselves of their upbringing or beliefs in pursuit of a wholly new identity.[44]

Even as they fended off foes in both the mainstream churches and the gay community, members of the gay religious movement asserted themselves as a crucial part of the liberation struggle. They made many inroads with gay political organizations, worked with gay newspapers to make sure their events were covered and their activities reported on, and showed up at gay pride marches to take their place as a central force within the gay liberation movement. At a gay pride event in Philadelphia in 1975 titled "Super Sunday," members of Dignity marched alongside the Gay Activist Alliance, the Gay Media Project, and the Women's Switchboard. Similarly, at the gay pride march in New York City in 1974—which was one of the most visible and potent illustrations of gay political activism—members of the Unitarian Gay Caucus, the Gay Synagogue, and Dignity marched alongside members of many of the prominent political groups of the day: the Gay Academic Union, the National Gay Task Force, and the Gay Activists Alliance of New York and New Jersey. In fact, the *New York Times* chose a photo of Rev. Tom Oddo, the national secretary of Dignity, to illustrate the march.[45]

But at the same gay pride marches where gay religious groups confidently paraded alongside more explicitly political groups, other gay activists delivered vitriolic critiques of traditional organized religion. One of the most significant denouncements of traditional religion happened at the Boston gay pride march on June 18, 1977, three weeks after Anita Bryant's antigay campaign led to the repeal of an antigay-discrimination bill in Florida; in the interim, gay people throughout the country had attempted to retaliate by boycotting orange juice. (Bryant was a longtime spokesperson for the Florida Citrus Commission.) Charley Shively, a leading activist, contributor to the newspaper *Fag Rag*, and college professor, stood in his academic regalia before a crowd of gay people and condemned the various power structures that both denied gay rights and inhibited their progress. As he later recounted in an article in *Fag Rag,* he first took aim at academic institutions. He told the crowd that, even though he had a PhD from Harvard and taught at Boston State College, he had recently received a letter claiming that he was unqualified to teach gay history. Showing the crowd the letter and his Harvard diploma, he told them that they were "only worth burning." He lit both papers on fire. The crowd roared.[46]

He then told the crowd that earlier that day they had marched by some of the richest and most powerful banks in the city. He noted that the John Hancock Insurance Company and the Prudential Insurance building "have one hundred, two hundred, a thousand times more space than all the gay bars and all the gay organizations in Boston." He then pulled a dollar bill and his insurance card out of his pocket and announced, "This is what they're worth: Burning." As the dollar and the card burned, the crowd cheered. Next, Shively took on a Massachusetts law prohibiting homosexual acts. Once again, he took a match to light the criminal code on fire, and even before he did the crowd began screaming, "Burn it, burn it!" Shively obliged.[47]

For his final act of resistance, Shively picked up a copy of the Bible and read a verse from chapter 20 of Leviticus that denounced homosexuality. He did not stop there, but continued reading the chapter, which also condemned witchcraft. By this point, the crowd was rumbling with excitement. They shouted, "Burn it, burn it!" Shively ignited the Bible and dropped it at his feet. But this time his act of defiance was met with resistance. A member of the crowd pushed his way through the rally, screaming, "You can't burn the Bible!" The demonstrator grabbed the burning Bible and tried to put out the fire with his feet.[48]

Shively continued with his speech. He claimed that countless witches had been burned to death because of those few lines in Leviticus and that many people had also been persecuted because of that verse, far more than would ever be known.[49]

Members of Dignity and Integrity in the audience were outraged. They began protesting, screaming for Shively to get off the stage. Among them was Brian McNaught, who had gone on a hunger strike in Detroit to get the Roman Catholic Church there to pay attention to the subject of homosexuality; he had since relocated to Boston to lead Gay Catholics there. He and the other religious members of the audience began marching to the stage, demanding that Shively's speech stop being filmed. Shively saw them coming. He dropped the microphone and ran off the stage. He then approached Elaine Noble, who was scheduled to dance after Shively's speech and was standing nearby. "The Catholics are coming over here," he said. "What should I do?" According to Shively's own account, Elaine replied, "Just get the fuck out of here as fast as you can."[50]

The religious gay people stormed onto the stage. McNaught ran up the stairs and grabbed the microphone off the floor. "What you see here is worse than Nazi Germany," he screamed to the crowd.[51] McNaught condemned Shively for his comments and then spoke about the importance of the gay religious movement. He refuted Shively's claim that "Christianity is the enemy" and argued that the main opponent of gay religious people was not the church but gay political activists who did not understand the symbiotic relationship between faith and sexuality.

The showdown between Shively and McNaught resulted from the tense atmosphere of the event, which took place just weeks after Anita Bryant's successful attack on gay people. McNaught heard parts of Shively's speech as a direct insult to the gay religious movement, but Shively himself seemed to be more focused on responding to Bryant's campaign. Shively mentioned Bryant's use of religious fundamentalists' ideas to indict and criminalize gay people and her claim that her political campaign was endorsed by the Bible. For his part, Shively, like many other gay people at the time, promulgated a gay rights ideology that was antagonistic toward organized religion. In this view, religion had been used to justify the social and legal subjugation of gay people and had served in certain historical moments as the driving force behind the persecution of gay people, which began, he argued, with the seventeenth-century burning of the witches and was continuing with Anita Bryant's "Save Our Children" campaign.

Shively fits into the traditional narrative framework of gay liberation: he rejected existing power structures; he voiced opposition to political enemies; he viewed religion as the source of gay oppression; and he cast himself and others as part of a historical narrative that began with witches. This is the history of gay liberation that people have embraced, promoted, and repeated over and over again. It even fits into the broader historical narrative of American protest and the radical tradition that runs throughout the major epochs of American history.[52]

Moreover, as a member of *Fag Rag,* Shively could direct what the newspaper covered and leave his own archival trail. He himself probably wrote the *Fag Rag* headline "Boston Bible Burning." Shively wrote himself into history, becoming part of the historical record and embedding his perspective in the public memory that would dictate the course of gay history for the next few decades.[53]

But Charley Shively, like his burning of the Bible and like gay opposition to religion in the 1970s, is only part of the story. The demonstrator who attempted to rescue the Bible revealed that some gay people disagreed with the antireligious remarks of many gay political activists. For the unnamed demonstrator, as well as for Brian McNaught and the other religious people in the audience who stormed the stage, there were certain lines that could not be crossed, certain actions that could not be tolerated. Laws could be burned and committee letters could be destroyed, but some gay people were not willing to allow their faith to go up in flames. They demanded that the gay religious movement be heard. They retrieved the microphone. Despite their efforts that day, however, and despite their decade-long articulation of their mission, they would be silenced by history.

Further, in the broader writing of the history of gay liberation, there is no room in a discourse that insists on promiscuous behavior to explain the spread of HIV for a counternarrative about gay people's spirituality and morality. According to the logic of sexual promiscuity as the cause of HIV, it makes more sense to portray gay people at a disco than in a church pew, in a crowded bathhouse than at an ordination ceremony, or even in a unified march to demand equality than in a debate over religion.

These divisions within the gay community have been forgotten, and so have many of the details about the period. In fact, the underlying implication of many of the critiques of the gay religious movement was that religious gays were prudes who refused to participate in the sexual revolution. Yet this too rings false. Larry Bernier, a gay man living in Boston in the midseventies who eventually became a leading minister in the MCC, offered perhaps the most pointed response to such thinking: "There is no conflict for me in worshiping Jesus at service and then running out and sucking cock in the shrubs at the Fenway."[54]

The nuanced ways in which many gay people embraced both their sexuality and their faith have also been flattened in favor of a critique that dwells on the antipathy of many mainstream denominations toward homosexuality. But even as mainstream Christianity disapproved of homosexuality, the Metropolitan Community Church did not. This fact has been lost to history, however, because many of the major religious institutions' attitudes and doctrines were attributed to the MCC. As one man explained in a letter to the editor of *The Body Politic:* "It occurs to me that you perhaps wrote the editorial without really understanding what MCC is about. When you talk about Christianity, you are perhaps talking about the religion you knew as children, about the churches your parents took you or dragged you to, when you were younger. Perhaps, this accounts for your strange notion that Christian belief and gay liberation are contradictory. I certainly don't feel a conflict within me."[55]

The MCC and the gay religious movement accelerated gay liberation. The movement offered refuge when none was in sight, and it helped to create a language, slogans, and a set of beliefs that brought gay people together in places as diverse as the Up Stairs Lounge in New Orleans, a basement in Washington, DC, and a rented Presbyterian church in San Francisco.

The gatherings and churches instigated by the gay religious movement would not be the only places, however, where gay people could go to define the meaning of liberation. Other activists would explore liberation in bookstores and literary circles, in novels and newspapers, and in poems about the past and history books written for the future.

3 THE BIOGRAPHY OF A BOOKSTORE

Like many New Yorkers, Craig Rodwell had a vision. He imagined a world where gay men would no longer be restricted to the bars and bathhouses in the city as the only places to congregate. A vice president of the Mattachine Society, a gay political group in New York, Rodwell wanted to open a store that would cater to the growing local gay community. "I was trying to get the Society to be out dealing with the people instead of sitting in an office," Rodwell recalled. "We even looked at a few store-fronts. I wanted the Society to set up a combination bookstore, counseling service, fund-raising headquarters, and office. The main thing was to be out on the street."[1]

When the Mattachine Society rejected Rodwell's vision, he resigned and decided to found a bookstore that would serve as a hub for the gay community. Rodwell had no experience in running a bookstore; his only training was in ballet. As he once explained, in a mix of humility and grandiosity, "I am not a bookseller businessman. I am a person who at the age of 13 set out to help change the world and primarily Gay people's self-images."[2] He believed that gay culture's overemphasis on sex had led to gay men's economic exploitation. Rodwell coined the term "sexploitation" to describe the focus on gay men's sexual lives and the commercialization of homosexuality. "When you're asked to pay $10 for a magazine of male nudes wrapped in cellophane, that's sexploitation. When you're expected to pay $5 and upwards to see a male movie in a heterosexually-operated movie house, that's sexploitation. And whenever, as a Gay person, you're asked to pay $10 for something that cost the establishment $1, that's sexploitation."[3]

Rodwell furthermore worried about what happened to gay men when they interacted with each other on a purely sexual basis. "Aside from the high cost to Gay males of sexploitation movies, magazines, and books," he wrote, "the real cost to our brothers is when we allow ourselves to be conditioned to think our being Gay as totally sexual phenomena. Another one of the stereotypes used against Gay people is that all we think of twenty-four hours a day, is sex. In other words, we are viewed as homo*sex*uals rather than as Homosexuals." This is also the logic that guided the homophile movement's decision to use the term "homophile" instead of "homosexual."[4]

Rodwell also did not like the fact that many heterosexuals accepted gay liberation as long as gay men remained isolated in ghettos, cut off from the rest of society. As he explained:

> In recent years, the larger American culture which we are all a part has "allowed" us to have Gay bars, baths, movie houses. The rationale being that since there are a lot of Homosexuals in the country, it is the public interest to keep us isolated in bars, baths, and movie houses where we are permitted to commit our "perverted" acts out of the views and minds of the general public. Did you ever wonder why the vast majority of Gay places are located in out-of-the-way areas within our major cities?[5]

Rodwell wanted to create an alternative, but without the Mattachine Society's support, he needed to finance the bookstore on his own. He decided to move to Fire Island, where he would work as a bartender to earn as much money as he could in order to rent a storefront. Fire Island had become a popular gay summer vacation destination in the midtwentieth century; thousands of gay tourists were attracted each summer to the sandy shore that ran parallel to the southern shore of Long Island.[6]

A historian exercising a novelist's imaginative privileges would evoke the fateful day in the early summer of 1967 when Rodwell left for Fire Island by ferry from New York City by describing the city streets, the conversations taking place among the men waiting in line for the ferry, and, most of all, the determination in Rodwell's eyes as he emerged from the subway and made his way to the ferry. Rodwell would have been wearing a golden tan jacket with a white interior and a dark brown shirt tucked underneath it, with a Navy backpack hanging from his shoulder and a duffle bag in his hand. His all-American boyish looks would belie the fact that he was twenty-eight years old. His brown hair parted to the side might have signaled an adolescence spent in boarding school, but little else about his appearance would have suggested the broken home, the night spent in jail, the devotion to Christian Science, the fiery commitment to black civil rights, and the years of training in ballet.[7]

Rodwell would have taken a deep breath, taken his seat on the ferry, glanced at his reflection in the window, brushed back his brown hair, and grabbed a handkerchief from his pocket to wipe the sweat off his forehead. As the ferry roared away from the port, perhaps Rodwell's face looked angelic. He would have closed his eyes and briefly meditated on his purpose. He would have smiled.

Novelists can do what historians cannot. Historians must rely on the records that people leave behind. The problem the historian often encounters is that when ordinary people do extraordinary things, they do not realize it at the time. So they do not save documents of their experiences or record their observations and feelings. Rodwell would eventually amass an extensive archive of material about his life's work, but there is only one single-sentence story of his fateful trip to Fire Island, from an interview he did years later. "The cheapest store-front in the Village that I could find was $115 a month, and they insisted on the first month's rent plus two months' security. That was $345, or one third of the money I had saved. But I did it!"[8]

Rodwell scheduled the grand opening of his bookstore for a few months later, on Thanksgiving Day, November 24, 1967. His mother flew in the day before from Chicago to help him set up the shop at 291 Mercer Street, between Waverly Place and East Eighth Street. They stayed up all night assembling the shelves and arranging the books, though the former task took more time: his selection was only three copies each of fewer than twenty-five titles. He stocked books such as Edward Sagarin's *The Homosexual in America,* published under Sagarin's pseudonym Donald Webster Cory. At the time, the book ranked as the leading sociological manifesto for gay rights. Rodwell also included lesser-known gay titles, like D. H. Lawrence's novella *The Fox,* set in the early-twentieth-century English country-side, as well as Oscar Wilde's plays and Hart Crane's poetry. Rodwell devoted a section of the store to periodicals that promoted the gay liberation movement, ranging from *The New York Hymnal* (which he founded to support the Homophile Youth Movement) to *The Ladder,* the newsletter of the Daughters of Bilitis, the first lesbian political organization. He would also distribute free pamphlets that tracked the progress of gay liberation outside New York (like "The Purple Report"), an article on "Homosexuality and Citizenship in Florida," and brochures from various gay religious groups.[9]

Rodwell's goal was to help establish a gay literary culture in New York City. At the time, most gay people's access to collections of gay-themed books and materials was restricted to the smut stores near Forty-Second Street, which carried only pornography. In the midtwentieth century, one could find books and articles by gay authors in libraries and mainstream bookstores, but they were never assembled together on the same shelf. The New York Public Library had copies of Oscar Wilde's plays and Hart Crane's books, but they were not cataloged as gay literature. Instead, they appeared on library shelves based on their subject. Further, the Mattachine Society may have had copies of, for instance, the article "Homosexuality and Citizenship in Florida," but one needed to know where the Society's underground headquarters was to be able to read it. And the Daughters of Bilitis newsletter that Rodwell stacked in his shop had often circulated through clandestine networks; it was difficult to get a copy of a particular issue without knowing someone in those networks. Rodwell's organization of these and many other scattered books, papers, and pamphlets into a single genre was revolutionary—it was the first time in American history that literature had been organized under the subject heading of "gay culture." The Library of Congress cataloged "homosexuality" under the subheading "criminality and medical abnormality" and had no subject heading for gay literature and culture. By placing just a few books and political pamphlets on a shelf, Rodwell, with his mother by his side, changed the world of letters' official definition of homosexuality. In his scheme, gay people were not criminals subject to sociological and psychological studies, but writers of a distinct genre of literature and creators of a distinct culture.[10]

As his mother neatly arranged the books on the shelves with the covers facing outward, Rodwell hung posters and T-shirts above the bookcases that promoted positive images of gay people. On a wooden desk, he set up a bin by the silver metal toolbox that served as register with buttons bearing popular gay catchphrases like GAY IS GOOD, ROOMMATE WANTED, and the names of Batman and Robin printed inside a heart. The buttons quickly became one of the store's signatures. Rodwell collected dozens of these buttons sporting popular and often political slogans that advocated for gay equality. He once recalled that the mailman in Greenwich Village wore a pin on his US Postal Service hat that read GAY REVOLUTION.[11]

Every inch of the store celebrated gay people. Even the name that Rodwell chose for the store reflected his vision and political commitment. "I wanted a name that would tell people what the shop is about. So I tried to think of the most prominent person whose name I could use who is most readily identifiable as a homosexual by most people, someone who's sort of a pseudo-martyr. And Oscar Wilde was the most obvious at the time, so I called it the Oscar Wilde Memorial Bookshop." The name gave the bookstore credibility, evoked the gay literary tradition, and embodied Rodwell's mission to promote positive images of homosexuality.[12]

The bookstore was the first of its kind in the nation, and one of the first public embodiments of gay culture. Up until the late 1960s, gay men had certainly dominated theater groups, antique shops, and certain restaurants, apartment buildings, neighborhoods, and even literary societies, but these places were not defined outwardly and publicly as gay institutions; instead, they were informally marked as "gay" over time owing to the large number of gay people associated with them. From Rodwell's perspective, this world was too inconspicuous. He might have been aware of the culture and history of this previous era, but the point of creating the bookstore was to make visible in the world the literary culture in which he lived. He founded the Oscar Wilde Memorial Bookshop as a visible institution whose sole purpose—at a time before liberation had become a common term among gay people—was to promote gay culture.[13]

The Oscar Wilde Bookshop's existence and success owed much to Rodwell's belief in the power of imagery and visibility—a belief that can be traced to his early activism in the black civil rights movement. To understand that influence, we need to briefly visit Chicago in the early 1960s, at the height of the American civil rights movement.

In his early and mid-twenties, Craig Rodwell had closely watched the movement unfold in the South from his Chicago apartment, and he wrote letters of protest to elected officials and local government. For instance, as a twenty-two-year-old, he sent a letter to the Chicago Board of Education about the "mobile schools" it had established; Rodwell claimed that these were a ploy to avoid integration in Chicago and had only increased "the ghettoization of Chicago's negroes." In 1965, in response to the civil rights struggle in Mississippi, he signed a petition that called for members of Congress to unseat Mississippi's members of the US House of Representatives. Observing the civil rights movement from his home on North Damen Avenue in Chicago, he saw that the newspapers' coverage of the civil rights struggle shaped what many people outside of the South understood about the movement. From this experience he learned about the power and efficacy of representations.[14]

It was during this period that he read a *Life* magazine article that featured an insider's glimpse into the subterranean world of gay male urban life. *Life* ran black-and-white photos of mostly silhouette images of gay men loitering on city streets, crowded together in smoky bars and wearing leather jackets, and handcuffed by undercover policemen. The article warned readers of the "gay world" and the increasing number of gay men "openly admitting, even flaunting, their deviation." And it went on to alert readers that "for every obvious homosexual, there are probably nine nearly impossible to detect." Although the article played on a number of damaging stereotypes, Rodwell saw value in it. In response to the story, Rodwell wrote a letter to the editor, stating: "The homosexual in this country has been a scapegoat for too long, as have the Negro and the Jew." But he did not condemn the article. Instead, he praised it because it offered him a chance to expose the oppression of gay people. There was no longer, according to Rodwell, a "conspiracy of silence in the public media" about homosexuality.[15]

The civil rights movement provided Rodwell with the framework to develop this argument. Having seen how the civil rights struggle became amplified when mainstream media reported on the movement, Rodwell knew that simple recognition can lead to political power. It was a virtuous circle. Gay people, influenced by the civil rights movement, were becoming more prominent in American society, and as that happened the press would cover them and thereby only advance their cause. As he put it in his letter to *Life* magazine, "The increasing awareness of the public and press regarding the problems of the homosexual and discrimination against him is indicative of the attitude of the new generation of homosexuals— those of us who have reached adulthood in the 60's, the 'civil rights' decade. The American homosexual is rapidly coming to the realization of his responsibilities to himself and to society by demanding full citizenship in the Republic."[16]

Throughout the late 1960s and early 1970s, Rodwell wrote many letters to US representatives to protest conditions in the South, all the while keeping an eye on how the mainstream press depicted homosexuality.[17] If a journalist even obliquely recognized the plight of gay people, he wrote a letter commending the journalist for his or her bravery and willingness to consider the challenges that gay people faced.[18] If, on the other hand, a writer presented a sensationalistic account of gay people that had nothing good to say, Rodwell fired off a letter of protest.[19] He saw even a negative portrayal as an opening to initiate a dialogue about gay people with journalists who had media power. He once wrote a letter of protest to Beverly Sills, an opera star and television host, who had interviewed two gay activists, Elaine Noble and Bruce Voeller, on her show. Rodwell accused Sills of making comments characterized by "blatant homophobia and heterosexism"; Sills replied with a postcard that read, "I think you should be informed that some silly son-of-a-bitch is writing letters to people and signing your name to them."[20]

Rodwell also gained insights about the civil rights movement from his involvement with leftist politics and homophile groups in the 1960s, as well as from reading radical writings that were circulating underground. He collected articles that appeared in the *New York Times* on the Black Panthers. Among his papers, Rodwell included information about a meeting of "Yippies, the Black Panthers, the Young Lords party, the Committee of Returned Volunteers (mostly from the Peace Corps), the Women's Liberation Movement and the Gay Liberation Front." This meeting, which took place in New York on July 19, 1970, was "historic," as Jean Cohen, a graduate student who was in attendance (and who would become a prominent political scientist at Columbia University), told a *New York Times* reporter.[21]

According to the *Times* article, "Willie Amarfio of Ghana, a follower of Kwame Nkrumah, the deposed head of state, in bringing the session a message from the developing nations, told the 130 Americans and 30 foreign guests that 'your attitude strikes me as not serious to be associated with such a frivolous organization, the homosexuals.'" Rodwell marked this section in the article. His efforts to become more educated about leftist and racial politics often brought him up against hostile and unwelcoming members of leftist groups who did not appreciate the involvement of gay people. Others in positions of power criticized gay people's political mobilization. Rodwell kept a copy of an address that Alfred Gross, a physician and ethics professor, delivered to medical students at Bellevue Hospital on the topic of the homophile movement in 1967. Gross noted that "Jews and Negroes . . . could proudly proclaim their identity as such. Homosexuals, if they had any sense, would do well to hide their lights under a bushel. Those who insisted upon publicly calling attention to their sexual propensities were either candidates for a martyr's crown or a place in Bedlam [mental institution]." Despite encountering activists who dismissed gay groups as valid stakeholders in social activism and others who encouraged gay people to remain closeted, Rodwell learned much from these forums, readings, and workshops, even if his presence as a gay man was not fully accepted or his political vision embraced. He intuited an important connection among various marginalized groups and learned to adopt civil rights strategies in advancing the cause of gay liberation.[22] Rodwell's views on civil rights and his interest in the media's depiction of gay life not only inspired his founding of the Oscar Wilde Memorial Bookshop but led him to promote the relationship between gay liberation and black civil rights at the store.

When Rodwell opened the store in 1967, it became an instant hit, attracting both gay men and lesbians. Within a short time, crowds began to show up on the weekends. Some patrons were locals, while others were tourists from elsewhere in the United States or even abroad. They had heard about the Oscar Wilde Memorial Bookshop at parties, from friends, from newspaper articles that Rodwell wrote, and from the journal *The New York Hymnal,* which he edited. Rodwell had personal relationships with superstar gay and lesbian writers like Rita Mae Brown, and literary luminaries like Tennessee Williams and Christopher Isherwood gave readings at the store. Rodwell hung photographs of them posing with the staff on the wall; in Isherwood's photo, the writer is holding Jonathan Ned Katz's book, *Gay American History.* In the corner of the store, Rodwell set up a table for free coffee and pastries. Regular customers returning from trips abroad would bring cookies and chocolates for other patrons.[23]

As part of his effort to promote positive images of gay people, Rodwell refused to stock pornography. He sold history books about the ancient Greeks, plays by Tennessee Williams, and manifestos like Sidney Abbott and Barbara Love's *Sappho Was a Right-on Woman*. As Rodwell emphasized, "My general policy was to be a shop where gay people didn't feel that they were being exploited either sexually or economically. . . . The reason I'm against most of the highly sexualized magazines, for example, is not the content particularly—although it's done rather leeringly—but the whole sexploitation angle. A ten-dollar piece in something that makes sex look dirty and furtive."[24]

Yet Rodwell was by no means a prude. As he once said, "People call me a puritan, and in a sense I have to agree with them. I don't mean I am puritan sexually—far from it." He cruised for sex in parks and on city streets. One night when he was out on the prowl for sex on the Upper West Side near Central Park, he met a young man who worked on Wall Street and whose conservative political views clashed with his progressive politics. Despite their political differences, they went on to have a romantic relationship. Each morning Rodwell's new boyfriend would phone him with a wake-up call and a joke. Yet one morning he did not call. Rodwell's boyfriend had discovered that he had contracted gonorrhea. Rodwell admitted that he had continued to have sex with other men despite being in love with his boyfriend.[25]

The boyfriend dumped Rodwell and eventually moved to San Francisco, which was a gay mecca. According to some accounts, Rodwell was so devastated by the breakup that he even contemplated suicide. Meanwhile, his boyfriend's politics moved to the left after his arrival in San Francisco. He ditched his conservatism and his suits and became a leading activist in San Francisco. He grew his hair long, wore beaded bracelets, and spoke the language of gay oppression. Perhaps Rodwell's politics had influenced him. His boyfriend opened a camera shop, which, like the Oscar Wilde Memorial Bookshop, soon became a political hub for the local gay community. Rodwell followed his ex-boyfriend's career, clipping articles that mentioned him and saving them in a neatly marked manila folder. Rodwell remained in love with him long after he left New York and always held a special place in his heart for this man, whom the rest of the world would soon come to know. His name was Harvey Milk.[26]

By both chance and inclination, Rodwell was at the center of gay liberation. On June 28, 1969, he and a friend were walking home from a bridge game when they heard noise coming from the Stonewall Inn; they dismissed it as another raid on the neighborhood's Mafia-run gay bars. But Rodwell soon realized that this was not a typical bar raid. A crowd of protesters began forming around the police wagon as the police handcuffed and hauled drag queens into the wagons. An irrepressible activist, Rodwell climbed onto the steps of the highest stoop and yelled, "Gay power!" and "Christopher Street belongs to the queens!" People in the crowd heard him and began chanting with him. Decades later, the historian Martin Duberman identified Craig Rodwell as one of the leading protagonists in the Stonewall uprising.[27]

The Stonewall riot may have signaled the start of gay liberation to the rest of the world, but Rodwell had been working hard for gay equality long before June 28, 1969. On April 26, 1966, for instance, in response to the New York Liquor Authority's prohibition on serving alcohol at institutions frequented by gay people, Rodwell, still a member of the Mattachine Society, had staged a "sip-in," along with Dick Leitsch and John Timmons. They went to a number of bars in the Village and boldly proclaimed that they were homosexuals and demanded to be served. Most of the bars obliged.[28]

For Rodwell, Stonewall represented not the start of gay liberation but a turning point in the gay struggle that gave gay people an opportunity to publicly cultivate a sense of community. In a letter that he wrote to gay people in New York about the importance of the Oscar Wilde Memorial Bookshop for the community, he explained: "Never before in history have thousands of people, such as yourself, begun the struggle to ease the effects of heterosexism from our world and to help create a society where men can love men instead of competing with them for power over women or money or government, where women can love women instead of competing with other women for approval of 'their men' or playing the role of servant to man." In an effort to capture the political momentum of the Stonewall uprising, Rodwell planned the first-ever gay pride march in New York City on Christopher Street, modeled after gay rights demonstrations that took place in Philadelphia in the late 1960s. He wanted the march to memorialize the Stonewall riot, so he proposed to hold it on the last Sunday of June in 1970. He emphasized that the march would be open to gay people of all ages and that there would be no "dress regulations"—a stark departure from previous gay protests and marches, which had enforced strict guidelines on who could attend and how they could dress. Some of the homophile groups of the 1950s and 1960s, trying to avoid the press's and the public's quick tendency to see gay people as deviant, adopted the practice of some black civil rights activists of appearing more "respectable" at marches. According to Rodwell, Stonewall had made gay people bolder and more open, however, and allowed them to be themselves. Many years later, Kay Tobin, a leading lesbian activist, wrote Rodwell a letter that captured the revolutionary fervor of the early marches in the 1970s and the new identity politics unleashed by Stonewall. "I feel the founding of the bookstore cannot be fully appreciated by today's activists, nor can they realize what a big step out of the closet the first pickets were. The squabbling over the dress code beside the larger issue keeping gay people from picketing—fear of the consequences. Thank goodmen we were all in the bandful of people with the guts to go public."[29]

Rodwell and Tobin would be comrades in the fight for gay liberation for many decades. Their alliance began a year after the Stonewall riot, when Tobin sent Rodwell a one-page typed letter asking him if she could interview him for a book, *The Gay Crusaders,* "on the leaders and foremost personalities in the gay movement." Tobin recognized the political significance of the Oscar Wilde Memorial Bookshop as a community center that embodied the hope and spirit of gay liberation. Her questions for Rodwell focused less on the books he sold and more on how his activism had inspired him to open the bookshop. Tobin and her coauthor, Randy Wicker, devoted a chapter to Rodwell's energetic contributions to the movement and his founding of the bookstore. In 1972, less than two years after the interview, Arno Press, a progressive publishing house, published *The Gay Crusaders*.[30]

The publication of *The Gay Crusaders* brought international recognition of Rodwell and the Oscar Wilde Memorial Bookshop. Rodwell had already been an active contributor to gay magazines, newspapers, and journals, but *The Gay Crusaders* turned him into a celebrity. Gay men, in particular, across the United States and around the world, responded to the book's portrait of Rodwell and the Oscar Wilde Memorial Bookshop. A reader from Wesleyville, Pennsylvania, a small borough in Erie County, was so moved that he wrote to Rodwell: "I bought the book 'The Gay Crusaders' and read it from cover to cover. I've bought a lot of books in my time, but 'The Gay Crusaders' has to be the best of them all." He added that, inspired by the authors' dedication to the "Gay Crusaders of the Future," "I long to be one of the future gay crusaders."[31]

The letter writer was also thrilled to learn that Rodwell "counseled young men." Rodwell intended the bookstore to serve many functions, including providing help to young men as they came to terms with their sexuality. The young reader sought Rodwell's advice as he navigated his way out of the closet and also thanked him for reading his letter. He went on to say that his own hobbies and interests were similar to those that Rodwell had mentioned in *The Gay Crusaders* interview. "I like most of all the things you do," he wrote. "I like beer, ballet, the beach, and reading. I am not interested in baseball, but I like to watch Buffalo Roller Derby on TV."[32]

The young man ended the letter by thanking Rodwell again for reading it. "You've been so kind to me, and I want to thank you again for taking time to read this. Please answer my letter soon." He signed the letter "Faithfully Yours" and enclosed a necklace for Rodwell. "Some necklaces stand for peace," he said in a postscript, "but this one stands for 'Gay Power!' and the friendship between you and I."

He ended with: "I've read about you, you've become my idol, and I look up to you with admiration."[33]

A few months later, Rodwell received a similar letter from a reader in San Francisco. This fan had also read *The Gay Crusaders* and had actually been to the Oscar Wilde Memorial Bookshop when it first opened. He began the letter by reminiscing: "I recall when you opened your shop. So many of my friends had visited you and encouraged you in what you were doing for all of us in those days. . . . [When] I first walked into your shop . . . I felt, at long last, [a] sense of belonging to a larger community." He explained that even in San Francisco there was no bookstore or any other place akin to the Oscar Wilde Memorial Bookshop and also criticized the degree to which sex dominated gay culture in San Francisco. "The market is glutted with the usual trashy gay sex novels and the ever present 'big dick' slick magazines. I suppose they all serve some sort of purpose as pornography, but they certainly don't install a sense of pride in the gay person. Actually, they contribute, at least from my point of view, to gay oppression."[34]

A college student from Allentown, Pennsylvania, wrote to Rodwell in 1969 offering to help the bookstore "in any way possible." "I have worked as a library assistant at school," he wrote. "I have been in NYC often, I know what it is like. I am butch, I get along with all people, I am honest and I am creative—I have ideas which I think may help our movement," he explained.[35] The dozens of letters like this that Rodwell received proved to him that the bookstore was important, and they inspired him to persevere when he faced rent hikes and other challenges.[36] He surely had similar conversations with customers who came to his store over its forty-two-year tenure in the Village. Those encounters undoubtedly reinforced one of the most heartfelt messages of these letters: that many gay men wanted more out of liberation than just sex.

In the spring of 1972, Rodwell received a letter from a customer from New Haven that delivered a polemic against the sexual culture of the 1970s. "What would happen if, instead of picketing City Hall and upsetting the Bourgeois with parades, we picketed the male theatres and dirty-book shops that reduce so many of us to blithering idiots and boycotted the bars and baths?"[37] For many gay men in the seventies, greater access to gay sex had not been the panacea for oppression that many had thought it would be. In fact, as Rodwell's correspondents suggest, the elevation of sex as the hallmark of liberation had replaced—at least for some men—one form of oppression with another. Many gay men were not comforted by sex, and some did not feel comfortable in a world that overemphasized physical appearance. Some were not interested in sex all the time and wanted more out of liberation than a night at the baths.

Rodwell himself walked a fine line between sex and politics. He did not oppose anonymous or frequent sex, but he did fear that sex could become the only way in which gay men interacted with one another. As he once explained, "Sex is damned important to everyone, hetero, or Gay. But the question we should be asking is, do we overemphasize the sexual part of our being Gay males at the expense of developing social, cultural and group contacts between us?"[38] Establishing the Oscar Wilde Memorial Bookshop was Rodwell's answer to this question.

The light of the Oscar Wilde Memorial Bookshop radiated around the world. It became a destination for Europeans visiting New York City, and even many people who did not make it to the store in person wrote from as far away as Iceland and Hungary, asking Rodwell for book recommendations. The store also had a following among American soldiers stationed in Vietnam. Gay soldiers read about the Oscar Wilde Memorial Bookshop in *Queen's Quarterly* and sent letters to Rodwell, requesting books and magazine subscriptions. Some soldiers learned about the bookstore from friends in the United States, who passed along Rodwell's name and address to them. "I saw the article about you and your bookstore in *Queen's Quarterly* and was very impressed," wrote one American soldier stationed in Vietnam.

> It's so good to know someone is really working to honestly improve the outlook for gay life. I feel especially interested in this because I've been cut off from gay life completely for 6

months now—I'm in the army in Vietnam and I have found life completely meaningless over here—the company I'm in is small and consequently everyone tries to outdo the other in masculinity, etc. I'm not sure why I'm writing you—I guess loneliness has something to do with it.

For this anonymous soldier, the Oscar Wilde Memorial Bookshop represented hope, possibility, and community.[39]

A radio and switchboard operator stationed in Long Binh, a military outpost near Saigon, wrote to tell Rodwell that he hoped to visit the Oscar Wilde Memorial Bookshop soon. He explained that he would be back in the United States for a month before he reenlisted and wanted to come by the bookstore "to buy some more things" before he returned to Vietnam. Books and magazines offered him solace, keeping him connected to "the movement" and to the people he knew in New York City who were fighting for liberation. Yet, for him, the New York City streets where gay men lived and congregated seemed more dangerous than Vietnam. "I'm probably safer here," he told Rodwell, "than in New York."[40]

Indeed, despite the political fervor of liberation—and perhaps because of it—it was not safe to be gay in New York City. In the middle of the summer of 1970, Rodwell started receiving multiple letters with no return address. He was accustomed to receiving letters from people he did not know, asking for advice and offering thanks, but those letters almost always came with a return address, since the letter-writers hoped Rodwell would respond. Little did Rodwell realize that the death threats in these anonymous letters would soon lead to an FBI investigation. One letter from July 30, 1970, read:

> . . . You white fucking pigs your both going to hell when I get done . . . You queers are going to die, no matter how long it takes, your both doomed to die. I'll blow your minds apart if I have to, but you pigs won't continue to fuck each other while I have any thing to say about it . . .
>
> . . . I hope I aint got none of your diseases cause your dead your dead any way.

We intend to put that fucking book store that you working at, out of biz, and we can and will do it. We'll ruin you . . . you dirty scum pig queer whore master dog fag.[41]

The letter did not end there. The letter-writer described cutting, burning, and torturing the staff of the bookstore, emphasizing that he would offer no mercy in killing them and would do everything possible to maximize their suffering.

Amid the deranged threats was one clue pointing to the motivation, if not the identity, of the letter-writer. In a July 23 letter, he had written: "When I get done with you, you ain't gonna get away with stealing my man." The writer leveled this accusation at someone named Jack; claiming that "Jack and Terry" were "fag lovers," he says throughout the letters that he will kill them both. At times, he suggests that he won't hurt Terry as badly as Jack, though he still plans to murder Terry. The letter-writer mentions in one of the letters that Terry answered the phone when he telephoned the store to threaten to kill Jack. There is no surviving evidence of what either Jack or Terry said when talking to the author of the letters.[42]

The letter-writer was apparently a scorned lover, but the reference to the lost relationship is mentioned only briefly—a few sentences in a collection of letters that span well over twenty-five pages. Over the course of the letters, the writer became less invested in avenging his lost relationship and more interested in destroying one of the few visible symbols of gay culture in 1970s New York: the Oscar Wilde Memorial Bookshop. Focusing his rage on the bookshop and the "queer whoremasters" who worked in it, he threatened to destroy the store for promoting gay liberation and to kill the staff for being gay.

After the first letter arrived, Rodwell contacted the New York City Police Department (NYPD). The police arrived at the bookstore, looked over the letters, and filed a report of the incident. Because the threats came through the mail and had crossed state lines (they were postmarked in New Jersey), the NYPD probably turned the case over to the US Post Office authorities and the FBI. The FBI sent Special Agent Thomas J. McCrystle to investigate the case and a few days later sent Rodwell a letter of its own, stating that it would not investigate the case any further.[43]

We will never know why the authorities refused to investigate the case, and we will never know who the anonymous letter writer was. But even more perplexing is that we will never know to whom the death threats were actually directed. The letters were not addressed to Rodwell, but to "Jack" and "Terry." No employees with those names are mentioned in the surviving records of the store. In fact, at the time Rodwell manned the shop himself seven days a week, from noon to 10:00 PM, because he was unable to afford additional help. As the store expanded, Rodwell would become seriously involved with an unnamed man, who eventually worked at the store with Rodwell, splitting shifts with him but sometimes working alongside him. Were "Jack" and "Terry" aliases for Rodwell and his boyfriend?[44]

"Jack" may have been a fake name that Rodwell used. At some point, Rodwell may have admitted to being Jack, as the letter from the FBI was addressed to him. If so, that might explain why the FBI refused to investigate the case further: if Rodwell admitted to being Jack, the FBI may have dismissed the case as an instance of gay drama.

The fact that Rodwell kept the letters raises more questions. It's surprising, for instance, that no other material relating to this incident can be found in the voluminous collection of his papers, which includes over a dozen boxes of correspondence, newspaper articles, and other documents. Rodwell consistently wrote about and documented anything and everything about gay life in New York City. If the *New York Times* ran an article that mentioned the word "gay"— whether about medicine, religion, the law, or any other subject— Rodwell clipped it and filed it away.[45] Among his papers are clips from the *New York Times,* the *New York Post,* and *The Village Voice,* ranging from full-page reports on gay men being mysteriously murdered in the Village during the seventies to an entire folder dedicated to the late 1970s film *Cruising,* about a gay serial killer in New York.[46]

Rodwell did not just collect articles about gay people; he also wrote to the leading papers in New York about gay life in the Village, often to inform editors about homophobic incidents and crimes. He did not shy away from controversy and on many occasions strenuously defended the reputation of gay people against the media's lurid accounts. He wrote to US representatives and municipal officials on a range of topics that affected gay New Yorkers, from crimes committed against gay people to the annual gay pride march. In 1970 he even sent New York mayor John Lindsay a complimentary subscription to the magazine *The New York Hymnal,* a periodical he founded to support gay youth. His prolific achievements and active involvement in supporting gay people in New York eventually earned him letters of commendation from Mayor David Dinkins's office in 1993.[47]

For someone who so assiduously tracked gay life in the city, it is odd that Rodwell's records reveal little about his own apparent brush with violence and crime. Rodwell may have been a public gay activist, but he seems to have kept his sexual activities private. It's possible he circulated as "Jack" in the underground sex world of the time to protect his public identity. When he was a fourteen-year-old in Chicago, he met a thirty-year-old dishwasher at a cruising spot. The two went to a motel to have sex, and on their way out they were both arrested. Rodwell was let go with minor charges since he was a youth, but the dishwasher was sent to prison. The experience haunted Rodwell for many years. "I've often wanted to find him and somehow make up for what the court did to him. I couldn't understand the governmental interference. It made no sense whatsoever to me at the time."[48]

Whoever sent the letters, and whomever they were addressed to, they do carry a larger significance. Stories of men feeling scorned by male lovers are probably as old as stories of men feeling scorned by women or women feeling scorned by men. What represents a seismic shift in this episode is the existence of the first-ever gay bookstore, which was founded not in the service of pornographic fantasy but as part of the broader mission of gay liberation. The Oscar Wilde Memorial Bookshop fostered a sense of community and culture that sustained thousands upon thousands of gay people. The bookstore was a major pillar of gay life in New York, and it served as a touchstone for gay people across the world.

Yet all of this attention came at a cost. As soon as Rodwell established the Oscar Wilde Memorial Bookshop, it became a public and immobile target for homophobic attacks, which historically had occurred outside of gay bars and bathhouses, in parks, and on city streets. The city's bars and bathhouses had unmarked doors and pitch-black windows, but the Oscar Wilde Memorial Bookshop was a public cultural site that made its purpose clear. It boldly proclaimed itself as an institution exclusively devoted to gay people.

The threatening letters probably would never have been written, much less delivered, if Rodwell didn't have a public mailing address. Rodwell's creation of a storefront quite literally made him and his employees much more vulnerable to attack.[49] Rodwell was often greeted in the morning by epithets written on the windows and storefront of the shop. A swastika was once chalked on the pavement outside the store. Rodwell frequently received abusive letters and phone calls that "usually consist of blunt sexual overtones (I want a blow job)," he explained, "or threats of violence (Cocksucking faggot, I hate you and I'm going to burn that shop down)." One year he had to cancel his trip home for Christmas because some person or group had vandalized the store. "I had just flown home to Chicago, and my mother met me at the airport, and she was in tears. She'd just gotten a call from NY that the shop was broken into and trashed, and I had to get on the next plane back."[50]

Attacks on the Oscar Wilde Memorial Bookshop continued throughout the seventies. One particularly violent attack occurred on August 1, 1977. On what was a warm summer day, an unidentified man stood and watched customers walking in and out of the store. His awkward presence—alone on Christopher Street observing the hustle and bustle of people on a Saturday afternoon—would not have struck Rodwell or his customers as unusual. It was the familiar behavior of men in the process of coming out of the closet. They would study a store, a bar, or a cruising park before making an entrance. However, unlike such men, who would fidget nervously with their hands in their pockets, avoiding eye contact with passersby and repeatedly checking the time on their wristwatches, this man held "a large jagged rock." He lifted his arm and hurled it at the large glass storefront window.

The window burst, sending glass shards into the store and bouncing off the sidewalk. Customers screamed and scrambled for cover. Nancy Jachim, a part-time employee, scanned the street, looking for the person who had thrown the rock. Spotting the likely culprit, she pushed through the dazed customers and chased him down Christopher Street. The man made a left onto Waverly. Jachim followed him. He sprinted down Waverly and then darted across Sixth Avenue, running between buses and honking taxis. Jachim did not let him out of her sight. He raced to Washington Square, where he attempted to hide among some of the old men playing chess, the children gathered near the fountain, and the aspiring musicians drawing a crowd. Jachim spotted him nonetheless. Knowing she could not approach him on her own, she noticed a police officer in the crowd and quickly explained what had happened. The officer approached the rock-thrower and arrested him.

The next day Jachim and Rodwell went to criminal court to see the man arraigned. They spent nine hours waiting for justice to be served. The rock-thrower told the authorities he was a "gay activist."

"A play on words," Rodwell muttered.

Rodwell and Jachim were not given the opportunity to testify in court. They did not get to explain to the judge that a customer in the store had been so badly injured by the attack that he had to be hospitalized immediately. They did not get to explain the sheer terror that everyone felt when the storefront window shattered, not knowing if it was a bomb or a bullet or a rock that had broken through the glass. And they certainly did not get to express how traumatized they remained long after the crushed glass had been swept up and they had gone home. The court did not hear any of this. The judge quickly imposed a small fine on the rock-thrower and had him released.[51]

Rodwell and the staff hoped that was the end of the saga, but the rock-thrower continued to show up at the Oscar Wilde Memorial Bookshop and terrorize the staff and clientele. Sometimes he would stand across the street from the shop, yelling derogatory names and slurs at anyone who approached the store. At one point he threatened to shoot the customers. A neighboring store owner called the police once to report him. The police did nothing.

Rodwell took measures to protect his staff. He installed shatterproof windows and hired a security guard. He coached his staff on what to do if another assault occurred. Despite these precautions, the men and women who worked in the store remained scared. They had signed on to working at a bookshop where they could talk about gay literature and work closely with customers who were seeking political solidarity and intellectual engagement. Yet they came to work every day frightened that they would be attacked.

The staff's anxiety could be all-encompassing. One night as the store was about to close, the only remaining customer, a tourist from Bethlehem, Pennsylvania, was browsing through the small section of albums and asked a female clerk about a particular record. She said that the store did not have the record. He continued to ask her about it. She could not determine if he was genuinely looking for the album or if he was "baiting" her. According to Rodwell, people would come into the store posing as interested customers but would ask for items that were not gay-related simply to antagonize the staff. This clerk sensed that this was the case with the man from Bethlehem. The two exchanged a few final abrupt words, and he left in a huff, saying that he hadn't thought the store would carry the album anyway.[52]

In the end, this customer proved to be innocent. He was not trying to bait the clerk, but the rash of assaults on the store had made her doubt his motivations. He wrote an irate letter to Rodwell complaining about her "rude" behavior. Interestingly, he knew about the assaults on the Oscar Wilde Memorial Bookshop and rightly assumed that her reaction to him was in large part due to the violence inflicted on the bookstore. Yet he thought that her fear was no excuse for her to be "discourteous." He admonished Rodwell, writing that antigay forces could claim victory when gay people suffered "from fear and/or paranoia."[53]

Characteristically, Rodwell wrote back. He first apologized for his "unpleasant experience," but then explained that with "the physical assaults and threats of assaults against our workers . . . all of us are a little edgy and wary." Rodwell maintained that "our need for strict security must override the occasional bruised egos we encounter." The customer's letter had ended by stating that he would never again shop at the Oscar Wilde Memorial Bookshop. This was not the first time Rodwell had heard such a comment from a gay customer. Telling the offended customer that he regretted that he would not visit his New York shop again, Rodwell encouraged him to visit Giovanni's Room, a gay bookstore modeled after the Oscar Wilde Memorial Bookshop in Philadelphia, not far from Bethlehem.[54]

Rodwell had opened the Oscar Wilde Memorial Bookshop because he wanted to promote the idea that "gay is good," in the words of the popular slogan, but such a simple message had invited violence and harassment, as well as a lack of sympathy from some members of the gay community. He was not terribly shocked by the violence committed against the store; as he once explained, "I expected some of that, so it came as no surprise." In New Orleans at the Up Stairs Lounge, at gay religious sites across the country, and at the first gay bookstore in the nation, violence became the uninvited companion to gay liberation. Those on the front lines who had devoted their lives to publicly supporting the movement, people like Rev. Troy Perry and Craig Rodwell, were particularly vulnerable to attacks by those who aggressively opposed them.[55]

Sometimes the battles that took place at the Oscar Wilde Memorial Bookshop were not so visible as a threat scribbled on a piece of paper and mailed to the store or a crazed stranger lurking outside the store and holding a rock. Instead, many battles were waged internally as gay men and women stared nervously into the bookstore from across the street and struggled to muster the courage to walk into it for the first time. No one crossed the threshold of the Oscar Wilde Memorial Bookshop who had not already been engaged in a battle against homophobia. But nothing inside the bookstore allowed them to conceal their identity or camouflage their desires. There was no bartender serving alcohol that could dampen their anxiety, nor were there any naked go-go boys who could distract them from feeling awkward; there were no darkened corners where they could hide or have sex.

Instead, the books on the shelf forced them to come face-to-face with their sexuality. Once opened, however, these books could offer comfort. The characters in the novels could inspire kinship, and the history books could connect them to the men and women who had gone down the same difficult path before them. But the initial foray into the bookstore still took courage, whether to brave the views of mainstream society or to engage gay culture by going beyond the unfettered sex granted by liberation.

Sometime in the early 1970s, a young man who had grown up in Greenwich Village and seen the changing world of gay liberation from his bedroom window on Bank Street summoned enough courage to walk into the Oscar Wilde Memorial Bookshop. As an avid reader, he realized that the only way he would come to terms with being gay was to read about it. So he walked a few blocks across the neighborhood to the bookshop, but he was too nervous to go inside. As he recalled, "I walked around the corner twice before going in the first time. I was just getting involved and investigating the gay movement. It was just the beginning."[56]

Even in a bohemian place like Greenwich Village, the only place for him to get his hands on a book about gay life was the Oscar Wilde Memorial Bookshop. How did he first come to know about it? Had the store run an ad in *The Village Voice?* Had a friend told him? Had he read about the bookshop in a leftist pamphlet? Years later, he would not be able to remember.[57]

He finally found the resolve to walk into the store. Within a few short years, he would become a prominent author, and his book would be showcased on the shelves of the Oscar Wilde Memorial Bookshop. His name was Jonathan Ned Katz, and his book, *Gay American History,* became an instant classic.

But the day he walked into Craig Rodwell's bookstore, he was just an ordinary gay person in search of a culture, a safe haven, and a book that would help him deal with his sexuality.

4 *GAY AMERICAN HISTORY*

Once inside the Oscar Wilde Memorial Bookshop, Jonathan Ned Katz began reading a pamphlet about gay liberation. It was not about the Stonewall uprising, but about a gay community in Germany in the midnineteenth century. He was dumbfounded. The son of political radicals and an avid bibliophile, Katz knew a great deal about history, not only from books but from discussions with his brother William, a writer and book editor, and his father Bernard, a labor activist who took classes with the preeminent radical historian Herbert Aptheker. But he had never heard about this community in Germany.[1]

Gay culture in the United States in the 1970s, Katz had assumed, was something new and revolutionary, something that had just begun in the wake of the black civil rights and women's movements. But the fifty-page pamphlet he held in his hands told a different story. It revealed that long before World War II, gay culture had thrived in a place that was viewed in the United States in the 1970s as the embodiment of oppression and evil. How was it possible that of all the nations in Europe, Germany, home of Hitler and the Holocaust, had given birth to a more radical gay world than that in Greenwich Village in the 1970s? As Katz turned the pages of the pamphlet, "The Early Homosexual Rights Movement (1864–1935)," which had been written by two gay American activists and scholars, he read about gay men fighting for acceptance, policymakers debating the meaning of homosexuality, and a doctor by the name of Magnus Hirschfeld, who had been one of the first and most vocal advocates for gay rights in the world.

By the middle of the nineteenth century, as Germany began to unite as a nation, it developed a legal code that made homosexuality illegal. A number of Germans protested this legislation, not only in the language of rights but in that of medicine. Hirschfeld, the son of a highly regarded Jewish physician, had trained to be a doctor at several European universities, including Heidelberg University, Germany's oldest university. He believed that science and medicine could help explain homosexuality. He began writing on the subject. One of the most famous treatises he produced, "Sappho and Socrates," focused on homosexual love and intimacy. Arguing that both sexes had the neural centers to be attracted to both men and women and that "sex was multidimensional, and 'male' and 'female' were abstractions," Hirschfeld began a massive effort to catalog various forms of sexual behavior.[2] In 1897 he founded the Scientific Humanitarian Committee and later, in 1919, the Institute for Sexual Research with the hope that scientific advancement could prevent the further criminalization of gay people in Germany. Urging gay men "to come out" and thereby emancipate themselves, Hirschfeld also organized a major petition to the German government to overturn legislation that criminalized gay people. The petition won the support of over 5,000 Germans, including notable scientists such as Albert Einstein.[3]

Deeply fascinated by this lost figure, Katz wanted to learn everything about Hirschfeld and the gay culture he defended and tried to help in nineteenth-century Berlin. Previously, Katz had "had no inkling that this world existed." Here was a highly prominent physician who only a century earlier had devised a scientific theory of homosexuality sympathetic to the plight of gay people. That doctor, as well as that theory, had supported gay people in developing a vibrant culture and identity in Berlin. *How do we not know about this?* he wondered.[4]

Katz soon learned that Hitler's emergence in Germany had spelled the end of this world. Hitler issued orders to his subordinates to hunt down and imprison gay people in the 1930s, summarily eradicating the culture that Hirschfeld had helped to create as well as many of the documents produced by his institute. The slender pamphlet that Katz found at the Oscar Wilde Memorial Bookshop represented one of the few accounts of this forgotten world.

It's a sunny day in late May 2012. Katz is still living in the Village, now in an apartment with a cracked cement stoop and a narrow Victorian door, tucked away on Jane Street, one of the few streets in New York City where trees cast a shadow on an entire row of brownstones. Katz sits in his living room facing the window, which looks out on the street. He is wearing a pair of shorts, a T-shirt, sandals. His legs are crossed. Silhouettes of male bodies that he has painted hang high on the walls in the living room and in the sitting room behind it. A late springtime breeze comes in from his studio in the back of his home.

Katz recalls that day at the Oscar Wilde Memorial Bookshop almost a half-century ago. He tries to remember the exact location of the store, but can't—was it the original location on Mercer Street or the second on Christopher Street? He can remember the anxiety he felt as he circled the block, trying to find enough courage to walk in. He smiles as he recalls his hesitation. Once in the store, he remembers, he saw *The Body Politic*, the now-defunct Toronto-based gay newspaper, on the shelf. He praises the newspaper for its intelligent articles, and the tone of his voice conveys his sorrow at the newspaper's demise. As his memories unfold of the first day he walked into the Oscar Wilde Memorial Bookshop, the past feels like a secret family heirloom passed on from one generation to the next.

He then stops reminiscing. Lifting his eyes to look out the window to the tree-lined street, he begins to speak again but his voice cracks and tears come to his eyes. He pauses. A frisson of indignation cuts through his emotions, and his voice steadies. He props his slender body up in the small wooden chair and firmly asserts that he wrote *Gay American History,* the first history of gay life in the United States, because "this might be our only chance."[5] To do that, he says, he read about the Nazis suppressing any reference to homosexuality in the past, destroying a scientific institute dedicated to the study of sexuality, and burning books about gay life in Germany. He had feared that something similar would happen in the United States.

Collecting his thoughts, Katz explains why he became a historian. He recounts a scene from *Life of Galileo,* Bertolt Brecht's short play about Galileo's imprisonment during the Inquisition. The Roman Catholic Church authorities have imprisoned Galileo for his belief in heliocentrism and are threatening to torture Galileo if he continues to promote this idea. Galileo ultimately gives in, but at the last minute passes along his thesis notes to his assistant, who spirits them out of the country.

"I find it so moving," Katz says, "because that's the way we felt. This might be our only chance to sneak everything we learned into this book. This might be the only chance. I find it extremely moving, passing on the information against the people who wanted to suppress it." He decided to become a historian to ensure that his people's history would not be forgotten.[6]

In the summer of 1975, Katz was living in a spacious apartment, rented for $150 a month, at Bank Street and West Fourth Street. He had grown up a few blocks away in a brownstone, where his bedroom window looked out onto a patio and down into the yard. Twenty-four years earlier, he had become a celebrity of sorts in that yard: at thirteen, he had directed a film version of *Tom Sawyer* starring the kids in the neighborhood. *Life* magazine even did a feature story on him titled "*Life* Visits a Back-yard Movie Set."[7] But by the 1970s his ambitions had shifted from film and fiction to preparing for a revolution. Now, every Saturday night, he met with a group of like-minded companions—members of the Gay Socialist Action Project (GSAP), gay intellectuals who discussed and debated how they could make their dreams of liberation into reality.

Katz waited all week for Saturday night to come. It was thrilling to be in a room with men who shared his desires and hopes. The tiny sliver of New York City where he lived was undergoing a rapid transformation. Greenwich Village had been home to scores of intellectuals, writers, artists, and musicians since the turn of the century, and in more recent decades it had given rise to the Beat poets and Bob Dylan. Katz had come of age in the neighborhood. As a young boy, his parents had sent him to the Little Red School House, an independent school that was a refuge for those targeted by Sen. Joseph McCarthy's Communist witch-hunts and other dissidents. Now, post-Stonewall, the neighborhood was being shaped by the promise of gay liberation.[8]

On his way to the Gay Socialist Action Project meeting in Morningside Heights, Katz would walk to the subway along West Fourth Street in the Village and feel the effects of the new transformation. More and more gay men crowded onto the streets where even months before they would have been too fearful to linger. On hot summer nights, some walked around shirtless, while others wore only leather vests, showing off their hairy chests and muscled bodies. Katz passed by Abington Square, where gay denizens watched the weekend tourists arriving wide-eyed, many of them having come expressly to stare at the men dressed in denim. These men sat and waited for the sky to darken, for night to fall, and for the chance to walk a few blocks west toward the piers and the abandoned trucks, where they would have anonymous sex. Katz would brush by them as he rushed to catch the subway. This was not his idea of being gay. "Everyone went crazy in the piers," he said.[9]

Instead, he read. In the early 1970s Katz was a textile artist, but the other artists he knew were "counterculture" and "liberal." "I was not part of the East Side arts scene, I was more scholarly," he explained. "The closet fosters reading," he added.[10]

Katz read everything that he could get his hands on, and Karl Marx became his intellectual and political companion. "I read every page of *Kapital* and made notes about every sentence. I asked questions. I educated myself by arguing with Marx." Despite his affinity for Marx, he struggled to find political alliances in Greenwich Village, or even among his artist friends in the East Village. So he took the subway to Morningside Heights, home to Columbia University, to be with a group of gay intellectuals. He would wait underground, where the air smelled of rotten food and urine, for the graffiti-painted train that would take him uptown. The weekend trains invariably ran late. When he finally arrived at the stop at 110th and Broadway, he would head to the apartment of John D'Emilio, a Columbia graduate student in history, overlooking Morningside Park. The meeting would already be under way, with about a dozen men gathered in the living room and a pot of spaghetti boiling in the kitchen. They sat on couches made of pillows and twin beds in a living room painted with bright yellow, red, orange, and blue stripes. A beaded curtain hung in the entrance to the room.[11]

The members of the Gay Socialist Action Project were activists, intellectuals, writers, and historians who understood how the past and their politics had shaped their identity. They had gathered to read and debate Marx because they were searching for a theoretical framework for what it meant to be gay and for instructions on how to launch a revolution. They hoped that Marx, as well as the burgeoning literature on civil rights and feminism, would offer guidance. Marx was the topic du jour among the political and intellectual left during the 1970s; his theories were taken up by marginal groups of all kinds that sought to upend existing power structures. At the time, the power structures that formed the primary opposition to gay liberation were religious and medical authorities. The medical community, like Magnus Hirschfeld's opponents, pathologized homosexuality as a disorder, while many religious organizations demonized gay men and women.[12]

From Marx, the GSAP learned to more closely examine the structures that produced power rather than refute the pronouncements of priests and doctors line by line. They learned that homophobia was less about what a priest declaimed from a pulpit and more about the fact that the priest had the power to make such a claim; similarly, it was less about doctors labeling gay people "degenerates" in medical textbooks and more about doctors having the authority to put forth a theory as verifiable truth. The members of GSAP came to see that gay people's alleged aberrance did not make them oppressed, but rather that their oppression made them appear aberrant.[13]

Katz described coming home from the meetings feeling discombobulated. It was "a huge, amazing change," he said. "I was experiencing a change in my self-conception and conceptions of gays in a very short time." Growing up, he and the other members had all been taught that homosexuality was a sickness that could be treated by psychologists, but as the Gay Socialist Action Project was now beginning to argue, that was not the case. *Oh my God,* Katz remembered thinking. *Was I stupid to fall for that idea that I was sick?* Sitting on secondhand furniture in a crowded apartment, members of the reading group came to understand that they were not sick, but oppressed. To make that distinction was "mind-blowing," Katz recalled. "I would get dizzy and have to lie down."[14]

Katz began to reach some other important conclusions. He soon realized that different "models" had been developed over time to explain the phenomenon of men being intimate with other men. The first was the religious model, under which authorities meted out "harsh penalties" to those who committed sodomy. Katz noted that the language reflected the model: religious authorities used the word "sodomy," whereas the medical model, the second model to be developed, invented a scientific lexicon to describe same-sex relations. The term "homosexuality" dated from the late nineteenth century. By charting how different periods defined same-sex relations, Katz came to further understand how those in power oppressed gay people.

Katz and his activist and scholar friends added their own model to the mix. They called it the "political" model, out of recognition that their predicament resulted from the various political structures that had power to define gay people. As Katz explained, when it came to discussing homosexuality in the 1970s, what mattered was "whose word, whose concept" informed the discussion. To disarm the exclusive power claimed by the medical community, religious leaders, and other powerful authorities to define gay people in the 1970s, GSAP members realized, they would need to invent their own definitions of gay identity and culture so that it would be their word, their concept, that defined homosexuality.

On April 6, 1976, Katz and the members of the GSAP decided to speak for themselves at a meeting sponsored by the Association for Psychoanalytic Medicine, which was holding a panel to explore "The Psychodynamics of Male Homosexuality" at the New York Academy of Medicine. As a group of over 200 gay activists protested in the streets outside the Academy's doors on the Upper East Side of Manhattan, Katz and his cohort, wearing suits, sneaked into the meeting through a back entrance. They took seats in the crowded auditorium acting as if they were meeting attendees. When one of the doctors used the term "misplaced fantasies," a GSAP member stood up from his chair and blew a whistle. The doctor paused briefly. When he continued to read his paper, another member popped up from his chair and heckled him. The panel speakers became silent. Katz and the other GSAP members took turns reading from a historically informed manifesto that they had written about the medical community's condemnation of homosexuality.[15]

> Did German Jews have a moral obligation to debate Nazi theorists' ideas of Jewish inferiority? Did Southern slaves have the obligation to meet with apologists for slavery and argue whether Blacks were really inferior? Do Gay men and women in 1976 have the moral duty to discuss with the psychological ideologues of homosexuality inferiority whether homosexuals are "diseased," "pathological," "immature," or only "neurotic"?[16]

Each reader of the manifesto cited a historical example of the ways in which the medical community pathologized homosexuality. When they neared their conclusion, one stated, "Some of us have died." Another said, "Despite the mad and evil scientists, some of us survived." Then, as a chorus, they all announced, "Some of us decided to revolt."

The doctors abruptly ended the program and stepped down from the stage. Katz and the Gay Socialist Action Project had made their point, exposing the prejudicial and unscientific history and nature of the medical model. They had challenged the doctors' medical authority and used history to demonstrate their oppression.[17]

To expose the oppression of gay people, Katz and others drew comparisons between the rising gay movement and the black civil rights struggle and the women's liberation movement. This analogy enabled Katz and the Gay Socialist Action Project to borrow the framework and language used by black people and by women in fighting for equality. Of course, the members of the Gay Socialist Action Project were not the first or the only gay intellectuals to make these comparisons. Craig Rodwell, as we have seen, understood the connections among oppressed peoples in the United States. Others did too. As a gay man wrote in *The New York Hymnal,* "Homosexuals are sick like Negroes are inferior. We realize now how absurd we were about races: we left no job open to the colored woman but scrubbing floors and then we looked down on her because she was a scrubwoman. We know now that inferiority was imposed upon the Negroes, it was not intrinsic."[18]

For Katz, drawing these connections hit home—literally. He had grown up in a household that constantly stressed the links among history, politics, and activism. His father's labor activism had resulted in his being marked by the FBI as a suspected Communist. When I asked about his father's affiliations and background, Katz hesitated and then quipped, "I come from the fifties, I should not give names."[19]

One of the names that he did mention was that of the historian Herbert Aptheker, whom he credited as a major influence on his father's political development. Aptheker ranks as one of the leading historians of the twentieth century, but when Bernard Katz met him in the 1950s Aptheker's affiliation with the Communist Party had gotten him blacklisted in academia. Eventually, Aptheker started teaching an evening course at the Jefferson School of Social Sciences, an institution designed to educate full-time laborers. It was there that Katz's father learned about the struggles of the marginalized and dispossessed. Aptheker had been an early pioneer in African American history and wrote his master's thesis on Nat Turner's slave rebellion of 1831—a subject that made its way into his lectures at the Jefferson School and then into dinner conversations in the Katz household.[20]

Katz and his brother, William, became enthralled with their father's history lessons. Their interest in black history developed alongside their interest in the civil rights movement. "Society was trying to understand why blacks were angry," Katz recounted. Studying the past became a way for the Katz family to understand the broader struggles that black Americans had faced in the four centuries since they had first been enslaved in the New World. Katz's brother published an anthology of black protest literature, *Eyewitness: A Living Documentary of the African American Contribution to American History*, in response to the race riots in the Watts neighborhood of Los Angeles in the summer of 1965. At the time, black history was still a marginal topic that did not appear in school curricula and was studied mostly by political radicals.[21]

Katz found much of interest in black history. He did not dwell on the horrors of slavery, which he found "overwhelming and depressing." Instead, following Aptheker's lead, he began to study black people's resistance to the institution of slavery. To him, the history of black people in America could not be narrated simply as a story of injustices and violence committed against them, but as a chronicle of how they fought back. Katz found the stories of Nat Turner and other leaders of slave revolts electrifying and soon began his own original research in nineteenth-century black history.[22]

To document compelling cases of resistance to slavery, Katz focused on runaway slaves from the South who fled to the North and were deemed "fugitives" by the US government. Drawing on archival documents at the New York Public Library, he wrote a play about fugitive slaves. It was the influence of the Socialist plays of a few decades earlier, which used theater to convey political messages, that led Katz to present his research findings in the form of a play that would reach a broad audience instead of an academic article for a history journal.[23]

In the play, Katz told the story of one enslaved man who escaped from plantation slavery but was eventually captured and returned to bondage, an ending that one of Katz's African American friends criticized. "We don't need more of those stories," he said. So Katz returned to the archives and found what was then a little-known story about some fugitive slaves who escaped to Pennsylvania. When their owner found them, the fugitives rose up in a riot and killed him. This incident occurred shortly after passage of the Fugitive

Slave Act of 1850, which required the North to return runaway slaves to the South, and became the basis for Katz's second play, *Resistance at Christiania: The Fugitive Slave Rebellion*, in 1968. "The importance of resistance—I learned that before gay history," Katz said.[24]

From the experience of writing the two plays, Katz recognized not only the need to tell "new kinds of stories" but also the power of archival history. So much history had not been studied, even though so many manuscript collections, old newspapers, and other materials were available to the curious historian—professional or amateur. At a time when mainstream white historians were just beginning to study slavery from the vantage point of resistance, Katz told a previously untold story by doing research at the New York Public Library archives, where he uncovered the accounts of slaves whose actions contradicted the prevailing characterizations of slaves as feckless and subservient. In 1973 he cowrote with his father a historical novel, *Black Woman: A Fictionalized Biography of Lucy Terry Prince*, about an eighteenth-century enslaved woman.[25]

A number of influences coalesced in Katz's life. Reading the pamphlet about gay culture in Germany and the Nazis' erasure of it prompted him to investigate gay history; researching and writing plays about black history revealed to him the critical importance of providing a historical context to a social movement; and his involvement with the Gay Socialist Action Project showed him that gay people needed to wrest power away from the authorities and define their own culture. These three threads combined to inspire him to document the gay past. "We needed to understand our history," he explained. Katz came to realize that a choice had been made not to tell gay history and that this decision was born out of a particular ideological view of gay people as insignificant. History was not a comprehensive accounting of everyone who ever lived, but a means of talking only about people and events that best represented the past in the view of those in power.[26]

When he first began researching gay history, Katz encountered patterns similar to those discernible in the history of black people.

The only gay history books in the late 1960s and early 1970s were, as he joked, about "Queens of England." These history books, some of which lined the shelves of the Oscar Wilde Memorial Bookshop, told stories about notable people in history and literature who were assumed to be gay, such as Alexander the Great and Walt Whitman. Most of these were not real history books, he explained, but part of a genre meant to entertain rather than make a particular argument about the past.[27]

Katz was determined to do just that: make an argument about the past. The sources he found in the New York Public Library, however, were problematic. When he found references to men as "gay" or "homosexual" in newspapers, diaries, pamphlets, and court cases, he learned, for the most part, about the social norms, regulations, and laws that vilified gay people rather than personal details about their lives. He learned about power structures, not the actions of gay people. He uncovered only fragments of the gay experience, not the lost gay utopias—like that in Germany in the nineteenth century—that he had hoped to find. "I moved through libraries like a detective, a tracer of missing prisons, following up clues, following trails from footnote to footnote, an explorer in an unknown land," he said. He "rummaged through library card catalogs and walked through library stacks, pulling out likely books and consulting indexes."[28]

He began to stitch together parts of poems, personal testimonies, newspaper clippings, sermons, and essays, organizing the materials chronologically. Again, he decided to use archival documents as the basis for a play, which he titled *Coming Out!* The play would be performed as a series of first-person narratives by a cast of ten actors, both men and women. Intended to advance the cause of gay liberation, the documents that Katz found and selected told of the long struggle faced by gay people. Although Katz wrote the play to provide a historical context for gay liberation, he also wanted, like Craig Rodwell, to provide gay people with a sense of culture and community based on a shared intellectual heritage. And as with his work in black history, Katz wanted to reach a large audience.[29]

Friends of his in the Gay Activist Alliance (GAA) produced the show. The GAA premiered the play at a firehouse that it rented in

Soho. On a warm and sticky summer night in June 1972, a predominantly gay audience sat in a tiny theater with no air conditioning and not enough seats. Some audience members sat in the aisle, while others crowded together in the back of the room.

Perhaps the most important aspects of that night went unrecorded. There are typewritten drafts of Katz's play, but no transcripts of the audience's conversations. There are newspaper reviews of *Coming Out!*, but no published reports of the audience's anticipation before the start of the play. We know that some of the actors were nervous about playing gay characters, because in doing so they would be announcing their identity, but we do not know how the gay members of the audience were affected when they heard those lines. Photographs from the opening night display the bare-bones set, the expressions of the actors, and the makeshift costumes, but we don't have an emotional barometer that indexed the range of feelings that filled the room as the actors took their places, the lights dimmed, and the play began.[30]

Five men and five women walked onto the stage, where ten boxes were arranged in a straight line parallel to the first row. Each actor took a seat on one of the boxes. The stage then lit up. Speaker I stood and announced, "The Stonewall Resistance, June 27–29, 1969," and read a poetic rendition of *The Village Voice*'s story of the uprising. Speaker II provided the police report. Next, all ten members of the cast recited the following chant, or, in 1970s gay protest parlance, "zap."

> *We are the Stonewall girls,*
> *We have our hair in curls,*
> *We have no underwear,*
> *We show our pubic hair.*[31]

From there, the play unfolded as a series of monologues narrating gay life from the colonial period to the present. Court cases on sodomy came alive as an actor read an excerpt from a minister's seventeenth-century journal. One actor called out, "Five beastly Sodomitical boys, who confessed their wickedness." Then another appeared onstage as the famous colonial Massachusetts leader John Winthrop and uttered the word "sodomy."[32]

The next speaker who appeared onstage offered the etymology of the word "faggot," charting its first recorded use in the *Oxford English Dictionary* in 1300, when it meant a "bundle of sticks," to its 1591 meaning ("a term of abuse or contempt applied to women") and beyond. Katz wanted to convey the sheer range of meanings assigned to same-sex desire throughout history. As he explained, "If you think of yourself as some sort of psychological mutant or biological freak, you have an ahistorical way of looking at yourself. Gays have a history, a society. And it's very important to me to show not only the ways in which Gays have been oppressed, but the ways in which they have survived and resisted."[33]

Coming Out! took every pathology assigned to gay people and proved how historically entrenched and hurtful it was. An actor representing an American subject of the nineteenth-century sexologist Havelock Ellis read the pseudo-scientific definition of gay people as "inverts." An actress read a modern-day manifesto, "The Woman-Identified Woman," that the lesbian activist group RADICALESBIANS proclaimed on May 1, 1970:

> *What is a lesbian?*
> *A lesbian is the rage of all women*
>   *Condensed to the point of explosion.*
>   *Lesbian is a word,*
>   *The label,*
>   *The condition*
>   *That holds women in line.*
>   *When a woman hears this word*
>   *Tossed her way,*
>   *She knows she is stepping out of line.*
>   *Lesbian is a label*
> *Invented by the Man.*[34]

By incorporating RADICALESBIANS' rejection of the term "lesbian," a term many in the audience embraced, Katz demonstrated that semantic battles were ongoing—and that gay people of the present should think critically about every term, even those that seemed to belong to them.

Along the same lines, even as he conjured the long history of homophobia, Katz interspersed current events throughout the play to prompt his audience to think hard about the political struggles of their own time. One present-day vignette featured two black men who were charged with "disorderly conduct" for allegedly engaging in sexual acts in a men's room at a New Brunswick, New Jersey, train station. One of the men arrested was a New Brunswick high school English teacher and director of the town's Afro Culture Club. When the news of his arrest reached his school, he was suspended. Learning this, his students organized a protest that challenged the school's decision. The students were arrested, and his suspension stood. This particular episode was intended to force the majority-white audience—and the majority-white movement—to think about racism. Informed by his knowledge of and commitment to the black civil rights movement and its history, Katz reminded his audience that gay blacks faced a double form of oppression.[35]

Katz worked diligently to include the experiences of lesbians, who also faced a double form of oppression. However, "it's particularly hard to find material about women," he explained. Their experience in both women's history and gay history had "really been suppressed. Families have destroyed letters, the people themselves have destroyed letters because they don't want to be remembered as gay." Katz did, however, come across some telling sources, including a few lines from a poem that the renowned early-twentieth-century American writer Willa Cather wrote about her partner Isabelle. With only a scrap of evidence, he imaginatively reconstructed their lives together. In one of the most moving parts of *Coming Out!*, two actresses appeared on the bare stage and told the story of how Isabelle, the daughter of a wealthy Pittsburgh family, met Willa. Isabelle convinced her parents to allow Willa to temporarily live with her, a provisional arrangement that lasted five years. They ate dinner with Isabelle's family every evening and then escaped to their bedroom in the secluded part of the house, which overlooked "gardens and shaded streets." There they "read together in quiet" and "spent many happy hours" without fear of anyone encroaching on their privacy. The actresses then lowered their voices and somberly told of the day Isabelle died. "Willa did not think she could go on living," they said together. When her grief eventually subsided, Willa realized that Isabelle "had been the one person for whom all her books had been written."[36]

In a play that had recounted so much about oppression and hatred, this love story offered a positive counterpoint. With a few poetic lines and an intimately staged set of scenes, Katz resurrected the tenderness between Isabelle and Willa. But the story of Willa and Isabelle did not end there. Katz used it to reveal a great irony of the histories of women and gay people. Even though Cather devoted her life to words and many critics later celebrated her as a lesbian icon, the actress playing her told the audience that "the hundreds of letters that had passed between the two women were destroyed."[37]

Coming Out! did not offer a happy ending; instead, it ended with a call to action. Eight actors appeared onstage, each reciting a stanza that summarized the play's plot about the history of gay people being silenced, criminalized, and pathologized, and then concluded by stating, "We will work and shout and fight, until we have our rights, until all gay people are free, until this society is changed."[38]

Katz wanted to move people, to bring them to tears, to anger them, to inspire them, to politicize them, and to challenge them intellectually. As one critic noted, "Katz embraces the philosophy of Sartre and marries it to the dramaturgy of Bertolt Brecht. In his writing, he tries to present the whole range of human feelings and experiences—both negative and positive—in a social context."[39]

Coming Out! proved a success. In June 1972, a few months after it premiered, it played at the Washington Square Methodist Church in the Village, and then again at the Nighthouse, a small theater a few blocks north in New York City's Chelsea neighborhood. It had a profound effect on many who saw it. As one audience member proclaimed:

It is a song of life, of gay life. It is a memory of things past, a view of things present, a promise of things yet to be. It is a drama, a comedy, a satire. It is beautiful, it is ugly, it is common, it is rare. It brought many to the point of tears, both from sadness and laughter. It reminded us that we are not alone in our struggle. . . . I cannot find the adjectives to describe what I felt during that evening.[40]

Many audience members took to the play's explicit political message. Katz had chosen to present his research in the form of a play not only to reach as many people as possible but also to contribute to the collective activist spirit that defined the Gay Activist Alliance. As Katz recalled, an elderly man who saw *Coming Out!* described it as resembling the community plays put on by the Communist Party in the 1930s. Through the play, Katz expressed a radical gay consciousness that had rarely been articulated in the arts. As he explained, the play "communicated our new militancy," adding, "We didn't want psychiatrists talking about arrested development. We wanted to speak for ourselves."[41]

What so many in the audiences for *Coming Out!* felt was a sense of kinship, of solidarity, of understanding, and most of all, of culture. When Katz wrote the play, he imagined his audience would be made up of gay people. "In my study of Walt Whitman in the nineteenth century," Katz explained, "it seemed to me his knowledge of the existence of an audience of men he was writing for allowed him to express himself." Knowing that there was an audience of critically engaged gay people, whom he may not have seen on the street or in his neighborhood but only imagined, nevertheless propelled Katz to continue with his research and writing. In the early 1970s, with the exception of a handful of gay religious associations and political organizations, and with the exception of Craig Rodwell's Oscar Wilde Memorial Bookshop, there were few places even in New York City where gay people could come together as a community and relate to each other on something other than a sexual level. Additionally, the bar and bathhouse scene segregated gay men from lesbians. Katz and the GAA hoped that seeing the play together would help foster a sense of community among lesbians and gay men. Although the history of the divisions between gay men and lesbians is long and complicated—and thus not easily overcome by a single play—some people did see the value of *Coming Out!* in this regard. As one critic wrote, "I must congratulate David Roggensack on his direction and I feel that he really succeeded in bringing together both parts of the Gay Liberation Movement; i.e., the boys and the girls."[42]

For all of its importance for gay liberation, the play's most profound impact may have been on Katz's own coming-out saga. When Katz first walked into the Oscar Wilde Memorial Bookshop, he had not yet come out of the closet. He walked in hoping no one he knew would see him. To his knowledge, no one did. As a man who grew up feeling that he was in "anxious exile," the possibility of his identity being publicly recognized made him uncomfortable. Even after he developed an understanding of homosexuality that demanded political action, he did not come out to his parents. While writing *Coming Out!* he planned on going by the pseudonym of "Jon Swift," even though he recognized the hypocrisy of such a choice. When it came time to publish advertisements and programs for the play, the director, David Roggensack, asked Katz which name to use. As Katz recalled, "In what felt like a daring, scary venture, I gulped and said, 'Okay, use my real name.'"[43]

He initially felt emboldened by his decision. Then his mother called. It was the morning of the opening, and *The Village Voice* had published an ad in the Friday issue about the premiere. His mother had seen the ad. Her voice trembling and sounding like she was about to cry, she asked:

"Is that you in *The Village Voice?*"
"Yes," he replied.
"Are you a . . . a homo-sexual?"
"Yes."
"Why didn't you tell me?"
"Because I knew you'd react like you're reacting," Katz explained.
"But why do you have to be so public?"
"Because I have to."[44]

Katz's response echoed the feelings of many in the cast: the fight for equality required that gay people become more visible to the outside world. The play became a way for gay people to explain to heterosexuals the struggles they faced—which was why Katz told his mother that he had to be public about his sexual orientation, no matter how difficult it was for him—or for her. In the early 1970s, most Americans had simplistic and negative views of homosexuality. The play set the stage literally and metaphorically for gay men and lesbians to define themselves to heterosexuals. As a reviewer for a gay newspaper wrote, "*Coming Out!* set the 'straight' community straight on the bad-mouthing and bad press homosexuals have so long received and how Gay Liberation has begun to change all of that."[45] Gay people were not only coming out, but they were bringing their stories and experiences out into the open as well. The play gave them the inspiration, and the language, to do so. As Katz put it, "My work on the play *Coming Out!* initiated my new life as an open gay person . . . with all their pleasures and, of course, their pains. My work on *Coming Out!* helped make me human." As he recounted later, "Seeing my ideas come alive onstage, it was just an amazing experience; it was stimulating. It was a collective experience. It wasn't me sitting alone in the library."[46]

By 1973, the play was still going, and Martin Duberman, a leading academic and activist, reviewed it in the *New York Times*. Duberman praised *Coming Out!* and in the process took a shot at the recent production of Al Carmines's *The Faggot*, which was playing a few blocks away at the Judson Memorial Church in Washington Square Park. *The Faggot*—not to be confused with Larry Kramer's yet-to-be-published novel *Faggots*—was a musical that included sketches of gay life with cameo appearances from the likes of Gertrude Stein, Oscar Wilde, and Catherine the Great. *The Faggot* was one example of a new genre of Off-Off Broadway productions that capitalized on being amateurish and experimental in their content and direction. Like *Coming Out!*, it was performed in a makeshift theater. Unlike *Coming Out!*, *The Faggot* was meant to chronicle the everyday lives of gay men without promoting a particular political message. However, the campy characters of *The Faggot* did not charm Duberman; they enraged him. "The one deals in lives, the other one in stereotypes," Duberman wrote. "The one stirs, the other lulls. The one suggests the need for unity and commitment, the other for bikinis and cocktails. The one demands an end to oppression, the other helps to reinforce it."[47]

Carmines defended his play in the *New York Times* a few days later, claiming, "My bored and depressed middle-aged homosexuals are not interested in pretending that they are not bored and depressed middle-aged homosexuals in order to gild the image of gay liberation. In short, Mr. Duberman, my characters are themselves with their and my very personal pain and joy in relating to the world." Carmines criticized Katz's play for being overly political and militant—a critique that many others launched against *Coming Out!* for its alleged lack of artistic sensibility and its overtly political agenda. Carmines went on: "I have spent a lifetime trying to see what I see—rather than what leftists, rightists, gays, straights, old or young tell me I ought to see. I don't believe the only acceptable plays about homosexuality are those which wallow in self-pity or sound the call to arms. I believe there are ways of being black or a woman, or gay, or anything else which are not comprehended in even your compassionate militancy, Mr. Duberman."[48]

The argument between Duberman and Carmines raised the question of which narrative would prevail—Carmines's account of the banality of gay life or Katz's story of revolutionary change? Implicit in Carmines's defense of his play was the idea that gay liberation was something new and thus, like a fad, something that might pass. His claim that many of his middle-aged friends remained "bored" and "depressed" seemed to reflect his belief about the perpetual condition of gay people. But while much of *Coming Out!* was indeed new and revolutionary, the play also reflected a familiar trope in American history: the oppressed rising up and demanding equality. The story of gay oppression tapped into this particular American sensibility and became a rallying cry. Accordingly, it is hard to imagine that Carmines could have been proven right, at least not in a post-Stonewall world.

As it turned out, Duberman's support of *Coming Out!* led to Katz receiving an offer from a publisher to turn his play into a book of primary sources. This book would become the defining statement on gay liberation, while Carmines's play would fade into the recesses of popular memory and become largely forgotten.

At first, Katz doubted that he could transform *Coming Out!* into a history book. The task seemed too daunting. He recalled sitting with his then-boyfriend at a pier on the Hudson River and asking, "Do I dare call this book *Gay American History?* Is there enough material? Can I assert by that title that there is such a thing?"[49]

Despite these concerns, Katz was more fearful about what would happen if he did not write the book. Apprehensive that there might be a backlash against gay liberation that would erase it from history, he felt that he "needed to find as much as I possibly [could]." Katz had grown up in a household shaped by anti-Communist hysteria and had witnessed how ideas could be censored and experiences erased from the historical record. Further, his study of black history had revealed that much of it remained unwritten and unknown, and he had also learned how the Nazis wiped out almost every shred of evidence of a gay past in Germany. Katz knew that he had to write the book so that similar erasures could not happen in the United States. The experiences of so many gay people had already been lost. If even Willa Cather's letters had been destroyed, what would happen to the experiences of ordinary gay people? If history provided a prologue to the present, chances were good that gay liberation in the United States in the latter half of the twentieth century would be forgotten if gay people did not document it.[50]

In 1976 Katz published *Gay American History*, which ran to about 450 pages and by its very publication offered symbolic proof of gay liberation. Katz had unearthed many more stories besides the ones he used to write the play. As he saw it, the more sources he could find, the more people he could document, the better the chance that gay liberation would be remembered.

Gay American History therefore not only serves as a documentary history of gay people throughout American history but also, more importantly, reveals the extent to which gay liberation unfolded on shaky ground. "We did not know if there [would] be any more books like this," Katz explained. It was unclear whether homosexuality would become a field of academic study and whether such studies would be considered legitimate. As Katz said, "I filled *Gay American History* with everything I found, because this might be our only chance."[51]

The sheer heft of the book testified powerfully to the historical experience of gay people. *Gay American History* also single-handedly created a subfield in US social history. During the 1970s, the history profession gradually turned toward social history—or as one historian famously explained it, the writing of history "from the bottom up." Historians narrated social history from the vantage point of ordinary people—laborers, working-class people, immigrants—and shifted attention to minority groups like women and black people. *Gay American History* reflected and furthered this vision of how history should be written.

Katz divided the book into six sections: "Trouble: 1566–1966"; "Treatment: 1884–1974"; "Passing Women: 1782–1920"; "Native Americans/Gay Americans: 1528–1976"; "Resistance: 1859–1972"; and "Love: 1779–1932." His commitment to the principles of social history had led him to start with Native Americans—a bold and deft move in the 1970s. His previous scholarship in black history had made him sensitive to issues of resistance, which historians had only begun to explore in the 1970s. Recognizing the need to document how oppression leads to resistance, Katz presented gay people as willful actors in their own liberation, which, he argued, had been going on for over four centuries. Many readers of *Gay American History* understood the political rationale behind this decision. Historian Jeffrey Escoffier paraphrased the Marxist theorist Antonio Gramsci in his review of Katz's book in *The Body Politic*: "Political liberation required a critical and coherent view of history and one's place in it. Otherwise, if our social consciousness is disjointed and episodic we have no chance of changing the world and giving ourselves a free place in it."[52]

Katz also took a cue from the emerging field of women's history, a subfield of American social history that had arisen alongside the contemporary social movement. Feminists' critique of objectivity, which shaped debates about the status of women in the 1970s, informed Katz's critique of gay men's objectification of one another as sexual partners—a theme of both his play and his book. Additionally, the work of women's historians guided his approach to gay history. In the 1970s, he reveled in historian Mary Ryan's caveat in her book *Womanhood in America* that her book dealt only with "heterosexual women." That Ryan thought it necessary to make such a distinction encouraged Katz as he pondered the possibility of a "thing called gay history."[53]

In one important respect it is amazing that *Gay American History* even exists. Katz approached his numerous historical models and sources of inspiration without a PhD. In other words, he had no experienced mentor guiding his research or fellow graduate students and professional colleagues helping him navigate the many questions that doubtless arose. He researched and wrote the book armed with only a high school education and the intellectual nourishment offered by the members of the Gay Socialist Action Project.

Gay American History turned Jonathan Ned Katz into a celebrity within the gay community, and he found himself an in-demand speaker. A month before publication, the Gay Alliance Toward Equality in Toronto held a dinner in his honor; he shared some of his research with over seventy people that night. For instance, he told the audience about a Native American from the 1960s who had claimed that he was "not against whites but heterosexuals who think everyone should be like them." He also read an excerpt from a love letter written to the anarchist Emma Goldman by her female admirer Almeda Sperry: "It is the wild part of me that would be unabashed in showing its love for you in front of a multitude or in a crowded room. My eyes would sparkle with love." *The Body Politic* reported on the event and praised Katz's book, summarizing its message: "Women have been loving women, and men have loved men, as long as this continent has been inhabited."[54]

Katz would eventually return to the Oscar Wilde Memorial Bookshop, no longer as a man anxious about walking inside but as a vindicated, published author invited to participate in the store's "Meet the Authors" series. Craig Rodwell may not have noticed Katz when he first walked into his store, but he certainly knew who he was in 1977. He referred to Katz's book as the "'Bible' of Gay Liberation for many years to come."[55]

Not often do historians find two of their subjects in the same room. Even though Katz and Rodwell lived in the same neighborhood and shared similar political agendas and intellectual commitments, they rarely crossed paths. This in itself reveals something fundamental about the making of gay liberation. Despite the arduous work and energy that activists like Rodwell and Katz put into the movement, the future of gay liberation remained uncertain in the 1970s. Indeed, despite the political groups and committed activists, despite all the meetings and conferences organized around liberation, fighting for gay liberation day in and day out was not easy, if it was even possible. Katz wrote a locally popular play and then published an internationally popular book. Rodwell organized political events at his bookstore and corresponded with gay people across the world. Yet the two men rarely found themselves in the same room because there were still few rooms where they could meet. There remained more bars, bathhouses, and pornographic theaters in New York during the 1970s than there were gay bookstores, coffee shops, and forums for political thought and engagement. It would require more than sex to advance gay liberation—it would require that Katz and Rodwell find a place where they could develop their ideas and reach large numbers of gay men and lesbians.

The place they would ultimately find was not a political institute or even the basement of a university library—the traditional shelters for the socially conscious and intellectually engaged. Instead, they, along with tens of thousands of other gay men and women, would turn to the pages of the gay newspapers and magazines that were proliferating in the seventies. There, in letters to the editor, feature stories, and investigative reports, they would find the space to theorize, to debate, to argue, to historicize, to mobilize, and, most of all, to find each other.

5 THE BODY POLITIC

First they forced him to dance, and then they chained his hands and his feet to a crossbeam and beat him. One of his contemporaries described him as "effeminate."

This is all we know of him.

There was a reference to another: a cultural attaché to a foreign embassy who, in a deep state of depression and hopelessness, "fell over dead for no apparent reason."

There was a story of a third: a young and healthy man who, after the evening roll call, was ridiculed, spat on, and beaten by soldiers. They put him in a cold shower and forced him to suffer "alone and in silence" on a "frosty winter evening." The next morning his fellow soldiers described his breathing as "an audible rattle." Despite his suffering, the soldiers continued to beat and kick him. They tied him to a post and "under an arc lamp until he began to sweat, again put under a cold shower." He died later that evening.[1]

These are fragments of stories about gay men in Nazi concentration camps recounted in the pages of *The Body Politic*, a gay newspaper founded in 1971 that reached readers across the United States, Canada, and parts of Europe. The article was published long after the defeat of Hitler and the end of the Nazi regime, and far away from the death camps, the torture, and the mass murder.

The article was nonetheless viewed as news by its readers. It was the first account that many of them had ever read about the Holocaust, let alone about the persecution of homosexuals by Hitler's regime. They learned that Nazis tortured those presumed to be homosexual, referred to gay people as "degenerates," "weaklings," and "congenital cowards," and branded homosexuals with a pink triangle, forcing them to wear it on "the left side of the jacket and on the right pant leg." *The Body Politic* included an illustration of the inverted pink triangle, which had yet to develop as a symbol within the gay community, on the first page of the article. This was probably one of the first places it was seen by many gay people.[2]

The article appeared in *The Body Politic* as part of a larger series on the history of homosexuality in Germany by the notable literary scholar and historian Jim Steakley. The series appeared around the same time as "The Early Homosexual Rights Movement (1864–1935)," the pamphlet that had been so influential in Jonathan Ned Katz's intellectual, political, and personal development. Steakley's series focused on tracking gay life in Germany from 1919 to 1933 (the Weimar period), through Hitler's persecution of gay people before and during World War II, and from the postwar period to the rise of gay rights in Berlin in the 1970s.

Steakley's interest in German history began when he was an adolescent and his family lived in Germany for four years. Visiting a concentration camp for the first time at age ten, he came into direct contact with the aftermath of genocide. His interest in German history was not limited to the war, however. He collected stamps of German leaders, learning their names and exploring the general history of the nation. In the summer between his junior and senior years in high school, he returned to Germany on a scholarship that sent him to Munich and to Dachau, the first Nazi concentration camp that held political prisoners. "It stimulated my thinking," he remembered.[3]

Steakley learned much about the Nazi regime from reading John Hersey's novel *The Wall*, about resistance in the Warsaw ghetto, and Leon Uris's *Exodus*, about concentration camp survivors. These books raised his consciousness about Jewish history and further piqued his interest in studying history more broadly. But he distinctly remembered never reading anything about gay people in the camps. Despite the fact that gay people formed a significant portion of the Dachau prisoners, they had not been included in the early histories of the concentration camps.[4]

After he had embarked on an academic career, Steakley returned to Germany in the early 1970s and began to dig up details about the Nazis' persecution of homosexuals. He came across a memoir that mentioned a homosexual inmate whose scrotum had been placed in boiling water. In the course of his research, he realized that what he was uncovering had implications for gay liberation in the contemporary United States, in the sense that, as he put it, the Nazis' persecution of gay people served as a "frightening prospect of what could happen." Although he defined himself as a Marxist and doubted that history "could repeat itself," he nevertheless believed that history "offered lessons." As he explained, "The Nazis brought something to an extreme point." The lesson was clear enough: "We had to show examples of oppression." According to Steakley, after the start of gay liberation, many nongay people doubted gay people's accounts of the struggles and oppression they claimed to experience. Steakley credited the work of Jonathan Ned Katz with inspiring him to look to history and with laying the groundwork for his own research, which he hoped would "advance the consciousness of society."[5]

Soon after Steakley returned to the United States from Germany in 1972 with bundles of photocopied notes, he went to Toronto to begin working on his series of three articles for *The Body Politic*. "Part of the oppression of gay people lies in the denial of our history," read the opening line of the first article, which appeared in June 1973 (the same month as the Up Stairs Lounge fire). Steakley launched into an in-depth analysis of gay life in Germany from 1860 to 1910, writing about Karl Heinrich Ulrichs, who disputed that homosexuality was a sin and instead likened it to uncommon preference, like left-handedness. Steakley chronicled the rise of the sexologist Magnus Hirschfeld and the unknown history of the gay movement in the 1930s. Unlike "The Early Homosexual Rights Movement (1864–1935)," the pamphlet that Jonathan Ned Katz read, Steakley's research went beyond the late-nineteenth and early-twentieth-century homophile movement and down to the rise of Nazism and the reemergence of gay liberation in Berlin in the 1970s.[6]

The second installment in the series, published in January 1974, detailed the persecution of homosexuals in the 1930s and during World War II. Steakley revealed that the Gestapo had lists of homosexuals. In 1933 the SS rounded up gay people and convicted 835 men of homosexuality. In 1937 the official SS newspaper, *Das Schwarze Korps,* called for the death of what it claimed were 2 million German homosexuals. Of those 2 million, Steakley reported, 50,000 were officially sent to camps, but overall "perhaps hundreds of thousands of homosexuals were interned in Nazi concentration camps." The official statistics mostly counted the men who went to trial, but many others were sent "to the camps without the benefit of a trial," and some of these men were "summarily executed by firing squads."[7]

Steakley's third and final article offered an account of the gay liberation movement in Germany in the early 1970s, focusing on how leftist politics, campaigns for workers' rights, and the student movement had paved the way for gay liberation. Throughout the article, Steakley compared German gay liberation to the American gay rights movement, noting how the success and power of the left in Germany had helped to promote gay liberation. As he explained: "The millions of women and foreign nationals in the German labor force were united on the issue of class oppression and escaped the separatism which vitiated the American left."[8]

Why did *The Body Politic* run a series in 1974 on the history of homosexuality in Germany, at the height of gay liberation, a period often hailed by historians as victorious?[9]

The reaction to the publication of Steakley's series signaled that many gay people in the seventies were looking for what historians refer to as a "usable past"—a connection to a previous decade or epoch that would provide legitimacy, meaning, and, most of all, a genealogy to their plight. For historians like Jonathan Ned Katz, finding a usable past became a life's work. Steakley, like Katz, showed readers that the gay culture that arose in the 1970s was not an entirely new phenomenon. "We were living in tremendous freedom in Toronto and New York City, and that seemed like a parallel to the Weimar Republic," Steakley said. Yet there was a "free-floating anxiety that America could become more fascist"—the awareness of "a frightening prospect," as he said of Nazi persecution, "of what could happen."[10]

In the 1970s, many gay readers turned to the pages of an ever-growing gay newspaper culture in order to historically situate their culture. This expanding culture and the articles, like Steakley's, that started to appear gave gay people a language with which to frame their predicament. In recounting the history of violence against gays in Los Angeles, for example, Rev. Troy Perry referred to the police as "the Gestapo." A reporter for *The Gay Clone* explained the connection between the persecution of Jewish people in Europe in the early twentieth century and the persecution of gay people in the United States in the 1970s: "There is a tolerance among good people of discrimination against homosexuals that is similar to the tolerance of anti-Semitism that was so pervasive in Europe before the holocaust and that, at least according to some scholars, created a hospitable climate for the destruction of European Jews." W. I. Scobie, a writer for San Francisco's *Gay Sunshine,* argued that "the so-called 'National Socialist League' is California's very own gay Nazi party." In his article "Death Camps: Remembering the Victims," he further asserted, "Today, gays suffer still under totalitarian regimes not very different from that so admired by our own 'Gay Nazis.'" Scobie bookended his exploration of the death camps with a political call to action.[11] The gay press made this history accessible to gay readers, partly by allowing journalists to spell out the political importance of the events they wrote about in a way that traditional history books could not. In fact, printed at the top of *The Body Politic* throughout the 1970s was an epigraph by the writer Kurt Hiller, written in 1921: "The Liberation of Homosexuals Can Only Be the Work of Homosexuals Themselves."[12]

Readers' interest in history helped to spur the development and growth of gay newspapers. In fact, the publication of Steakley's articles on the history of gay culture in Germany turned *The Body Politic* into one of the leading gay periodicals of the 1970s, if not the most prominent one, and it launched the paper into international markets, across Europe and into Australia. *The Body Politic* would acquire a reputation for intellectual seriousness, an international focus, an emphasis on the gay artistic, cinematic, and literary worlds, and a commitment to reviewing the latest academic scholarship. As Jonathan Ned Katz once remarked, "*The Body Politic* was the gay community's version of the *New York Review of Books*."[13]

For instance, *The Body Politic* published the "Our Image" series, which offered lengthy reviews of popular films, books, and plays with gay and queer themes. In the July 1, 1977, supplement issue, Thomas Waugh, a film critic, in his extensive review of Soviet filmmaker Sergei Mikhailovich Eisenstein, claimed that many art historians never acknowledged Eisenstein's homosexuality because they did not think it mattered to his work; Waugh argued differently, unpacking various scenes in his films that disclosed a gay subtext. Another 1977 issue contained reviews of essay collections by Gore Vidal and the feminist Robin Morgan, as well as a critique of the collected work of the poet and artist Frank O'Hara. When Steakley's series was published, it provided a kind of genesis moment. As Jerald Moldenhauer, one of the founding editors of *The Body Politic,* noted, Steakley's "series on the history of homosexuality in Germany elevated the paper to an even higher level and gave it promise of becoming something that all people interested in gay history and politics would want to read." After the series, *The Body Politic* created a special features section devoted exclusively to gay history and literature.[14]

Print culture—newspapers, magazines, and journals—became a means of establishing gay communities in the 1970s. Periodicals allowed people to communicate across regional and often national boundaries, to share ideas and experiences, to advance political causes, to report on the violence and crimes committed against gay people, to connect to the past, and to report and advertise more ephemeral matters, such as news of new gay businesses and notices about political groups' meetings. Craig Rodwell, for example, noted the importance of gay newspapers to the development of the MCC; he explained, "Gay publications aided the founding of gay institutions, for example, the Gay Metropolitan Community Church in LA. In 1968, Rev. Troy Perry advertised in *The Advocate* for formation of a gay church. From modest beginnings and through the aid of gay media, MCC grew to 20 missions in cities across the United States." The many gay newspapers, journals, and magazines that appeared in the 1970s often literally encompassed within a page or two the vast experiences of the gay community.[15]

It is nearly impossible to determine the actual number of the hundreds of weekly and monthly newsletters, quarterly journals, and annual magazines that proliferated in the 1970s—many were short-lived and not subsequently archived—but roughly four dozen newspapers and journals spanned most of the decade. These ranged from Boston's *Fag Rag,* Arizona's *Gay News,* and San Francisco's *Gay Sunshine* to Philadelphia's *Gay News* and *Lesbian Tide* in Los Angeles. Among the many other short-lived publications were San Francisco's *Join Hands,* a newspaper devoted to prisoners' rights, and *The Gay Clone,* which only appeared annually on May Day. The *Austin Gay News* began as a newsletter of only a few pages but developed into a full-blown newspaper. Rodwell further noted, "Some gay lib newspapers, such as Boston's *Lavender Vision* and Philadelphia's *Gay Dealer,* ceased publication, and New York's *Come Out* published only two issues in its 1971–72 year. Detroit's *Gay Liberator* suspended publication for six months in March 1971, but resumed as an independent gay radical paper after Detroit's GLF [Gay Liberation Front] folded."[16]

Although there had certainly been regional and national gay communication networks and political alliances before Stonewall, it was the start of gay liberation that led to the founding of so many gay periodicals.[17] At the time of Stonewall in 1969, the movement was scattered. There were committed activists in San Francisco and Boston and activist groups on college campuses in the United States and Canada that took their cue from the revolutionary fervor of the black civil rights and women's liberation movements. Gay rights activists and leaders struggled to remain in touch with one another and reach others outside of the major urban centers. Craig Rodwell's establishment of the Oscar Wilde Bookshop was a response to this dilemma, as was Jonathan Ned Katz's decision to write plays and books about gay history. With the exception of some religious organizations, gay people who lived in the American South or in tiny towns in the Midwest, however, were stymied when it came to developing more robust and inclusive networks.

Faced with similar challenges, other social movements in the 1960s created an underground press. According to one historian, "Underground newspapers educated, politicized and built communities among disaffected youths in every region of the country."[18] In Berkeley, California, activists founded the *Berkeley Barb*; in New York City writers founded *The East Village*; and Texas activists founded the *Austin Rag*. The vast underground print culture that emerged in the 1960s comprised mimeographed pamphlets, underground newsletters, and literary magazines that reached millions of readers across the country and the world. Throughout American history—from Thomas Paine's *Common Sense* and William Lloyd Garrison's *The Liberator* to *The People's Advocate*, which endorsed the Populists in the late nineteenth century—political publications had proven vital to the movements they supported.[19] The gay press would serve a similar role.

Gay print culture grew in tandem with the movement itself. When news of the Stonewall riot reached Boston, John Mitzel, a contributor to Boston's *Fag Rag*, remembers gay students, both men and women, creating homophile organizations on college campuses. According to Mitzel, a crucial part of starting a political organization was starting a periodical. In Boston this was a coed enterprise at first: gay men and lesbians came together to create what Mitzel defined as a "69 publication": *Lavender Vision* was a magazine in which half of the pages were devoted to men and half were devoted to women. But shortly after the first few issues were published, the lesbian writers and editors, seeing a need for a separate publication devoted to lesbian issues, decided to leave the magazine. However, the new magazine, known as *Lavender Vision Two*, had a short life. When the lesbians left *Lavender*, the men debated the title of their new publication. Some wanted to name it "Surrender Dorothy," and others wanted to change it to "Kumquat Times." They eventually settled on Mitzel's suggestion, "Fag Rag," which Mitzel said had the benefit of being "to the point."[20]

Many of these periodicals began as local papers and newsletters that reported on gay life, culture, and politics in their cities and towns. A new gay periodical quickly became the mouthpiece for the local community. In the founding issue of Boston's *Gay Community Newsletter,* the editors explained, "There has been a long-standing need in the Boston gay community for improved communication between the various gay organizations and the gay individual." The editors pointed out that the lack of coverage given by "the straight press" to gay issues only exacerbated the problem of keeping gay readers informed about relevant news and events.[21]

In its inaugural issue, the *Gay Community Newsletter* offered a panoply of articles and announcements and ads: information about a "Gay Women's Rap Session," ads about events sponsored by both the Metropolitan Community Church and Dignity, and ads for the Boston showing of Jonathan Ned Katz's *Coming Out!,* which the newsletter claimed "effectively creates a sense of Gay Pride." An announcement for a "Transsexual and Transvestites workshop" asked, "Where are we in the gay movement?" In the 1970s, transgender issues remained marginalized even among the most radical gay and lesbian activists, intellectuals, and community organizers. This ad is an early sign of a debate that would soon become prominent within the gay community.[22]

The burgeoning gay press provided a political forum for gay people to communally and publicly grapple with the direction of the movement. Further, the rise of the notion that gay people had rights revealed the impact of the gay activists of the early 1970s, like the members of the Gay Socialist Action Project, on fostering a sense of political identity. Once gay people embraced "gay" as a legitimate identity—and not as signifying religious, psychological, or physiological aberration—they could begin to consider its political and legal dimensions. "What can be done?" asked a column on law and politics in *Gay Community Newsletter* titled "How Do the Laws

Oppress Gays? The Why and How of Political Change." And "what is being done?" it added. The gay press became a medium for articulating and spreading these questions.[23]

Underscoring their deep commitment was the fact that most editors, writers, and contributors to the gay press worked as volunteers. "They did it . . . for love," Rick Bébout, an editor on *The Body Politic* staff, said about the early years of the journal. "Their status came from what they could give away: to each other, to themselves, even to people they'd never meet," he explained. Of the hundreds of people who worked at *The Body Politic*, "only a handful" were ever paid. Similarly, the *Philadelphia Gay News* began with a modest budget of $5,000 (from borrowed funds) and was run by a group of volunteers who met in the apartment of a gay couple, where they taught themselves how to produce a paper.[24]

Organizational structures were egalitarian. Many periodicals functioned as "collectives" in which all volunteers were involved in every stage of the decision-making process. Jerald Moldenhauer recounted "a supposedly horizontal power structure" at *The Body Politic*. Every word of every article was read aloud at group meetings "for approval, revision, and rejection." This process may have ensured democratic and transparent decisions, but it did not promote efficiency. The minutes from a meeting of *The Body Politic* on April 1, 1974, noted that "no decisions were reached." Although the staff understood that this was a "cumbersome way to run a paper," to them it was effective in the ways that mattered. At *The Body Politic*, Bébout explained that the collective structure "kept people involved, committed; kept them working out of no more than passion."[25]

In keeping with the volunteer and community ethos, the staff members of a periodical often collectively funded its production. Fortunately, costs were minimal. The three founders of *The Dallas Voice* each contributed $250 to cover expenses, $500 of which went to renting office space for the first month. As John Mitzel recalled, "it was so damn cheap" to publish *Fag Rag*; he remembered that it cost $500 to print 5,000 copies of the quarterly at a printer in Worcester, Massachusetts. When distributing copies of *The Body Politic*, Rick Bébout boasted that "no one owns any of this; our work lines no one's pockets." According to Bébout, some privately owned gay publications failed because they were intended as moneymaking ventures and the founders were liable to walk away. *The Body Politic* avoided this problem by "creating" an owner in 1975: a nonprofit company called Pink Triangle Press.[26]

The gay press offset production costs just as the mainstream press did: by running ads. At first, however, this practice was a point of contention. Initially, the collective at *The Body Politic* refused to allow commercial advertisers, but they changed course by the end of their first year. As Rick Bébout recalled, "Many ads were from businesses gay owned if not gay in name: a pet shop, a restaurant, a hairdresser; boutiques for cloths, plants, personal grooming and housewares; travel agents; a few theatres and the occasional publisher, usually in league with Glad Day." Unlike the Oscar Wilde Memorial Bookshop, many of these businesses did not have a name that signaled, implicitly or explicitly, their purpose or the identity of their owners. The ads thus served as a guide to a clandestine network of gay businesses spread throughout North America. The December 1, 1975, issue of *The Body Politic*, for instance, included ads for hotels in Fort Lauderdale and Miami, a jewelry store in Toronto that specialized in "Navajo" silver and turquoise pieces, and a custom furniture and upholstery shop.[27]

Bars and clubs emerged as the leading advertisers. Since many of these institutions were located in secret locations and bore names that did not publicly announce what they were, their ads in gay newspapers allowed gay people to find each other. In effect, the ads supplanted the gay "guidebooks," which had first appeared in urban centers in the early decades of the twentieth century and by the 1960s had extended their geographic reach—which remained limited, however, compared to the periodicals of the 1970s.[28]

The ads for bars and clubs indicate that sex was not divorced from or in conflict with the mission of the gay press. In 1978 *The Body Politic* ran an ad for "Rush," or "poppers," a chemical drug, alkyl nitrites, taken during sexual intercourse. Thus bars, bathhouses, and other advertisers selling sex facilitated the political objectives of the newspapers by funding their circulation. In the

September 1, 1976, issue of *The Body Politic*, for example, a reader could find ads showcasing The Barracks, a bathhouse in Toronto, and even an ad for "Accu-jac," described as "the world's finest and most sophisticated masturbation machine." But adjacent to this ad appeared an article about eighty American, English, and Canadian women—"black, white, lesbian and straight"—who gathered for a conference in Toronto to strategize about the "Wages for Housework Campaign."[29]

This article represented the broad demographic reach of *The Body Politic* and its commitment to more than just the interests of gay men. Not only did *The Body Politic*'s staff include lesbians, but they also regularly brought to light and commented on the struggles of domestics, who could be both lesbians and heterosexual women, of any race. As the article in the September 1, 1976, issue stated, "The Wages for Housework Campaign can unite lesbian with other women without ignoring differences, because lesbian women have their own autonomous organizations within the Campaign to put forward their specific needs." The article revealed that many lesbians felt left out of the promise of gay male liberation and as a consequence felt the need to begin organizing across class, racial, and gender lines.[30]

On a foundation of ads that promoted sex and sex toys, *The Body Politic* covered a wide range of issues. On the same page of the September 1, 1976, issue that featured the ad for "Accu-jac" and the article on the Wages for Housework Campaign, another article reported on Jonathan Ned Katz's visit to Toronto to discuss *Gay American History*. At the top of the page, an ad selling pink triangle pins offered a brief history of the origins of the pink triangle, explaining that "homosexuals wore it to their death in the concentration camps" and had since co-opted it as "a symbol of the international gay movements" and "struggle for full human and civil rights."[31]

When an advertiser's politics clashed with the mission of *The Body Politic*, the collective dropped the advertisement. For example, *The Body Politic* refused to post ads for the Carriage House, a gay bar and hotel in Toronto whose policy prohibited women from entering "the two lower floor bars" and allowed them to enter "the upstairs lounge [only] if they are properly attire[d]." The collective noted that "the Carriage House has deliberately adopted a policy intended to discriminate against women." Not only did *The Body Politic* refuse ads from the Carriage House because of its discriminatory policies, but the collective published a story about it to explain their rationale to readers. In this and other ways, the collective's transparency extended to its readers. *The Body Politic* later formulated a policy that it would "not accept ads we consider representative of businesses which promote sexism, or whose ads are exploitative in appearance."[32]

When given the chance, *The Body Politic* also tried to shape sexual relations among men in its classified sections. *The Body Politic* wanted to promote a positive message about sex, relationships, and intimacy and did not accept ads that included discriminatory or hurtful comments or that drew superficial boundaries between gay men. Submitted ads that made statements like "No fats, no fems" were not printed. If an ad stated, "Straight looking, straight acting," the collective would accept it, but as Rick Bébout remarked, "with a wince at self oppression." He remembered that "ads caused endless contention" and that the ongoing battles over classifieds "would be the beginning of the end of *The Body Politic*." In an effort to avoid further debates, the collective published guidelines for would-be ad posters, revealing its views of the sexual mores of the period:

> If you're interested in meeting people it's best to be positive. Tell them about yourself and your interests—not about what you *don't* like. Specifying exclusions on the basis of race or appearance (saying "no fats or fems" for instance) is just plain rude, and being rude doesn't make friends.[33]

The Body Politic's code of sexual mores and political vision reached readers across North America and around the world. Initially, members of the collective personally distributed copies during their travels. As Jerald Moldenhauer explained, "Each year I managed a trip to Europe, usually Germany, Italy, England, and France. I carried copies of the *BP* with me to give to activists and bookshops that might be interested in selling the paper. I believe at least one other collective member did this kind of personal distribution, but only in England and Scotland." Moldenhauer credited Jim Steakley's series on the history of homosexuals in Germany with increasing "the international distribution of the paper, which early on had sales across Europe and in Australia."[34]

The staff at *Fag Rag*, by contrast, initially struggled to distribute their paper widely. John Mitzel remembered encountering problems with the post office when he requested a bulk mailing permit. When a post office clerk asked Mitzel what he was planning to mail, he replied, "A gay male anarchist publication." Mitzel's permit request was denied, but later a friend at the post office assisted him in dealing with the bureaucracy. Mitzel recalled mailing the journal to readers from New Orleans to Salt Lake City. In its early years of publication, *Fag Rag* had between 400 and 500 subscribers. The other 4,500 copies in each printing, according to Mitzel, were sold for a dime on newsstands in gay bookstores or given away.[35]

The geographic reach of *Fag Rag*, which was more of a northeastern periodical than *The Body Politic*, revealed a fact about the gay press, and the gay liberation movement, overall. Both publications connected people across great distances. The gay press in the United States promoted one another as well as papers in other countries. The January 1972 issue of *The Body Politic* listed the names and addresses of more than three dozen other gay newspapers across the world—from papers in Detroit, Houston, and Milwaukee to papers in France, like *Revue Littéraire et Scientifique,* and Berlin's *Pickbube.* By mid-1973, ads for the European gay newspapers had started to appear in *The Body Politic.*

That the gay press was a worldwide phenomenon indicates that gay people in the seventies did not see themselves simply as citizens of Canada or of the United States or even of Europe, but as a people transcending place and time. The impact of Steakley's series, for instance, revealed that sexual orientation trumped citizenship and nationality for many gay people. From the vantage point of many who read the series, the Nazi persecution of gay people was not just German history, but their history.[36]

The Body Politic and other gay newspapers did not merely embody the international spirit of many gay people, but helped to create it. Similar to pan-Africanism—the movement that encouraged black people across the globe to see themselves as part of a shared political struggle—gay people, too, in the seventies understood liberation as a universal struggle that affected gay people beyond their home country. Technological advances in publishing that allowed for cheap mass production of printed material, combined with the rise in aviation and other forms of travel, enabled gay newspapers to foster international connections in ways that would have been much more difficult in previous decades. Still, some observers saw differences in how gay publications fostered those global connections. According to Moldenhauer, who was born in Ohio but moved to Toronto to work on *The Body Politic,* the paper owed its global perspective to its location: Toronto "was well positioned," he said, "to produce a serious gay journal with a more global perspective." To him, US papers at the time were susceptible to notions of American exceptionalism that prevented them from looking beyond national borders. Canada's French and English history prompted *The Body Politic,* Moldenhauer recalled, "to look more to Europe for its cultural identity."[37]

Gay readers of *The Body Politic* were kept up to date about the plight of their gay brothers and sisters across the world. Articles appeared on gay political struggles throughout Europe and the fights for equality in Australia and New Zealand. A single page in the December 1, 1975, issue of *The Body Politic* reported on the organization of gay political activists in Israel, a recommendation by Polish doctors to send homosexuals to labor camps, and efforts to censor the Brazilian press's references to homosexuality.[38]

Violence was never far from the front page. The January 1, 1975, issue of *The Body Politic* reported on a death squad that targeted gay people in Chile. According to the article, this group was "designed to physically eliminate homosexuals" and had been responsible for numerous murders in Santiago. The article described two victims: an "executive of an automobile firm" who was found dead in his home with "multiple head wounds," and a French teacher, also found dead in his home, his skull fractured. The article noted that in both cases the assailants "turned up the victims' radios full blast in order to drown out any screams for help."[39]

The article did not represent original reporting but rather the collegiality and shared sense of purpose among gay periodicals across the world. A group of Argentinian gay activists heard of the death squad and made contact with a gay group in Australia. The Australian gay liberation press then sent the story to *The Body Politic*, which reached readers across Canada, Europe, and the United States. The paper also reprinted a letter from the Argentinians to the Australians next to the story. The Argentinians explained that they were publishing the fifth edition of their magazine *Somos* (*We Are*), as well as distributing flyers throughout Buenos Aires announcing the publication of their book *Letters to a Homosexual.* They described "the political environment" in Argentina as "very complex" and claimed that there was the "danger that we may still be turned against as scapegoats." The Argentinians ended the letter by emphasizing the shared struggle for liberation that connected gay people across national borders. "We must get together and stay in close contact," the letter read. "We are in constant contact with the most important people around the world. . . . Every gay liberation group is connected with its own country—and we never forget ours—but we know that in a way we all have a fatherland only in the abstract."[40]

Although *The Body Politic* and other publications in North America published stories about gay people across the globe, they tended to focus their attention on the English-speaking world, continental Europe, and South America. Few references to Africa or Asia appeared in its pages. *The Body Politic* reported on the formation of the Gay Liberation Front in Bombay in 1977 in response to the criminalization of homosexuality and police brutality against gay people in India. An article in *Gay Sunshine* in 1977 featured a critical analysis of the Japanese writer Yukio Mishima that analyzed his sexuality, work, and death. Other articles, problematically, such as an article on prostitution in Africa and particularly an article on Muslims, perpetuated a troubling fascination with queer people of color. In the article on Muslims, the writer recited poetry and reproduced photographs that celebrated homosexuality and emphasized "boy love." The poems embraced pedophilia in exploring the meaning of romance between boys and men in the history of "Arab civilization." Readers did not seem to object to the subject or to *Gay Sunshine*'s framing of homosexuality in Muslim history and culture.[41]

In reifying stereotypes about Muslim sexuality that offended few if any of *The Body Politic*'s readers, this article, with its Orientalist framework, may have obfuscated the subject of pedophilia enough to head off any reaction to it. A few months later, however, when the paper published an article on pedophilia all hell broke loose.[42] A few weeks after *The Body Politic* ran "Men Loving Boys Loving Men" by Gerald Hannon, a member of the collective since 1972, the Toronto police raided the offices of *The Body Politic* and seized twelve boxes of materials and the paper's subscription lists. The police charged the collective with "use of the mails to distribute immoral, indecent or scurrilous material."[43]

The article aimed to defend the rights of men who had romantic and sexual relationships with boys. Its publication appeared after Anita Bryant's campaign that attacked gay people as child molesters had gotten under way and after numerous columns had been published by Claire Hoy, a conservative journalist and critic of the gay community in Toronto. It also followed in the wake of the murder of a young boy who many believed was killed by a group of gay men.

Three months before the publication of Hannon's article on pedophilia, Emanuel Jaques, a twelve-year-old shoeshine boy in Toronto, was raped and drowned in a sink. Four men were charged with the murder, and the mainstream press labeled Jaques's death a "gay murder," causing a public outcry against homosexuality. As Gerry Oxford, a member of the collective, recalled, "People were tying us [homosexuals] to the whole Emmanuel Jaques thing, which was horrifying that people would associate every homosexual in the street with what happened to Emmanuel Jaques."[44]

The collective waited to publish Hannon's article out of fear of being associated in any way with Jaques's death, but they soon realized that the time would never be right to publish an article on pedophilia. "We have had it on hand, typeset and laid out, for nearly six months," the collective explained, "but we have hesitated, sensitive to the feeling that 'the climate was not right' after the antigay media barrages which followed Emanuel Jaques' death." Although many within the collective had argued against publishing it, the collective eventually agreed to run it. The article was intended as a starting point for a conversation. As the staff noted in the preface to the article, "The tide must be resisted, the discussion must be opened up."[45]

The preface was entitled "1977 Has Been the Year of the Children." The writers cataloged the many ways in which children had appeared as subjects of both debate and concern within the gay community—namely, in lesbian parents' custody issues, in the murder of Emanuel Jaques, and in Anita Bryant's campaign to "save our children" from gay people. Claiming that "children are to be the last frontier of heterosexist bias," the collective viewed youth sexuality as part of the larger fight for gay liberation. The collective argued on behalf of two positions: First, in a direct riposte to Anita Bryant's campaign as well as the growing criticism across the United States and Canada that aimed to prevent gay people from working as teachers, counselors, or child care workers, they maintained that gay people had the right to work with youth. And second, they argued that gay youth deserved to have access to positive representations of gay culture.[46]

In some ways, Hannon's article foreshadowed one of the best-known twentieth-century debates surrounding freedom of speech. A year later, in Skokie, Illinois, the American Civil Liberties Union defended the right of neo-Nazis to march in a neighborhood where many Holocaust survivors lived. Even though many members of the ACLU strenuously disagreed with neo-Nazism, they valued freedom of speech above all else and fought to protect the neo-Nazis' right to assemble. Similarly, despite the fact that many gay people in the collective objected to pedophilia on both legal and moral grounds, they believed in Hannon's right to publish the article and in *The Body Politic*'s responsibility to moderate the debate.

The collective understood many of the risks involved in publishing Hannon's article. At the end of their preface, they wrote about a boy who had called the office of *The Body Politic*. Sounding about nine or ten years old, he had asked to speak to Hannon, who had written on youth and sexuality in a previous issue, to ask him where to have sex. The collective member who picked up the phone realized that it was a setup. "The prompting voice of an adult male," the preface noted, "was audible in the background." As a disclaimer, they wrote that "it is illegal even to advise people under the age of 18 (and gay people under 21) to have sex," then added: "We can only speculate about the character of someone who would rather manipulate a child into an act of fraud than have him know anything real about the lives of men who love men and women who love women." Thus, the collective decided that the need for an open and public forum where youth sexuality could be discussed and gay youth could have an outlet to connect with the gay community outweighed the risks.

Yet there was a discrepancy between the collective's argument that young gay people should have access to gay people, gay newspapers, and gay culture, on the one hand, and Hannon's promotion of intimate and sexual relationships between men and boys, on the other. Despite the collective's goal of using the newspaper as a form of community outreach and a social service for young gay people, Hannon's article conflated sex with mentorship and confused romance with support.[17]

In its intense concern over the article, the collective failed to perceive this problem. Hannon argued that society had demonized pedophiles and that the word "pedophile" had become misunderstood. The actual meaning of this Greek-derived word, he claimed, was "lover of boys." According to Hannon, "People use it [pedophile] as a label for a disease," and he noted that "pedophile," like "homosexual," was a clinician's word for a kind of pathology. The collective had also introduced this argument in the preface, where it claimed that men who loved boys had been called "child molesters," "chicken hawks," and "dirty old men" . . . "just as all of us are 'pansies,' 'lezzies,' and 'queers.'"[48]

To prove that pedophiles were not "psychopaths who prey on hapless boys and then murder them" or "wealthy citizens [who] make clandestine use of a well-organized 'boy bordello,' one that recruits runaways and waifs," Hannon offered vignettes of three men and their relationships with boys. Both in his descriptions of these relationships and in his definition of "pedophilia," Hannon asserted that the sex between minors and adults did not involve force, coercion, or any other kind of abuse. In fact, in his view, heterosexual pedophiles were abusers. Hannon's stories of men and boys going bowling, watching TV, and cuddling were meant to convey innocence, yet he did not once acknowledge the power dynamics that govern relationships between men and boys. Hannon never suggested that the boys might not have been equipped to make decisions for themselves.[49]

Hannon's article was problematic in other respects too. The collective's preface argued for the need to provide youth with a forum to learn about their sexual orientation at a time when gay teachers and counselors were being prohibited from working with youth and gay youth often had no contact with the adult gay community.[50] According to the collective, the gay press could offer support, encouragement, and an opportunity for young people seeking to learn more about themselves and the history and culture of gay people. Conversely, Hannon did not emphasize that gay adults could be mentors to young people, but instead described romantic friendships, courting rituals, and sexual contact. Furthermore, he told the stories from the vantage point of the adults, thus foreclosing the voices, and agency, of the youth involved. In essence, Hannon defined mentorship as sex and romance—and in so doing caused a maelstrom of controversy.

Journalists at the *Toronto Sun* skewered *The Body Politic,* claiming, "Kids, not rights, is their craving." Claire Hoy led the attack by publishing three editorials in the *Sun* that condemned *The Body Politic.* One headline read, "Our Taxes Help Homosexuals Promote Abuse of Children." This was not the first time a Toronto newspaper had attacked *The Body Politic.* In 1974 the *Star* claimed that gay people "have the power to convert others to their own way of life" and that *The Body Politic* advocated for the "homosexual seduction of children."[51] The collective sent a letter of rebuttal to the *Star,* but it was not printed. In 1977, in the context of Anita Bryant's campaign and Emanuel Jaques's murder, it was inevitable that the response to Hannon's article would be quick and vicious.

Hannon had taken direct aim at Bryant. In the final paragraphs of his article, he wrote that her campaign to "save our children" was actually a rhetorical device that people in power had employed throughout history to further oppress dispossessed populations.

> They tried to save our children from witches, and turned the middle ages into a charnel house of burning and innocent flesh. They tried to save our children from Jews, and almost succeeded through twelve years of methodical and monstrous savagery. They tried to save our children from communists, and sat with Senator McCarthy in judgment upon heroic lives trying to salvage some dignity, some integrity from that degrading exercise. Now they want to save our children from homosexuals. They want to save our children from us.

The last sentence was meant both figuratively and literally: the collective had been drawing attention to gay parents who lost their children in custody battles as a result of their sexual orientation. And indeed, this passage represented Hannon's most powerful line of reasoning—yet it failed to consider the power relations involved in man-boy relations.[52]

The following month, after the police raid, the collective published a special issue titled, simply enough, "Police Raid Issue," which included the editorial "Crisis: In the Midst of Danger: A Chance to Unite." The editorial began by explaining that the word "crisis" in Chinese is made up of two characters; the first means "danger" and the second means "opportunity." The collective, which continued to support Hannon's article, saw the crisis at *The Body Politic* as an opportunity to advance the movement. "[We have] the chance to clarify issues, to renew allegiances. To fight back." Noting that a thousand people had taken to the streets in the freezing cold to protest Anita Bryant's visit to Toronto to support antigay activists there during the controversy, they wrote, "There were probably as many lesbians and feminists there as gay men, and that has never happened before."[53]

Yet many readers had disagreed with the original article and wrote letters to the editor insisting that pedophilia not be seen as part of the gay liberation movement. One reader wrote, "I don't believe that children's liberation should be a priority for the gay liberation movement. I think we will find it very difficult to defend that article in public, though defend it I do." Another wrote, "To paraphrase *TBP*'s masthead slogan, 'The liberation of pedophiles can only be the work of pedophiles themselves.'" The writer continued: "Why should gays stick out their necks for them? What have they done, or are they doing, or are they going to do, for us?" Others argued that it set the movement back. "That stupid article about teachers and Big Brothers loving boys (and glorifying them for it) has set us back several years." One letter-writer indicted *The Body Politic* for not realizing that some gay people like to keep a "low profile" and "don't need noisy idiots like you to harm us."[54]

Other readers supported the article. They endorsed Hannon's arguments and praised *The Body Politic* as the vanguard of the gay liberation movement for bravely discussing issues that others dared not touch. "I appreciate a great deal your finally publishing the article 'Men Loving Boys Loving Men.' The debate within the Collective mirrors the debate within the gay movement itself on the approach toward youth sexuality. I'm glad you chose to inform us and challenge our views on young people and sex." Some of the supporters understood that criticizing the article and condemning Hannon would lead to sharp divisions within the gay community that could jeopardize the larger aims of the movement. The collective had recognized that the likes of Anita Bryant and Claire Hoy were looking for any reason to launch a case against gay liberation. "The forces of reaction are organizing fast," the collective wrote in the special issue. "There is no doubt that we are in danger. But the danger is not, as one might think, simply that protection for gay people may not be included in the Human Rights Code in Ontario. The real danger is that we'll do what our opponents want us to do. Become confused. Attack each other. Be divided."[55]

Interestingly enough, however, what did more than the outside world's response to the article to promote divisions within the gay community was the article itself. According to Pat Leslie, a writer

for *The Body Politic,* Hannon's article "put many lesbians in a difficult position." Although initially she criticized her male colleagues
for not being sensitive to how the article affected lesbian mothers
and their relationships with their children, the arrival of Anita Bryant in Toronto compelled Leslie and other lesbian feminists—as well
as straight feminists—to throw their full support behind *The Body
Politic.* "Feminists know many of the gains we have won over the
past years will be lost if we chose to ignore Anita Bryant." As Leslie argued, "The question of sexuality is a feminist one with a feminist perspective and an attack on gay men is at the same time an
attack on women, forcing us back into traditional sex roles." Leslie
reported that gay men and lesbians came together in response to the
Anita Bryant demonstrations "successfully—for a moment." But she
worried that the coming together of lesbians and gay men might be
short-lived. "It will take a strong lesbian presence to teach gay men
about the need for a unity that is more than a pretense," she wrote.[56]

In the following month's issue, *The Body Politic* more directly
addressed Leslie's concerns and published an in-depth feature story
on "former separatist and Lesbian Theorist" Charlotte Bunch, who
analyzed the dynamics among lesbian and gay men, feminism, and
civil rights. Then, that spring, Chris Bearchell, author of a column
called "Dykes," explored "female child–adult relations in the pol
itics of the lesbian movement." Like Hannon, Bearchell began her
article by telling the story of a few female relationships in an effort
to underscore that younger females were not always coerced into a
relationship with older women but actually often initiated it. Unlike
Hannon, however, Bearchell did not eroticize these relationships, nor
did she detail physical and sexual interactions. Instead, she analyzed
how social structures, laws, and the policing of gender oppressed
young girls' sexuality. According to Bearchell, young girls "are forming meaningful relationships outside the confines of biological definitions and are stepping outside the bounds of parental authority. If
a young woman rejects not only parental authority and anti-sexual
attitudes but compulsory heterosexuality as well, she may be thrice
condemned."[57]

By using feminism to frame her argument, Bearchell developed a more sophisticated critique of social norms than Hannon had. "There may be feminists and lesbians who, because of their experiences with male power," Bearchell wrote, "suspect that child-adult relationships have more serious consequences for male children. As a feminist I have to remind any woman with those hesitations that male children, unlike their sisters, are the inheritors of male privilege. They will out-grow the oppression they experience as children." Whether the collective viewed Bearchell's article as an extension of or redress for Hannon's article, its publication demonstrated *The Body Politic*'s potential not only for incisive social and political commentary but for introspection and self-critique.[58]

The police raid on *The Body Politic*'s headquarters and the paper's impending trial for "use of the mails to distribute immoral, indecent or scurrilous material" made news across the gay world. The January–February issue of *Join Hands,* a gay periodical based out of San Francisco, led with the headline "Gay Press Attacked" and stamped "Final Issue?" on a reproduction of *The Body Politic*'s masthead. *Join Hands* reported that the police raid resulted from the fact that the "Ontario Human Rights Code is presently under consideration" and "a number of government ministers are known to oppose protection for gay people in the Code." *Join Hands* quoted Edward Jackson, *The Body Politic* spokesperson, who explained, "This is only one article in a paper that has been in publication for six years, and it is about the lives of only four gay men. That the government sees it as an excuse to refuse recognition of the rights of hundreds of thousands of gay people is simply further evidence of how much we need legal protection. . . . The real intent of the police raid," Jackson suggested, "was to shut this newspaper down."[59]

In Texas, *Gay Austin* reported that "the warrant used to seize material from the newspaper's office" permitted the police to take "almost anything." The Texas paper quoted Jackson's claim that the police filled twelve large crates with "subscription lists dating into the past, distribution and advertising records, corporate and financial records—even our chequebook." Jackson further stated, in the *Gay Austin* account, "It was an obvious attempt to terrorize the readers of a newspaper by seizing its subscription list. It has the effect of intimidating subscribers of a publication of which the government does not approve."[60]

Gay Austin placed the police raid on *The Body Politic*'s office within a broader global context of attacks against gay newspapers. In Britain, the *Gay News* had been sued for "blasphemous libel." As *The Body Politic* itself commented on the case: "In England, gays have also been sensitive to the parallels between the *Gay News* case and that of *The Body Politic*. Both papers are fighting charges which appear to have been trumped up in an attempt to intimidate or silence the gay press."[61] *Gay Austin* also reported that Diana Press, a feminist publishing house in California, was "viciously vandalized" and that two Toronto men were being criminally charged "for hanging gay posters." For readers of gay periodicals, the raid on *The Body Politic*'s headquarters meant censorship, surveillance, and, for some, a concerted effort to shut down newspapers and free speech altogether.[62]

As the trial approached, activists across the world publicly protested the raid of *The Body Politic*, and some Americans issued statements defending the paper to the US attorney general. The list of supporters ranged from activist groups in France and Australia to prominent leaders in the gay community, including Jonathan Ned Katz and Harvey Milk. Craig Rodwell spread word of a fund-raising event hosted by historian Martin Duberman in his West Village home in New York City to support *The Body Politic*.[63]

The trial began on January 2, 1979, a year after the publication of Gerald Hannon's article. Claire Hoy appeared as a witness for the prosecution, while Hannon, Ken Popert, and Ed Jackson represented the collective. The trial quickly moved beyond the legal concerns as the prosecution turned it into a vehicle to denounce homosexuality. James Long, a psychologist for the prosecution, told the *Globe and Mail*, a national newspaper in Canada, "It might be possible for some homosexuals to be perfectly normal people, but I haven't met any." The following day the *Toronto Star* reported on the trial's proceedings with the headline "Trial Told of Socrates' Sex Life." Ken Popert, who had been arrested along with Hannon and Ed Jackson in the raid, said that the trial sometimes felt "like a well-organized circus rather than a juridical proceeding."[64]

The collective was ultimately acquitted, on February 14, 1979. The judge's opinion stated that Hannon's article was "not written in a prurient style nor does it have the typical hallmarks of hard-core pornography—it is not lascivious, sexually stimulating nor titillating. It does not use gross explicit language calculated to cause sexual arousal or stimulation." The judge's description of the article as part of a series on "youth and sexuality" signaled his understanding of the broader intellectual and political objectives of the collective as a forum for thought.[65]

But the court battles did not end there. There were six appeals, two of which made it to the Supreme Court of Canada, and a range of other court activity over the course of six years. The scandal that began in 1977 finally ended in 1983: the county court judge in Toronto upheld the decision in favor of *The Body Politic*.[66]

Despite the victory, the whole episode probably raised more questions about the meaning of gay liberation than it did to guarantee its future. Many readers of the gay press were surely left to wonder what aspects of their sexual lives would be accepted by society and what aspects would land them in court. Did they have to educate their families, coworkers, and neighbors about the differences between homosexuality and pedophilia? Did gay people need to explain to each other that even though they might cruise parks for sex they were not members of sex rings that would gang-rape and murder a shoeshine boy? And what of one of the intended audiences for the article: young boys struggling with their sexuality? Did the article reach them, and if so, what effect did it—and the backlash—have on them? The concerns of readers of *The Body Politic* may have been more immediate. What would the government do with the seized subscription lists? Would they be accused of being pedophiles because they subscribed to *The Body Politic*?

The answers to these questions are lost to us, but we can be more certain about the answer to another question. How did the article affect *The Body Politic?* In the aftermath of its legal victory, the collective was in debt for legal fees of over $100,000. They had placed ads in the paper asking for money to pay for the legal defense, but the costs ultimately contributed to the paper's death in 1987. Ed Jackson's 1978 warning, as spokesperson for *The Body Politic,* that the case against Hannon's article was designed to shut the paper down entirely would prove to be prescient.[67]

The controversy surrounding the article nevertheless reveals the central role of the press in the gay community. As a forum, *The Body Politic* fostered important discussions about the meaning of sexuality. Gay newspapers made it possible for writers to explore controversial issues, and readers from across the globe were able to join the conversation. At a time when not every gay person had access to, or even interest in, joining a political organization, the gay press proved to be a critical conduit of information and ideas and a means of forging a community that would not have otherwise existed. Some of those who wrote letters to the editor, for example, remarked that they viewed themselves as politically conservative, or as uninterested in the everyday workings of gay politics, and preferred to keep a low profile. As one reader noted, "Most gays are not involved in gay lib organizing or lifestyles where they meet other gays often. . . . These magazines are often their only resource for making contact with their peers."[68]

It is notable, however, that though *The Body Politic* published thousands of articles on a dizzying number of topics over the course of the twenty-plus years of its existence, both the stories that catapulted the paper to international fame and the story that led to its downfall involved sexuality, violence, and government power. In other words, a line can be traced from Jim Steakley to Gerald Hannon, however problematic the latter's article was.

The Body Politic and its readers made this connection themselves. While members of the collective were never sentenced to labor camps or tortured or killed by death squads, they consistently compared their plight to the experience of gay people in Nazi Germany. And at the height of the controversy over Hannon's article, the collective feared that they were becoming the scapegoats for general economic and social problems, including rising unemployment. As the collective explained, "Homosexuals were among Hitler's scapegoats too, and his solution to the economic and social crisis of that time included a war to save that world from decadence." On the very same page, *The Body Politic* published a letter from Ronnie Allen, a reader from Somerville, Massachusetts, that referred to Ernst Roehm, a member of the SS, and to the infamous Night of the Long Knives, when Nazis murdered a number of political and military leaders, including Roehm, who was known to be a homosexual. Allen's letter proved the extent to which gay people in the 1970s drew analogies to Nazism to frame their own experiences during the period of the trial. The following month an article appeared in *The Body Politic* warning readers that the National Front, Britain's "leading far-right organization," had said that "homosexuals will be exterminated in gas chambers" if the political party with which gay people were affiliated came to power. And shortly after *The Body Politic* printed a special issue on the police raid, it ran a history of gay liberation in Germany in 1864—further aligning their plight with the history of homosexuality in Germany and the looming threat of state-sanctioned persecution.[69]

Gay people embraced the history of the persecution of homosexuals by the Nazis because it spoke to them and offered a much-needed analogy to their own experience. Gay liberation is often retrospectively characterized as a period of victories and celebration, but the tenor of the 1970s was in fact one of contingency and often fear. Many gay people didn't believe that gay liberation would last.

The history of the gay press reveals this and much else—such as the frank and serious debates about the meaning of gay sex among gay people. Talking about sex could be just as revolutionary as engaging in it, and the gay press facilitated and, at times, created that conversation. The story of the gay press therefore is not only about the creation of a vast communication network for gay people but also about how they talked and thought about the meaning of freedom. The press reported on liberation's discontents and on the movement's setbacks and struggles. As the December 1, 1978, issue of *The Body Politic* explained on the eve of the trial, "The law books will record a decision; they may record an appeal. What they won't record is a struggle, nor will there be any mention of the real forces of oppression."[70]

The Body Politic and other periodicals did, however, name the forces of oppression. In issue after issue throughout the 1970s, the gay press gave voice to the emerging gay body politic. The gay press succeeded in its stated mission, even if many papers, like *The Body Politic*, didn't last. And it succeeded because it left behind a remarkable and invaluable record of the intellectual ferment, and contradictions, that accompanied gay liberation.

6 "PRISON SOUNDS"

In popular memory, the 1970s soundtrack is a particular set of sounds: of crowds marching down city streets, of people chanting protest slogans, of late-night discos. Many who lived through the decade can still remember those sounds and feel the beat. They can close their eyes and return to the cruising parks, the abandoned waterfronts, and the dance floors, and they can still hear the faint whispers about all-night orgies, the grunting in the dark, the shaking of tambourines.[1]

But there were other sounds too—the sounds of those who could not dance until dawn at Studio 54, who could not join the loud parades.

When they heard the sounds of sex, it was often not consensual sex. A man's arms were pinned down to his sides, his head smashed into a cot, his legs spread open. No tambourines jingled. There were no political victories in sight.

The men making these sounds were in prison.

Some of them may have been attending one of those all-night outdoor orgies, but the cops showed up while their shirts were off and their pants were down. They were then handcuffed, pushed into a paddy wagon wearing someone else's T-shirt, and silenced.

The journalists of the gay press wanted to reform the practices that had led to their arrest, but most of all they wanted to hear from them. They wanted to give prisoners a voice.[2]

The gay press encouraged prisoners to write about their experiences and the abuses they suffered at the hands of a criminal system that pathologized them. Prisoners were also encouraged to write poetry, to express themselves in a genre that could capture what it felt like to be a gay prisoner. The gay press understood that gay prisoners had been writing poetry in jail since Oscar Wilde got locked up for indecent behavior. In stolen moments when Wilde was not doing manual labor, he wrote "De Profundis" about his time in jail, about his love, Lord Alfred Douglas, and about damaging his family's name.

Gay journalists in the 1970s wanted gay prisoners to follow in this tradition as best they could. Prisoners scribbled poems on whatever paper they could get—a stack of loose leaf from the library, a donated notebook, a paper towel. Gay editors published their poetry in the foldout sections of specialty newspapers devoted to gay prison life and also sometimes in popular gay newspapers, like San Francisco's *Gay Sunshine*.[3] That is where the following poem was found—in the bottom left-hand corner of a page in *Gay Sunshine*. It was surrounded by other poems that experimented with form, or spoke of loneliness, or otherwise revealed something about the decade in which they were written:

What are the sounds that echo through the tiers of a prison?

The sound a man crying in the quiet of the night
. . .
The sound of a man hanging himself
because he is too damn tired to go on living
the sound of a human being giving up.

The sound of a young inmate being raped
by an older and rougher inmate
the sound of blood and tears
and guilt and shame.

. . . And the worst sound of all
the sound of moving steel
the sound of a cell door slamming shut
and confining a human being in a cage of cement and steel.[4]

—**RONALD ENDERSBY** (a gay brother recently released from prison)

Endersby explained how prisoners felt and offered a counter-narrative to the triumphant discourse of gay liberation. Accomplishing what protests could not, poetry could reveal the interiority of the gay experience at the height of liberation. It exposed the fear, loneliness, monotony, sadness, and violence that shaped the lives of those farthest from the pride parades and political marches.

The language of protests was focused on broad critiques of structures of power, chants like "Two, four, six, eight, smash the Church, smash the State." Remembering only the protests of the seventies forecloses a discussion of the emotional experience of gay individuals and, more fundamentally, suggests that gay liberation was all about its adversarial and often combative relationship with heterosexuality. Put another way, the traditional narrative of gay history tells of gay people screaming, yelling, and critiquing the state.[5]

Yet gay people were invested not just in changing the laws but also in creating a culture. The gay poetry of the 1970s tells the hidden history of gay liberation as it reveals loss rather than victory, loneliness rather than community, restriction rather than liberation. It is no wonder that it has been forgotten. Even at the time, poetry was on the margins of gay liberation. "Poetry has been the poor country cousins in the gay liberation movement," noted a writer for *Fag Rag*. "Even among our own we live unwelcome." To counter this, *Fag Rag* devoted an entire issue to poetry in 1973, publishing dozens of poems by gay writers, both white and black. The periodical featured the work of Gerald Malanga, a noted poet and photographer who worked closely with Andy Warhol, and printed a three-page feature article on the poet W. H. Auden, in keeping with the commitment of gay writers and activists of the period to situating their work in historical context. *Fag Rag* also published—long before the scholarly and mainstream literary presses—snippets of Auden's poems that revealed his participation in the gay community in Berlin in the 1930s, as well as a few of his homoerotic stanzas.[6]

The plight of gay, lesbian, and transgender prisoners was another concern of the gay press. Exactly two years after the Stonewall uprising, a headline in *Gay Sunshine* read, "The Forgotten Ones: Gays in Prison." The article was written by gay and transgender people in a prison in Washington State. They wrote: "There is no protection for the Homosexual from the guards and administration, from the morbid prejudism and discrimination, name-calling and psychological anguish the Homosexual must endure from the guards and administration." As gay activists fought to improve mainstream attitudes about homosexuality, gay inmates reminded the gay community that discrimination and prejudice prevailed inside prisons despite the many changes occurring outside of them.[7]

Poetry became gay inmates' main vehicle for expressing their feelings and raising awareness; moreover, this unconstrained genre facilitated the publication of numerous writers in a single periodical. Gay activist groups solicited poems from gay inmates because they wanted them to feel part of the community, and also because they wanted to extend that community from the bars and bathhouses and churches and bookstores into the prisons. For instance, *Join Hands*, a newspaper founded in San Francisco in 1972 to support gay prisoners, advertised a poetry contest sponsored by the Illinois Prisoners Organization, which was seeking submissions to be compiled into an anthology by "Brothers and Sisters incarcerated in this nation's prison kamp system." "We want to hear from as many prisoners as possible," *Join Hands* announced. "We want your ideas to be expressed in the newsletter. We don't necessarily have to agree with your views in order to print them. You don't have to send in a polished statement to have your views published."[8]

The incarcerated gay poet Paul Mariah helped to bridge the gap between the burgeoning poetry movement within gay liberation and prison culture. While incarcerated, his ability to express himself was often limited. He told a reporter for *Gay Sunshine* that he "could not write anything in prison and send it out" because "it had to be censored." He could not even take books from visitors.[9] Neverthe-less, he would emerge as one of the most prolific imprisoned poets of his generation, writing over 500 poems during his lifetime. He also founded both *Manroot* magazine and Manroot Press, a publishing company devoted exclusively to poetry that published a number of leading gay poets in the seventies, giving each over thirty pages in a single issue to feature their work.[10]

Mariah wrote a great deal about his time in prison. It is unclear how much of his poetry he wrote in prison, hiding it in his cell, and how much he wrote after he was released. His poetry reflects both a commitment to prison reform and an attempt to develop a canon of imprisoned gay writers. In "The Swimmer Who Never Swam," Mariah yearns for life beyond bars, while in "The Holding Compa-nies' Company," he describes the bleak conditions within a prison.[11] He also tells the story of a public execution of a gay man and the isola-tion that his bereaved lover felt in the poem "In Quarry/Rock: A Real-ity Poem in the Tradition of Genet." Mariah's reference to Jean Genet reflects his keen historical sensibility. Genet was a popular twentieth-century French gay poet and writer who was locked up many times for lewd acts and for petty crimes. Mariah's "reality poem" was inspired by Genet's famous poem "Le Condamné à mort" ("The Man Sentenced to Death"), about two lovers separated by the death sen-tence imposed on one of them. Throughout the seventies, many gay people read Mariah's poetry and recognized his effort to use *Manroot* to create a canon of gay literature. Mariah also reclaimed the work of Robert Ingersoll, the Civil War veteran and friend of Walt Whitman who was a leading social critic and advocate of prison reform.[12]

The history of incarcerated gay writers and leaders became a popular topic in many gay newspapers in the 1970s. *The Body Politic*, for example, featured a story on the imprisoned Soviet poet Gen-nady Trifonov.[13] Sentenced to a labor camp in the Ural Mountains in 1978, Trifonov gained international attention owing to the robust efforts of the gay press to report on what had happened to him. The gay poet, though highly regarded by the "Russian literati," had been "brutally beaten and carried off" to prison. While incarcerated, Tri-fonov wrote a poem to the gay community.

All of you tell me: I alone
sang—as no one's allowed to sing—
of how we love without response
him who's our sole necessity[14]

By writing "we," Trifinov acknowledges a collective struggle that gay men across the globe were waging in the name of love. "Him who's our sole necessity" evokes an intimacy, a love, that for Trifonov is the essence of being gay. During his incarceration, which lasted at least six months, gay newspapers followed his struggle and relayed updates during the Cold War, signaling how gay people's allegiance often transcended national conflicts. A reporter for *The Body Politic* wrote that Soviet officials claimed to have released Trifonov from prison in early 1979, but the reporter remained skeptical about whether this was really the case. According to other sources published in the 1980s and later, Trifonov was released in 1980.[15]

Many gay prisoners wrote, like Trifonov, about love and romance. "There was something unforgettable / In the slender way you stood there," wrote one gay inmate in a poem titled "To Rickie." Poetry became a way for incarcerated gay people to evoke the memory of lovers whom they no longer could see. In "To Rickie," the poet continued: "I felt that quickening emotion. You would always arouse in me."[16]

By writing about past relationships and romance, incarcerated poets offered a rare glimpse into homosexual culture at the time. Poetry functioned as the "hidden transcript" of the gay liberation movement—it circulated primarily if not exclusively among gay people in gay periodicals and anthologies. The archives of the gay liberation movement are replete with notes about political strategies, minutes from organizational meetings, and newspapers that show the multifaceted culture of the period. But what about love and romance, which propelled many to join the liberation movement in the first place? Where are the stories of intimacy? We have photographs of happy couples holding hands at a march or embracing in a bar, but where are the accounts of the longing and desire that accompanied intimate relationships? Where are the expressions of the emotions that kept those relationships together or drove them apart?[17]

Ironically, perhaps, gay prisoners offered some of the richest and most nuanced narratives about intimacy in the form of poetry and lyrical prose. When alone in their cells, thoughts of love, romance, and desire often provided inmates with their only solace. And not only men were moved to write poetry. A lesbian prisoner in Clinton, New Jersey, asked, in "Ode to Vera":

> *Will I think of you?*
> *Only when I feel warm and wanted.*[18]

Poems allowed gay and lesbian inmates to call their lover's name, and thereby became, in another sense, a "hidden transcript" of gay liberation.

In publishing gay and lesbian prisoners' romantic poetry, the gay press revealed many of the secret struggles experienced by many gay people, not just prisoners: unreciprocated romantic gestures, loneliness, the lack of love. There was little room in the political discourse of liberation to announce that one was struggling to find a date or was lonely. Poetry allowed this kind of declaration, enabling gay people to fully express their emotions and, in so doing, offer a different narrative of liberation.[19] In a poem titled "Loneliness," Harvey "Gypsy" Lerner, an inmate at a prison in Somers, Connecticut, wrote:

> *Wrapping little gifts*
> *Then giving them to self*
> *Opening a closed door*
> *And knowing no one's knocked.*[20]

Although prisoner poetry, in telling of quiet moments and internal turmoil, offers a direct contrast to the conventional narrative of loud, rambunctious, protest-oriented gay liberation, these poems were not solely about feelings and romance. Some incarcerated gay prisoners wrote to promote awareness and to critique prison culture. In "Responsibility," Gregory A. Mack, held in Florida State

Prison, wrote about the lack of solidarity among gay black inmates. "A conflict in progress . . . Black gays neglecting other Black Gays while others stridently interact." Other poems in the same issue of *Join Hands* highlighted Native Americans' and women's experiences in the prison system.[21]

Indeed, gay newspapers committed to prison reform frequently published stories about women and people of color in prison. *The Body Politic,* for example, reported on the meeting of a multiracial group of gay prisoners in the Washington State Penitentiary who were advocating for safe cells for gay inmates and organizing against sexism in prison, and the cover of the December 1976–January 1977 of *Join Hands* featured a photograph of black and white inmates embracing.[22]

The gay press's coverage of gay people of color in the prison population arose from a larger social reality in the 1970s. Its solicitation of prisoner writing can be traced to the gay liberation movement's study of the black civil rights movement, which had produced important black prisoner writers. A decade before the founding of *Join Hands,* Martin Luther King Jr. wrote his now-canonical "Letter from a Birmingham Jail," on April 16, 1963, in which he justified nonviolent action to break unjust laws. In the following decade, an even more radical genre of prison writing began to surface in the black power movement. The gay press would take its cue from black political leaders like Malcolm X, Eldridge Cleaver, and Angela Davis, who all wrote from prison or about their prison experiences.[23]

Gay newspapers published stories that featured the plight of imprisoned black activists. *Join Hands* followed the case of Assata Shakur, a member of the Black Panther Party and the Black Liberation Party, who was accused of killing a New Jersey state trooper in 1973. The November–December 1977 issue of *Join Hands* began with the headline "Shakur Tried Again." Featuring a photograph of Shakur, the article claimed that she had been a victim of racism and concluded, "During her four year confinement Shakur has been continually placed in solitary, illegally held in men's prisons and denied privacy, and has come to court in chains."[24]

A few months later, *Join Hands* republished a remarkable article written by Shakur about the status of women in prison that had originally appeared in *The Black Scholar*. Shakur described the struggles of women in prison and claimed that many of them had been incarcerated for prostitution, drug offenses, and other nonviolent crimes. Shakur also explained how sexuality functioned in prisons. "About 80 percent of the prison population engages in some form of homosexual relationship. Almost all follow negative, stereotypic male/female role models." Shakur went on: "Women who are 'aggressive' or who play the masculine roles are referred to as butches, bulldaggers or stud broads. They are always in demand because they are always in the minority. Women who are 'passive,' or who play feminine roles are referred to as fems. The butch-fem relationships are often oppressive, resembling the most oppressive, exploitative aspect of a sexist society."[25]

Shakur made it clear that she was writing in order to raise political awareness both within and outside prisons. "There is no connection between the women's movement and lesbianism. Most of the women at Riker's Island have no idea what feminism is, let alone lesbianism. Feminism, the women's liberation movement and the gay liberation movement are worlds away from women at Riker's. The black liberation struggle is equally removed from the lives of women at Riker's." She issued a call to action similar to what had motivated the gay press to give voice to gay prisoners in the first place. "Let us rebuild a sense of community," she exhorted. "Let us rebuild the culture of giving and carry on the tradition of fierce determination to move on closer to freedom."[26]

Join Hands also covered the story of Joan Little, a black woman charged in 1974 for using deadly force to protect herself against sexual assault from a white prison guard in North Carolina. Her case gained worldwide coverage when she was acquitted. It was the first case in which deadly force was justified in response to sexual assault. As had happened when readers of *The Body Politic* and other gay periodicals linked pink triangles and the history of the Nazis to their understanding of gay identity, the stories of black women and stories about racism in prisons began to serve as frameworks for many gay readers' conceptualizations of incarceration.[27]

The articles about Shakur, Little, and other black prisoners thus point to another untold story of gay liberation. The predominant form of gay people's political activism, we are often told, was the struggle with homophobic people, often through intense screaming matches for political rights. The gay press's coverage of prison life reveals a story that was unfolding on the margins, a place where gay people found common cause, and conversed with black people. They spoke among themselves, not to those in power, creating an alternative space in their own lives and in the political life of the nation.[28]

The gay press witnessed how the black power movement gave Shakur and Little a platform to highlight their struggle and a community to call their own. For many gay men, lesbians, and transgender people in the 1970s, being incarcerated usually exacerbated their already tenuous ties to their families and communities. The isolation felt by gay prisoners thus had multiple dimensions. One way the outside gay community attempted to address these feelings was to refer to gay people behind bars as their "brothers" and "sisters." In the poem by the gay inmate Ronald Endersby that appeared earlier in the chapter, a parenthetical note identified him as "a gay brother recently released from prison." While other minority groups and people used the term "brother" in the 1970s to assert a particular cultural and political solidarity, for gay activists the term not only carried that meaning but also gestured toward an intimacy that folded strangers into the embrace of a family.[29]

Of course, despite the fictive kin relations that gay prison activists forged, courts and parole boards hewed to traditional definitions of family. In many cases, gay people would be paroled only if they could prove that they had stable family connections, such as parents, children, or even a wife. And those who didn't have these ties were often doubly unlucky: not only turned down for parole, they were also allowed minimal contact with the outside world. Charley Shively, a leading writer for *Fag Rag*, recounted the difficulty of trying to reach a gay inmate imprisoned for sodomy. Shively could not gain access to the inmate because he was not recognized as a family member. "Several of us from Boston's gay liberation front did what we could but our ties were simply weaker than those of his brother and sister."[30]

Gay prisoners with few connections to the outside world saw the gay press not only as a place to give voice to their emotions and experiences but as a potential source of aid. It is unclear what Ricky Bohannon actually wanted readers of *Fag Rag* to do after he wrote them a poignant letter about his incarceration, but the contents of his letter, and his plea, were not uncommon. Nicknamed "Bo-Bo," he told readers that he was serving a life term for killing another inmate. He recounted how the man pulled a knife on him and told him that he had two choices: "either let him screw me—or he would stab me—(so you can picture what state of mind I was in)." Bohannon stated that he consented to sex, but when the inmate put the knife down, "I took the knife and stab [*sic*] him in his chest." Bohannon described not being "happy or pleased at all about the killing but what's left for me to do except keep my head together and seek help!" Bohannon was transferred to another prison, where he made many friends because of his "age and youthful" looks, but when he realized that his friends wanted sex, he found himself alone. "It all ended up that I found out the hard way that you have no true friends in a place like this." Bohannon eventually found one friend, with whom he soon fell in love. His friend was black, however, and according to Bohannon, "a white person accepts *any* black person is the lowest thing in the prison in the eyes of the guards and all the inmates." He asked readers for help in a few places in his letter, but it was unclear what kind of help he needed. It seems that he just wanted someone to listen. *Fag Rag* not only published his account but included Bohannon's address in case readers were moved to write to him.[31]

Some newspapers offered special classified sections devoted entirely to developing pen pal networks to support gay inmates. *Gay Sunshine,* which was based in San Francisco, published ads from prisoners in London, Ohio, and San Luis Obispo, California. Some ads lamented abandonment by family and friends—such as one that read, "Lost Outside Contacts. 24 black Sagittarius"—while others expressed loneliness ("Very Lonely") and the need to connect to the larger gay community ("I Need a Friend"). *Gay Sunshine* encouraged prisoners to continue writing: "Please write us to stay on our mailing list free. Include your release or transfer date. If we don't hear from you, we'll presume you have been released and we'll delete your name from our list."[32]

In addition to offering a forum for gay inmates to articulate their troubles and ask for help, gay newspapers informed the larger community about the struggles of those who were incarcerated. In 1976 *The Body Politic* reported on protesters at a rally in Toronto who carried signs that read, END OPPRESSION OF GAY PRISONERS. Earlier in the decade, in an article titled "We Are All Fugitives," Don Jackson, a writer for *Gay Sunshine* identified a transformation that he believed was already under way: "The main thrust of the militant gay movement has shifted from the introspective philosophizing and analyzing of gay liberation" to "focusing on the thousands of brothers incarcerated in prisons, jails and mental institutions. Most gays realize we are all fugitives: the only reason some of us are free is because we have not been caught in our many felonies." Whether or not Jackson's assessment was accurate, he offered a moving argument for why other gay people should see the struggles of gay prisoners as central. Gay men incarcerated in the prison system, he noted, ranged from those arrested for sex offenses to those imprisoned in mental hospitals by judges who regarded homosexuality as a "loathsome disease." He also noted that many gay servicemen and veterans were locked up in administrative prisons that the Veterans Administration called "mental hospitals." Jackson wrote of the inadvertent effects of gay liberation. Many young men inspired by gay liberation had told their parents that they were gay, and many others had been outed by their parents because of articles in popular magazines about how "to detect homosexuality in your child." The end result, he argued, was that a larger number of younger people were coming out to hostile and unaccepting parents who were forcing them out of their homes and into juvenile institutions.[33]

Many in the gay press made it their mission to show what life was like behind bars. Some publications ran articles that showed prisoners living in squalor, and others explained that gay people got locked up for minor, nonviolent crimes. In fact, as a headline in *Gay Sunshine* announced, "The next gay prisoner we may help may be

you." Just as gay people were reading about the history of Nazi violence and stories about arson attacks on gay churches, the specter of
prison figured prominently in their imaginations.[34]

Gay newspapers served as a leading liaison between gay inmates and
the broader gay community, but they were by no means the only
group within the liberation movement that rallied for those who
were incarcerated. Gay religious groups became energetic advocates
for gay inmates and, like the press, often published accounts written
by prisoners. For instance, the Roman Catholic organization Dignity
published a story from a gay inmate in San Luis Obispo, California, in the Dignity newsletter in 1974. "I am a prisoner here," the
writer explained, "and I have no one on the outside world who cares
whether or not I ever get out. I am a Gay male and really need the
friendship of someone who could write." This inmate felt the need
to debunk what he believed were the many assumptions held by the
outside world about prison life. "Being Gay in prison is not the bed
of roses as some people think. We are not the elite society in here
believe me." He detailed the abuse, intimidation, and loneliness that
he experienced. His reference to prison as "a bed of roses" seems to
derive from the popular pornography of the period, which eroticized
homosexual sex in prisons. He ended the letter by urging readers to
write him, and he promised he would write back.[35]

But it was the Metropolitan Community Church that most consistently fostered connections with gay inmates. The MCC created
a special publication devoted to gay inmates called *Cellmate,* which
often appeared as an insert in the MCC's periodical *In Unity.* The
magazine served many functions, chief among them to encourage
MCC ministers throughout the United States to expand their ministries to the incarcerated. "Prison ministry is clearly a Christian social
action mandated by Scripture," Rev. Bud Bunce explained to readers
in *Cellmate.* Working with the National Council of Churches, the
MCC vowed "to be committed to working for change in the criminal
justice system." MCC members across the country organized groups

of members who visited prisoners, offering them a sense of community and connection to the outside world.[36]

Yet some MCC ministers were so overwhelmed by the many responsibilities of maintaining their own churches that they did not have the time, resources, or training to work in prisons. In December 1975, when Rev. Elder Carol S. Cureton addressed MCC ministers' doubts about developing a prison ministry, she explained the absolute necessity for this work. She submitted that "prisons have failed" to meet the needs of gay prisoners and that there "is a negative and condemning attitude toward gay people and at the same time a very limited knowledge and considerable lack of skills for dealing with their specific problems." She reminded MCC congregants of their mission: "Let us remember the words of our Lord as recorded in Matthew, . . . 'When [did] we [see] you sick, or in the prison, and [come] unto you? And the King shall answer and say unto them, Inasmuch as you have done it unto one of the least of these my [people] you have done it unto me.'"[37]

Reverend Cureton, along with other MCC leaders and congregations, began a massive effort to reach gay people by organizing prayer groups and religious services as well as many other types of support, such as legal advice, pen pal networks, and parole planning; she even sent cookies to prisoners and put on shows for them. Like the gay press, the MCC published poetry by gay inmates—not poems that highlighted romance or loneliness, but poems that illustrated gay inmates' relationship with God.[38] In a poem titled "The Wisdom of God's Plan," Mike Turpin, an inmate at Arizona State Prison, wrote:

> We wouldn't love the sunrise if
> We hadn't felt the night
> And we wouldn't know of weakness if
> We hadn't sensed God's might.[39]

After this poem was published, Steve Quesnel, a member of the MCC in Albuquerque, New Mexico, corresponded with Turpin and began collecting more of his poems to be published in future issues of *Cellmate*. Quesnel was far from the only MCC member who joined the clergy in creating prison ministries. Groups of committed volunteers sprang up from Philadelphia to San Diego, and in the Midwest in Indianapolis and Kansas City. "Our work has just begun," Rev. Jay Neely reported on the pages of *Cellmate* about his congregation's work in the New York prison system. "It is a big project. It is a great need. The volunteer response has been unlike any other project we have undertaken."[40]

During the Christmas season in 1975, the MCC in Seattle baked cookies and provided entertainment for prisoners at Monroe State Prison. Meanwhile, thirty members of the choir of the MCC church in Los Angeles "presented a two-hour program of gospel music for 150 prisoners" at Terminal Island Federal Prison in San Pedro, California. The group offered three two-hour performances: one in the morning, one in the afternoon, and one in the evening. According to the prison's periodical, the prisoners were surprised to hear "a choir that was inter-racial, musically diversified, and so relaxed." The prisoners enjoyed hearing the familiar sound of gospel and Christmas music sung by a group of gay men and lesbians who came in the name of God. According to the prison newspaper, some of the inmates claimed that they became believers after hearing the choir.[41]

A central preoccupation of the MCC's prison ministry was to reach nongay prisoners as well as gay prisoners. Ministers found that during services and other events nongay prisoners sometimes stumbled into the gathering and became engaged by the sermon. So ministers often focused on conveying a message that would reach even nongay inmates. They were further encouraged to reach a broader audience after being told that some heterosexual men who typically tormented gay inmates had been seen sitting next to their victims in the pews.

Most of the information about these events comes down to us from the MCC ministers and members who put them on. There is relatively little testimony from gay inmates. How did the arrival of a gay choir, for instance, affect their thoughts on gay liberation? How did they understand a choir that came in the name of both God and homosexuality? Given that some of the prisoners may have been incarcerated since the 1960s or earlier—before the explosion of organizations, parades, and other public displays of the gay community—a gay mass or choir may have been their first engagement with gay culture and their first inkling that being gay meant more than just sex. Certainly, some gay men incarcerated during the 1960s participated in the gay communities that predated Stonewall, but the visit of a gay minister or gay choir may have struck some as something entirely new—as exemplifying how gay men and women were creating an interracial community and fostering a sense of culture based on sexual orientation.

Unsurprisingly, the prisoners' reactions that were recorded focused on more immediate matters. Some prisoners contacted the MCC and conveyed how much they valued the work of the prison ministry and how the choir's music had affected them. One prisoner wrote to *Cellmate* in 1975 to express his gratitude to the MCC.

> I can see the need of a service for mainly gay men and would like to leave prison this time knowing that I have done something to get myself together in here. I took my first Communion at the November 6th MCC service. I am more and more into reading parts of the Bible, and listening to the sermons, and I've been attending all the regular chapel services as you advised. All in all, I find more happiness in this than just sitting around my cell.[42]

Scott Winans, an inmate in Orlando, Florida, also thanked the MCC for its support. Prior to his time in the Orlando prison, he spent two years in a federal prison in Indiana where he came in contact with an MCC member who wrote him and sent him a copy of *Christian Sexuality,* an MCC publication. After being transferred to Florida, he reached out to the local MCC church, and members of the congregation began visiting him. He wrote to *Cellmate,* "These people are taking good care of me!"[43]

Although many gay inmates not only appreciated the MCC's ministry but came to rely on it, some prison officials eventually banned MCC members from visiting inmates and offering religious services. Some prisons even prohibited inmates from receiving copies of *Cellmate* and the MCC newsletter. Prison officials in both

Canada and the United States claimed that the MCC was not a legitimate religious organization and therefore could not have access to
inmates in the way that mainstream religious orders did.[44]

The MCC responded by taking legal action in California in
1975. The church hired the attorney John Wahl, who had experience
arguing cases in front of the Supreme Court and had gained recognition early in his career for his work in making it mandatory for
California prisons to establish libraries stocked with law books for
inmates. Wahl went on to fight the MCC case for over two years on a
pro bono basis. The federal court ruled that MCC neither presented
a case of "clear and present danger" to the inmates nor disrupted
"the good order" of the prison. The Department of Corrections thus
recognized the MCC as a bonafide Christian denomination and
allowed the church to offer religious and social services to inmates.
The MCC credited Wahl for "following his calling to serve God's
people behind bars."[45]

In spite of this victory, the bigger fight continued. The MCC,
along with other gay prison advocacy groups, struggled to underscore the unique challenges, prejudices, and violence faced by gay
inmates, from both prison administrators and other inmates. At the
First National Conference on Alternatives to Incarceration, held in
Boston in 1975 (sponsored by the National Task Force on Higher
Education and Criminal Justice of the National Council of the
Churches of Christ in the USA), gay prison activists fought to have
sexuality included in the conference proceedings. According to the
activists, as plans for the conference developed no one was addressing the subject of homosexuality in prisons. When these activists
broached the issue, the organizing committee responded that "the
subject was too threatening." The gay activists suggested organizing
a session on "sexuality in prisons," a topic that seemed to include
homosexuality in an unthreatening and benign way. The conference
organizers accepted this proposal.[46]

The conference drew over 1,300 "correctional personnel, crim-
inologists, ex-offenders, lawyers, activist ministers, legislative aides,
and community organizers" from across the country. The organizers assigned the session on sexuality to a room that sat only twenty

people, so when more than one hundred showed up, the panelists had to open the adjacent room to accommodate the large audience. Afterward, MCC activists were excited about the outcome of the session. As Rev. Joseph H. Gilbert, pastor of the MCC in Providence, Rhode Island, explained, "There was sensitizing and I believe those who attended the workshop will be more attentive to gay needs in the agencies they represented." That said, the MCC also conveyed its concern that the conference did not provide enough opportunities for former prisoners to participate formally as panelists or as organizers on the program committee.[47]

In its prison ministry, the MCC recognized the critical importance of the individual experiences of inmates to its mission. The church used the knowledge it gained in creating pen pal networks and visiting prisons to refine these and other outreach programs. The MCC chapter in Indianapolis hosted a special seminar on how to train volunteers to engage inmates; they wanted not just to proselytize but to improve the quality of life for gay inmates. Some inmates, probably inspired by the MCC's attention and model, took it upon themselves to found activist and religious groups of their own. Harvey Alter, who served three and a half years in a state prison in Massachusetts and then worked as an activist in various religious and political organizations focused on incarceration, explained: "Gay prisoners need to find themselves; they need to develop a sense of strength, dignity, and solidarity with fellow inmates." After talking with only a single inmate in the women's division at Riker's Island Facility in New York, for instance, Dee Jackson, an MCC activist, was flooded with letters from other women in the prison who wanted to discuss sexuality. The MCC realized the need for outreach to many prisoners, as well as the need to seek information from them about the problems they faced behind bars.[48]

By putting inmates' experiences at the center of their intervention efforts, the MCC, along with activists and the gay press, came to learn of the rampant sexual violence in prisons. Inmates told about gays often being violently raped and abused. "I remember this one boy was gang raped 13 times," an inmate told a reporter from

Gay Sunshine. "Can you imagine being gang raped by these men 13 times, you know, 13 times not 13 men, but 13 different times by many men!"[49]

The struggle to imagine the sexual violence recounted by inmates reflected the broader difficulty that inmates had in speaking about sexual abuse among men. Developing the language to talk about forced, violent anal and oral sex as rape proved to be one of the most vexing problems faced by gay prison activists. At the time, according to both law and custom in the United States, only women could be raped. Men could only be charged with sodomy. Gay advocates had to fight to add the adjective "forced" to the term "sodomy" in order to distinguish acts of sexual violence from the consensual sex implied by the term.[50]

At the helm of the crusade to draw attention to sexual violence in prison was Stephen Donaldson. Donaldson was born Robert Martin in upstate New York to a middle-class family. He made his first forays into activism when he applied to college. In his undergraduate application to Columbia University, he declared he was gay. Despite the university's initial reluctance to accept him, it did admit him, but stipulated that he undergo psychological counseling and that he "not attempt to seduce other students."[51]

Once on campus, Martin became a leading member of the Columbia Homophile Organization in the years before the Stonewall uprising. He changed his name to Stephen Donaldson to avoid the possibility of his activism reflecting negatively on his family name. This may have been when he acquired his interest in pseudonyms. Later in his life, when he became more involved in the punk culture of the East Village in New York City, he went by "Donny the Punk." And in his personal correspondence as well as in his public writings and interviews, he used not only Robert Martin, Stephen Donaldson, and Donny the Punk, but yet another name, Donald Tucker.[52]

After graduating from Columbia, Donaldson enlisted in the Navy and was later discharged because of "suspected homosexual involvement." But his discharge only inspired him to further political activism. He went public with the case and demanded an honorable discharge. Although he did not succeed, he received the support of leading members of Congress.[53]

Donaldson became a leading critic of sexual violence in prisons after his own experience in jail. In the summer of 1973, he was working as a journalist in Washington, DC, and joined a Quaker group on the lawn of the White House protesting the US involvement in Southeast Asia. He was arrested, and when he refused to pay the $10 bond, he was jailed. He later claimed that because he was an activist and journalist, the guards purposely placed him in a group of violent inmates. By that time, gay prison activists had made headway in their demands that superintendents allow gay church groups to minister to inmates and to allow gay men, at the very least, to receive mail from gay newspapers. Thus, it's possible that the guards not only had Donaldson's antiwar protest in mind but also were suspicious of an openly gay activist.

In his second week in jail, a group of inmates lured Donaldson into a cell during the recreation period. "My exit was blocked," he recalled. "My pants were forcibly taken off me, and I was raped. Then I was dragged from cell to cell all evening." As a nonviolent Quaker activist, he refused to fight back. The next night the inmates came for him again. He claimed that he was gang-raped by forty-five to fifty men in total. He tried to escape from the group, but they pinned him down on the bed and "covered his head and face with sheets." His attackers eventually gave him a respite since he was alternately gagging and vomiting, and in that moment he escaped. He made his way to a guard who brought him to the infirmary. He was hospitalized and underwent surgery to repair extensive anal tears.[54]

The next day a Quaker posted his bail and Donaldson was released. He made a public statement about being brutally raped and became the first male victim to call attention to the epidemic of male rape in prison. Simply by saying that men could be raped, he offered a vocabulary for shedding light on and discussing sexual violence in prison. Donaldson started writing about rape in gay periodicals, appearing as a guest on radio shows, and working with police and

community groups. In all of his writings and appearances, he reinforced the idea that men could be raped, especially in prisons. In
a broader sense, he also attempted to shift the discussion of sexual
violence from being a crime only committed against women to one
that affected men as well.[55]

When Donaldson rose to prominence, the public discussion
about men raping women had only begun to surface as part of a
larger feminist discourse. In fact, the signal moment in that discourse was the publication of Susan Brownmiller's *Against Our
Will: Men, Women, and Rape* in 1975. To use the feminist parlance,
the book "broke the silence" about rape two years after Donaldson
announced that he had been raped. Donaldson's experience in the
DC jail made it into Brownmiller's book as an example of male rape
in prisons, and in so doing it helped to contribute to a wider understanding of sexual violence.[56]

Throughout the 1970s and even into the 1980s, Donaldson
continued to draw attention to rape in prisons. As Wayne Dynes, a
member of the Mattachine Society as well as an editor-in-chief of the
Encyclopedia of Homosexuality, noted, "While Donny is generally
acknowledged to be the foremost authority in the United States on
jailhouse rape, he is one of the most knowledgeable people in the
country on issues of prison sexuality in general." Beyond the scars left
by being violently raped, Donaldson argued, most male victims perceived their rape as an indictment of their manhood. Because rapists
often referred to their male victims by female names and described
their body parts using slang associated with women's anatomy, male
victims struggled with the psychological consequences of rape. Donaldson claimed that the assaults on their masculinity proved even
more damaging than the physical violence, and he fought to disman-
tle the assumption that rape resulted from a limitation or weakness
in the victim. Not surprisingly, when prisons began to systematically
document male rape, the statistics did not match reality because
many victims did not self-report out of shame.[57]

When interviewers asked Donaldson how he himself managed
to survive such a brutal rape, he explained that he went to psychological counseling but also emphasized that his spirituality gave him the

strength to survive and to lead the crusade to reform prisons. He had long been a seeker of spiritual experience. As both an undergraduate and a graduate student, he had studied Buddhism, and later, in 1971, he was briefly a member of the Psychedelic Venus Church. Donaldson understood spirituality as a crucial part of his identity. But by claiming that his spirituality both enabled him to survive the trauma of being raped and inspired him to lead a crusade, Donaldson also elided his earlier work for the homophile organization at Columbia, which points to an important aspect of his advocacy: he did not make his identity as gay or even as bisexual part of his testimony about being raped or use it in his advocacy work for sexual assault victims.[58]

There are numerous possible explanations for this erasure, but two seem most likely. First, as an advocate for victims of sexual violence in prisons, Donaldson emphasized that prison rape was about power: men raped other men to demonstrate their dominance. By making this argument, Donaldson deftly shifted the focus away from the victims to the attackers. If he had acknowledged his bisexual identity, the resulting focus on him, and other victims, could have led to the pernicious idea that his sexuality had in some way caused the rape—an idea that Brownmiller and other feminists addressed by asserting that rape did not result from the way women dressed or behaved. And if Donaldson had outed himself, he would have substantiated the argument advanced by prison officials that sexual violence was an isolated problem that only affected gay people and undermined one of his main points: that heterosexual men were both attackers and victims.[59]

Second, Donaldson may have avoided bringing up his earlier gay political activism in order to construct a straightforward and affecting narrative in which being gang-raped had politicized him. Raising the subject of his earlier political activism would have lent credence to the prison officials' assertions that he refused to pay bail because he wanted to gain a firsthand view of the conditions in prison. Also, while he was in the jail, he met one of the Watergate conspirators, G. Gordon Liddy, who later wrote in his biography that he thought Donaldson was sent to spy on him and write a story for the *Washington Post*. Given the many suspicions circulating about

Donaldson's character and motivations, it is no wonder that he did not talk much, if at all, about his earlier political activism.[60]

Although Donaldson did not explicitly acknowledge his earlier activism or his sexuality, both nevertheless shaped his campaign to raise awareness about sexual violence in prison. As a leading member of the homophile movement at Columbia, he had learned how to network and create a platform. After his dishonorable discharge from the Navy, he had publicized his discharge and pitched stories to the gay and mainstream press, both of which followed his case. Thus, by the time he was raped, he was able to draw on his experience and skills to help make visible what had been the invisible problem of rape in prison.[61]

Donaldson's activism and the efforts of many other gay activists, newspaper staffs, and religious groups highlight a forgotten thread of gay liberation. All of these groups created a political platform and fostered a public discourse about sexual violence and rape. All were discussing sex, not as a means of sensual release or political triumph, but to draw attention to the seemingly timeless practice of rape in prisons. Their efforts led to revised definitions of sexual violence and reconsideration of the legal codes that offered no rhetorical space to talk about the epidemic of male rape that they had only started to identify.[62]

In an interesting narrative turn of events, poetry remained one of the main ways in which prisoners discussed their plight. In his voluminous collection of newspaper clippings, cassettes of radio appearances, and correspondence about trying to change the legal definitions of rape, Donaldson kept a copy of a poem titled "What a Letter Can Mean," written by an anonymous prisoner. The poem described the loneliness and isolation of being incarcerated. It is unclear why Donaldson held on to the poem for years in his collection of printed materials, whether it reminded him of his mission to reform prisons or spoke to him on an emotional level that triggered his own experience in jail. What is certain is that poems became a narrative force during the 1970s that enabled gay prisoners to reckon with the meaning of liberation.[63]

Gay liberation gave way to massive organizing efforts, from the rise of the print culture to the upsurge of gay political, social, and religious groups. Many of these efforts turned at some point to the crisis in prisons. Gay activists did not forget about those left behind bars. Despite the common understanding of liberation—pride marches, protests for equality, gays dancing to the sound of victory—the success of gay liberation revealed a contradiction for many gay people. It unveiled the looming specter of prison, the threat of being arrested, and the large number of gay people in jail. As one prison activist recounted, "So it hit me and it began to eat at me. 'Why should I be walking around *free,* and not be involved in ministry to these people in prison?' . . . Some are imprisoned simply because they are gay."[64]

Many gay people understood that their success was connected to their incarcerated brothers and sisters' struggles. Many spent long hours as volunteers, organizing pen pal networks, forming prayer groups, editing articles, distributing newspapers, talking to lawyers, soliciting poems, staging choral performances, and visiting those in prison. They provided inmates with religious services, newspapers, and other forms of community and comfort.

Much of this activism and outreach only became possible because gay liberation had fostered new understandings of homosexuality. There had been sex between men in prisons prior to the 1970s, but prison officials dismissed it as either immoral or aberrant, or both. Gay liberation shattered the characterizations of men who had sex with men as immoral or pathological and demonstrated that gay people had a culture and a community that formed a distinct social group. By claiming that sexual orientation constituted a crucial aspect of identity, gay activists showed that being gay carried the possibility of creating a gay culture. In their efforts to share that culture with incarcerated gay people, gay activists accomplished one of the major goals of liberation: they fostered a sense of cultural identity among a group that otherwise felt dispossessed.[65]

But as the decade came to an end, these concerns would soon fall by the wayside. As gay liberation advanced, gay people were beginning to redefine masculinity, femininity, and the very meaning of being gay. Unlike the prison movement, which reached out to gay people in the most distant and confined places, the focus of these new ideas was turned inward. Many gay people became more obsessed with themselves than with others or with their community. By the end of the 1970s, new forums for community and cultural expression would begin to lose out as being gay became strongly connected to a particular—and barely attainable—body type for gay men.

7 BODY LANGUAGE

He is the one they have been waiting for.

He has cut the sleeves off his flannel shirt and refuses to button it. He is wearing Levi's 501 jeans, a black leather belt, and aviator sunglasses. He is hot.[1]

Against the prevailing styles, he cuts his hair short. He goes to the gym. He takes off his flannel shirt every chance he gets. He has broad shoulders, chiseled forearms, biceps the size of cannonballs, and a flat stomach, but he does not have abs—the sculpted washboard stomach has yet to come into vogue. But he does have pectoral muscles. That is the focal point. Not overly muscular, but beefy, virile pecs—a chest that represents his manhood.

Although he has a body that looks like it was made for sex, it is not. He is by no means a prude, but sex is not his priority. Being him is his priority. Having others look at him is his priority. He can be seen at the bars and bathhouses. Images of him appear on posters and in newspapers and magazines. There are even contests in which men compete with one another to look just like him. Someone has even created a thirteen-inch doll modeled after him, named "Gay Bob."[2]

Another important fact about him: he is white.

He may have come of age in New York City or San Francisco or another major urban center, but his look transcends a particular regional style. When he walks into a bar or down the street, everyone knows who he is. They don't know his name, nor do they need to. He is an icon. To those who admire him, he is "macho." To those who critique him, he is a "clone." He now embodies the meaning of gay liberation.

For writers and scholars, like Jonathan Ned Katz, who shattered earlier stereotypes of gay men as weak and degenerate, as even a third sex, the "macho" gay man embodied a version of masculinity often thought to be the sole province of heterosexual men. For the journalists and social leaders, like Craig Rodwell, who attempted to create a distinct form of gay culture, this icon was created specifically for the gay community. Heterosexuals might have noticed him and some may have understood him, but he was not on display for them. Many gay men assigned masculinity to his physique and power to his pectoral muscles; they grafted their own aspirations onto his body, and most of all, they identified him as their own.

Masculine gay men had been recognized in the gay community since the early twentieth century and even earlier, but the icon of the "macho" man or the "clone" emerged as something entirely new in the 1970s. He grew out of a transformed gay consciousness. Prior to the 1970s, there were masculine men who identified as homosexual, yet for the most part masculinity in the early part of the twentieth century was associated with a disavowal of homosexuality or gay identity. Many masculine men who had sex with other men often denied that they were homosexual. The gay community, in turn, often referred to them as "wolves" or "rough trade" or used other terms that distinguished them from men who were out.[3] By contrast, the macho clone who emerged in the 1970s was undoubtedly, unapologetically gay.

Touko Laaksonen's drawings, which he drew under the pseudonym Tom of Finland, represent an early example of the gay community's fascination with "beefcake"—the shirtless men who began to appear in the 1930s in men's magazines that featured male physiques. In the 1960s, gay men ordered physique magazines that emphasized masculine bodies and catered to a gay readership.[4] These early examples of homoerotic images, however, were more

representations—cartoons, comics, photographs—than actual people, and the degree to which they were recognized as gay varied.[5]
Although some gay men before the 1970s were indeed masculine and
"butch," and others were part of the underground leather community, the macho clone would popularize a form of identity that had
otherwise been mostly clandestine within the gay community.[6]

Unlike the earlier masculine men, who stereotypically wan-
dered into a gay bar or showed up drunk at a bathhouse and who
sometimes were married, the macho clone lived in a gay neighborhood and could be seen in the middle of the day walking the streets.[7]
The "out and proud" macho clone began to dominate the cultural
landscape of the 1970s, emerging as the leading representation of
gay male identity—unlike his historical antecedents, who had been
part of a larger constellation of gay male portrayals. The macho clone
could write for The Body Politic or be a member of the MCC. Dr. Tom
Waddell, for example, who emerged as an icon within the gay community in the 1970s, was both a physician and a former US Olympian. He had gone on to earn a medical degree after placing sixth out
of thirty-three competitors in the decathlon at the Olympics in Mexico City in 1968. After Waddell attempted to found the "Gay Olympics" and was sued by the US Olympic Committee, he changed the
name to the "Gay Games." The combination of his fit athletic body,
mustache, athletic prowess, and career in medicine represented the
ascent and embrace of gay masculinity.[8]

By embodying both masculinity and homosexuality, the macho
clone showed that the two attributes were not contradictory, but constitutive of one another. Even if critics found the clone's masculinity
artificial and constructed, his outward performance of masculinity
represented a shift in gay identity in the wake of liberation.

The new body type drew criticism, however, from gay men who
detested its homogeneity, which they believed would have quite
damaging consequences for the gay community's representations of
itself. Post-Stonewall, the representations of gay people were many
and varied as the gay community articulated its concerns, hopes, and
dreams. Harvey Milk gave political speeches. Lesbian journalists,
like Chris Bearchell, wrote provocative and probing articles for The

Body Politic. A plethora of political meetings—from church gatherings to panels on prison reform to workshops devoted to transgender concerns—expressed the missions, ethos, and meanings of gay liberation. By the end of the decade, however, the clone was effectively speaking more loudly and more gregariously than anyone else.

The clone also foreclosed on many other discussions. Gay liberation had begun at the Stonewall Inn with people of color, lesbians, drag queens, and transgender people, but the popularity of this white, muscular, male icon reduced their presence within the movement and within the gay community. The macho clone became the symbol of gay identity and eclipsed the otherwise increasing diversity that defined the gay community in the latter part of the 1970s.[9]

From the beginning of gay liberation, women and people of color had figured into the movement. Writers, activists, and intellectuals like Craig Rodwell and Jonathan Ned Katz acknowledged the major influence of the black civil rights movement on gay liberation, and both Rodwell and Katz included black gay people in their political projects. Katz wrote about black people in *Gay American History,* while Rodwell carried publications and other ephemera in the Oscar Wilde Memorial Bookshop on the black gay experience. In fact, Rodwell kept a copy of Carl Wittman's 1970 "A Gay Manifesto," which addressed gay people's response to black liberation: "This is tenuous right now because of the uptightness and supermasculinity of many black men (which is understandable). Despite that, we must support their movement, we must show them that we mean business; and we must figure out which our common enemies are: police, city hall, capitalism."[10]

Meanwhile, organizations like the MCC and the prison reform movement included women, transgender people, and people of color as part of their congregations and their organizational work. As Michael Bronski, a member of the Gay Liberation Front recollected, many activists understood fighting racism as central to gay liberation:

> The Gay Liberation Front talked a lot about racism. We understood that racism was about the lives of all US citizens black or white. Even our name reflected anti-racism battles: the National

Liberation Front of Vietnam and the Algerian Liberation Front. We understood that the Black Panthers had a political force and a vision that made sense in our times. GLF was hardly perfect in dealing with racism, most of its members were white, much of its discussion about racism involved breast-beating and platitudes. But we understood that racism was part of our fight, both for our sake as well as theirs.[11]

Activists writing in the *Arizona Gay News* echoed this concern, calling for all minority groups—"blacks, Latinos, women, Gays"—to come together to fight oppression. The macho clone rose to prominence despite this awareness of a shared cause.[12]

The macho clone also diminished the presence of lesbians in the history of the 1970s. It is true that many lesbians left the gay liberation movement because gay men did not take their concerns seriously, but the macho clone also probably drove many lesbians out of the gay liberation movement as the 1970s turned into a period that emphasized men. There is little direct archival evidence to explain how and why an icon may have caused lesbians to separate themselves from gay men, but it is likely that the male power embodied in the clone imbued him with aspects of patriarchy that led many lesbians to develop their own community. Some lesbians and lesbian feminists stayed in the movement and continued to contribute to the creation of gay culture—like Chris Bearchell at *The Body Politic,* or the women working in the gay prison reform movement and the MCC, or the women who inhabited the gay literary world created by Jonathan Ned Katz and Craig Rodwell. The rise of the macho clone icon, however, erased the presence of these women activists and turned gay culture into an environment exclusively populated by white men by the end of the decade—a development that contributed to the image of the 1970s as a decade of unfettered gay male sex.[13]

At the start of the decade, many gay men did not adhere to strict body types or styles. Early on, many gay men had emulated the hippie style—sporting long hair and beards and wearing tie-dye shirts and peasant blouses, folksy headbands with beads and flowers. Images of the gay male hippie body fill the pages of the inaugural issue of *Gay Sunshine*, whose cover features a naked male angel descending from the sun onto a bed of flowers.[14] He is thin rather than muscular; in fact, the only noticeable curvature in the image is that of his penis. His slightly askance position seems intended to mimic the pictorial conventions typically associated with femininity.

The second issue included an article with the headline "I Hate Macho," written by a woman named "Laurel," presumably a lesbian. Laurel wrote about personal experiences, from going to a nervous male dentist to dealing with a "macho" woman who owned a motorcycle repair shop. Claiming that she hated macho, regardless of who embodied it—whether men or women—she explained that she did not "hate all men," as many of her "sisters" did, because she tried to allow nuance into her thinking. Which was why she detested "macho" in the first place: "I know there are shades of pain and love, good and evil—I hate 'macho' wherever I find it."[15] In 1973 *Gay Sunshine* also published a lengthy feature article that explored the relationship between macho behavior and sports and went so far as to argue that "the homosexual S&M experience and the macho straight's sports obsession . . . are overwhelmingly masculine oriented in conventional terms"—further signaling how gay people wrote and read about the meaning of masculinity in the wake of gay liberation.[16]

Critiques of macho behavior were common within the gay community in the early part of the seventies. Over fifty men gathered in Boston in 1973 to participate in a discussion about masculine behavior sponsored by the Effeminist movement, a growing campaign among gay men to reflect on the meanings of masculinity, femininity, and sexism. According to the *Gay Community Newsletter*, "The male participants dealt with their inability to relate to other males on anything but a superficial level." The newsletter mentioned that straight men attended the event as well, which, according to the paper, was an "encouraging sign for the straight male consciousness in Boston." The Effeminist movement in Boston went on to sponsor a number of lectures in 1973 that addressed a range of issues, including "Men and Our Bodies," "Living Without Couple Relationships and Without Loneliness," and "Our Relationships with Women."[17] Effeminism spread across gay culture in the 1970s. As Craig Rodwell explained, "Revolutionary Effeminism is a new political movement being formed by faggots across the country who want to struggle with their male supremacy and fight their oppression. It is both an analysis and a plan of action."[18] While an actual "plan of action" did not seem to surface in any material way beyond the creation of workshops and thought pieces, Rodwell and other gay men witnessed the beginning of gay liberation as an opportunity to evaluate gender identities.

Lesbians and lesbian feminists, meanwhile, continued a discussion that had begun before the 1970s about the ways in which masculine behavior and identity—not just sex—oppressed women. As a result, a growing number of gay men in the wake of liberation took seriously the charge that they embodied forms of patriarchal power and strove not to perpetuate the same habits—often disguised under the "macho" or "masculine" identity—that oppressed women in the heterosexual world. As Craig Rodwell explained, "Faggots have been developing the effeminist analysis in recent years, both by reading and listening to the growing feminist analysis of sexism and male supremacy, and by doing consciousness-raising in small groups." He added, "As faggots we are oppressed by sexism and heterosexism . . . as men we are male-supremacist and thus oppress all women." Rodwell favored the use of the term "faggot" because "it embodies our choice to be un-masculine and we affirm our effeminateness."[19]

Gay men also began to explore how the economic structures and social norms associated with masculinity underwrote patriarchal power. In a newspaper article entitled "Masculinity as an Oppressive Ideology," Jim Chesebro, a gay activist and intellectual, explained, "Capitalism is built upon masculine ideology. Socialism requires sharing—it is the foundation for a feminine society. Self-reliance is built upon the masculine ideology . . . we need a revolutionary change from a masculine to a feminine society."[20] Chesebro's critique resonated throughout the gay community.[21] In a series of four forums held in Toronto in March 1976, members of the Gay Alliance Toward Equality met with the Canadian Women's Educational Press to examine "the sexist oppression of women and gays."[22]

Consequently, many gay men were thinking hard about how certain male attitudes and postures codified patriarchal power. In *Male Armor*, a series of plays written in the 1970s, the writer, activist, and historian Martin Duberman grappled with the question, "What Does It Mean to Be Man?" (which was also the name of one of the plays). Many of Duberman's gay characters wrestle with the meaning of masculinity in the context of gay liberation.[23] In *Elagabalus*, the main character rejects traditional notions of masculinity, while *Payments* valorizes the masculine performance of gay prostitutes.[24] Ads for Duberman's published collection of plays with the question "What Does It Mean to Be Man?" appeared in the gay press; clearly, Duberman and his publisher realized that they could tap a market for the book by directly addressing an uncertainty in the minds of many readers.[25] Meanwhile, the cover of the March 1971 issue of *Gay Sunshine* announced, "Women's Liberation Is Our Liberation."[26] Five months later, the cover of *Gay Sunshine* featured a naked man and woman breaking chains around their arms with the headline "Gay Brothers and Sisters Unite! Free Ourselves and Smash Sexism."[27]

Thus, the image of the naked male angel on the cover of the inaugural issue of *Gay Sunshine* suggests that the efforts to appear feminine reflected an inward-looking assessment of masculinity informed by lesbian and lesbian feminist critiques as well as by ideas circulating among gay men themselves. Before the 1970s, gay men's effeminacy had often signaled weakness, inferiority, or aberrance. Yet after Stonewall many gay men embraced effeminacy for political reasons. Gay liberation forged the opportunity within the queer community to construct the male body on new terms separate from and in opposition to those of the heterosexual world.[28]

The *Gay Sunshine* editors continued to test the visual boundaries of gay male identity in their early issues and tended to move toward more and more feminine imagery.[29] The November 1970 issue featured three naked men, all with shoulder-length hair, some wearing makeup, lounging on plush furniture.[30] Like the male angel from the previous issue, the postures of their bodies are feminine: one tilts his head, another is looking at the floor, and the third lies on his side and rests his hand on his head.[31] Gay men had engaged in various forms of gender performance before the 1970s, but gay liberation expanded both the scope and the range of these endeavors.[32] The headline that accompanied the photograph read, "Gender Fuck," articulating the militant kind of rebuttal of gender stereotypes that became increasingly popular and visible in the wake of Stonewall.[33]

Further, unlike pornography, these bodies—many of which appeared nude or seminude—did not specifically connote sex, lust, or desire. Although some readers may have been attracted to the three men who appeared in the November 1970 *Gay Sunshine,* the point of printing this image was to revel in the possibilities of gay liberation. No longer would gay people be hidden. Just as Craig Rodwell lined the shelves of the Oscar Wilde Memorial Bookshop with books representing gay people's literary aesthetic, *Gay Sunshine* and other periodicals ran images that represented a range of gay people's body aesthetics. Gay liberation gave newspaper editors, photographers' models, and readers across the world an opportunity to craft an identity more in accord with their own political sensibilities, artistic desires, and definitions of gender, and then to promote and circulate these sensibilities, desires, and definitions widely and relatively openly.

The period of relative heterogeneity in gay body aesthetics did not last very long. Early in the decade, there had been images of masculine and muscular gay men appearing alongside images of many other types. By the mid-1970s, the masculine, muscular gay male body was on the rise. By the end of the decade, many of the critics of masculinity and sexism within the gay community fell silent as the expansion and deepening of gay consciousness seemed to lose momentum and the macho clone emerged in full force. No longer did newspapers focus on political and social issues. Now they published more and more flashy, glossy images of gay bodies.

The macho clone appeared in newspapers, in ads for gay bars and bathhouses, on the covers of pornographic magazines, and in every other conceivable place that offered the opportunity for a sketch, photograph, or even cartoon image of a shirtless stud. For example, in one issue of *Gay Sunshine*, a photograph of two muscular, naked men is featured below a serious "rap session" about the politics and polemics surrounding gay liberation. No caption accompanies the photo, nor does it have any direct relevance to the rest of the page: an ad for the largest comic bookstore in San Francisco and an excerpt from a German gay newspaper. The image of the two muscular men serves no clear purpose.[34]

The macho clone was simply omnipresent. It appeared, for instance, on the cover of a comedy album, *God Save the Queens*, in a sketch of a shirtless, muscular cartoon character coming out of a treehouse surrounded by animals. It was showcased on travel guides to various cities and in cartoons; one cartoon depicts a group of identical men wearing blue jeans, no shirt, and a vest with a caption that satirically asks: "Do you think there is anything to this cloning stuff?" There was even a magazine called *The Gay Clone* that was published from 1976 to 1981. It covered familiar topics that could be found in other gay periodicals, like commentaries on socialism, histories of Nazism, and sections devoted to poetry submitted by readers, but it also published images of the clone throughout its pages: photographs of naked muscular men on beaches, sketches of shirtless Roman gladiators and beefcakes, and other illustrations of the emergent macho clone in the late 1970s.[35]

Although many gay men certainly desired and fantasized about the macho clone, many gay men also wanted to be him and tried to emulate him. The object of their sexual fantasy also became the subject for their own identity. Many gay men devoted more time to developing their bodies to appear more muscular. They went to the gym and took their shirts off at bars and on city streets in gay neighborhoods. They imitated the clone's look—short hair, denim jeans, and boots. Sometimes they added a Stetson hat to look like a cowboy, or chaps to look like a biker, or even shaved their bodies to look like a lifeguard. Some of them did drugs, and many of them listened to disco.[36]

For some gay men, the macho clone was a playful identity, a costume they wore at night, an ensemble they put together to get the attention of others. It was a performance. In fact, in a telling example of how art imitates life, in 1978 the musical group the Village People released the song "Macho Man," which became a national hit. Established by Jacques Morali, the Village People embodied the various performances of the macho clone. Morali studied the men on the streets of New York City's Greenwich Village to create the look for his group. He came up with a cowboy, an Indian, a leather man, a construction worker, a cop, and a sailor. For nongay American listeners, "Macho Man" and the Village People represented the eccentricities of disco and its predilection for musical theatricality. When the Village People appeared on the cover of *Rolling Stone* in 1979, they presented themselves as a group that defied categorization in terms of their music, ethnic diversity, and sexual orientation.[37] As David Hodo, the "construction worker," explained, the group did not like labels, whether "black-white, straight-gay, disco–rock & roll."[38] But for many gay American listeners, the song served as a harbinger of the changing notions of gay masculinity. "Macho Man" became the anthem of the new masculinity of the gay community.[39]

Reinforcing the macho clone and many gay men's desire to be him, contests to determine who came closest began to be held. Held in bars and clubs, these contests were similar to beauty pageants. In Los Angeles, for example, *Data Boy*, a biweekly publication, hosted a contest in 1978 in which over seven hundred men gathered at the Century Theater to watch thirty-six shirtless men compete for the title of "Data Boy." In Tucson, Arizona, gay men gathered at a local bar where they watched their contemporaries participate in the "Cycle Slut Contest." Taking their cue from the biker icon, men competed with one another to be the one who seemed most like a "cycle slut." Although the word "slut" certainly connotes sex, the point of the contest was less about sex and more about style. Men were judged on who looked the sexiest when shirtless and wearing biker pants.[40]

Shirtless men soon became a weekly feature of the bar scene in Tucson. One bar reserved Sundays for just this kind of patron, referring to the event as "Beer Blast and Bare Chest Sunday Nights." An ad for these weekly events appeared in the *Arizona Gay News* alongside articles with meeting information for two religious organizations—the Catholic gay organization Dignity and the Gay Church of Mind Science, which brought together gay spiritualists and those interested in metaphysics—and articles about community events throughout Arizona, mostly in Tucson and Phoenix. The photograph of the macho clone–beer blast ad may seem to have been at odds with the religious articles and the calendar of community events, but by the mid- to late 1970s many gay people had begun to accept the macho clone as part of the social landscape. He was everywhere, even in the newspaper where one found the time and location of the next Dignity meeting.[41]

By the end of the decade, the macho clone had been decapitated. No longer were there ads of men wearing cowboy hats or decked out in leather chaps and harnesses. Instead, the chest became the main feature. Often photographed or sketched without a head, images of muscular, hairless chests started to appear frequently. The ad for the best body contest held by the Mr. His bar in Phoenix in 1978, for example, showed only a muscular body clad in a speedo, unlike previous contests that featured cops, sailors, and Indian chiefs in their advertising. The model's muscular arms seemed almost inflated, his powerful shoulders framing defined pectoral muscles and sculpted abs. Muscularity became the one sign—the one proof—of masculinity. The costumes no longer mattered. Nor did the face. Just the headless torso.[42]

Many gay men protested their culture's emphasis on the macho clone. The writer and activist Arthur Evans asked, "Afraid You're Not Butch Enough?" in a widely circulated pamphlet that responded to the rise of the macho clone in San Francisco in 1978.[43] "Worried that the feminine half of your personality might be showing through?" he asked. "Then join Zombie Works! With our scientifically designed devices, you can make your body look just like a 1950s stereotype of the butch straight male. These wonderful machines were designed by government scientists in Germany during the 1930s. With your Zombie body and Clone clothes, all that remains is to build up your middle class values."[44]

Some gay men worried about the emphasis on the body promoting only sex and precluding any other type of human connection. As noted by Carl Wittman, a member of the New Left group Students for a Democratic Society (SDS) and coauthor with the 1960s political leader Tom Hayden of "An Interracial Movement of the Poor":

> Face it, nice bodies and young bodies are attributes, they're groovy. They are the inspiration for art, for spiritual elevation, for good sex. The problem arises only in the ability to relate to people of the same age, or people who don't fit the plastic stereotypes of a good body. At that point, objectification eclipses people, and expresses self-hatred: "I hate gay people, and I don't like myself, but if a stud (or a chicken) wants to make it with me, can I pretend I'm someone other than me."[45]

Others attempted to revive the earlier link between gay men's identity and effeminateness. The Body Politic rejected ads in its personals section from men who stated, "No fats no fems," and opposed the valorization of the clone, in part out of concern over the reaction of lesbian readers. The paper voted not to accept one particular advertisement for a bathhouse that featured a macho clone because it was "stereotypical," "sexist," and "might offend women" readers. According to a member of the collective that ran the paper, "Gay male feminists were ever willing to wield guilt by proxy." The gay men at The Body Politic thought that lesbian readers would take issue, not with the bathhouse, but with the macho clone, which emphasized the masculinity and muscularity—the patriarchy—that many lesbians opposed on principle. As The Body Politic explained in 1975: "Lesbian feminists have also argued that male nudity is subject to . . . exploitation. . . . The sense of outrage they feel at the systematic de-humanizing of the female body is transferred unaltered to a male context."[46]

Yet gay male readers disagreed with lesbian critiques of the male body. In response to the ad about the bathhouse, one reader wrote, "I understand that we must guard against sexism, ageism and exploitation, but to me pictures of men's bodies in publications are simply pictures, with no -ism. If I want, as the viewer, to put an -ism into my vision, that is my problem, not the publication's. Personally, I find the ad . . . very sexy." The reader further disagreed with the argument that men's bodies were sexually objectified in the same way that women's bodies were. He concluded his letter to the editor by stating, "Lesbians and gay men have a lot in common; but it is our oppression from straights that unites us and our sexuality that separates us."[47]

Indeed, lesbians and people of color often found themselves at odds with white gay men during the 1970s over their feelings of marginalization; as a result, many went on to form separate organizations to meet their particular needs. The emergence of the clone made the lines between gay men and gay women, and between white gay men and black gay men, clearer than ever. Lesbians and people of color could—and often did—fight for recognition in the gay community, but the macho clone did not foster discussion or even open the opportunity for a rebuttal. In many ways, it left no room for debate.

By promoting and emulating the macho clone, many gay men both wittingly and unwittingly sent a message to lesbians that their presence in the movement no longer mattered. Throughout the decade, gay politics and culture had functioned symbiotically. *The Body Politic* created a sense of culture and community and promoted an awareness of gay issues. Similarly, the gay religious movement provided an alternative cultural and political space for gay people. Yet the macho clone, even if it emerged out of a critique against the stereotype of gay men as inherently effeminate, by the end of the decade functioned on an aesthetic if politically coded level and thereby divided the gay community, separating men from women.

It did the same for relations between gay whites and people of color. As a graduate student in San Francisco in the 1970s, Clarence Walker, a historian, remembered that the macho clone signified whiteness and excluded gay men of color: "The Castro clone was a white boy. It did not refer to me or other gay men of color. Black men were present in the Castro, but they did not define the culture."[48] A man we know only as "Jason" voiced a similar concern in a panel discussion on ethics and being gay hosted by a local newspaper in 1979 in California. Jason explained to a group of other racial and ethnic minorities that as a young man growing up in Hawaii, he felt that society privileged whiteness. "I remember when I first came out when

I was 16, I peroxided by [sic] hair and looked absolutely ridiculous. The rest of my body had dark, curly hair and my head was totally blond." Still, Jason looked in the mirror and said, "That's the ideal I want." Also part of that conversation was a man named Xavier, who was born in Texas and self-identified as "Chicano." He posed a question to the group that he often asked himself: "Is it that we ethnics see the masculine image only in white people and not in themselves?"[49]

While some gay men of color tried to fit the mold of the macho clone as best they could, others resisted it. Along with lesbian and feminist groups, many gay men of color organized a movement, called "Third World," to combat the growing racism and sexism within the gay community. On October 13, 1979, over five hundred people gathered in Washington, DC, for the first national conference of "Third World Lesbians and Gays." The black lesbian poet and activist Audre Lorde delivered the keynote address, titled "When Will Ignorance End?" Wearing a dashiki and a head wrap, she congratulated the crowd of "Asians, American Indians, Latins and Blacks" for having the vision and strength to unite as a community. She then asked the crowd, "What does the responsibility of community mean? Does it mean only a trick-handshake, the latest fashion in cruising clothes?" By "the latest fashion in cruising clothes" Lorde meant the macho clone and the artificial boundary it created.[50]

As the macho clone symbolized a restriction of gay identity and culture, Lorde expressed hope for a better future. Like many others in the seventies, she understood the power of the past in shaping the present. Lorde called on the spirits of those who came before her and her audience to help redefine the community. As she said, "So while we party tonight, let a little drop fall, call it a libation, which is an ancient African custom, for all our sisters and brothers who did not survive. For it is within the contexts of our pasts as well as our present and our future that we must re-define community." She added, "I ask that each of you remember the ghosts of those who came before us; that we carry within ourselves the memory of those lesbian and gay men within our communities whose power and knowledge we have been robbed of, those who will never be with us, and those who are not here now."[51]

Despite the fact that the macho clone posited a homogenous gay identity, Lorde, like gay people in the early part of the decade, remained aware of the diversity within the liberation movement. "Some are absent because they cannot be here because of external constraints . . . our sisters and brothers in prisons, in mental institutions, in the grips of incapacitating handicaps and illness. . . . Others are not here because they lived a life so full of fear and isolation that they are no longer even able to reach out." Lorde recognized the myriad ways in which oppression affected gay people, and in her recognition of those affected by disabilities, she showed the power inherent in the gay liberation movement to be a pioneering force for change in society at large. As Lorde put it, "Not one of us is free until we are all free." She promoted a sort of proto-multiculturalism— the early 1990s movement that would extoll the virtues of diversity, inspired in part by Lorde's writings and those of other radical women of color. In the late 1970s, the prevalence of the macho clone in the gay community seemed to forestall any discussions of diversity, but Lorde called on her audience to embrace it. "We must not let diversity be used to tear us apart from each other, nor from our communities. This is the mistake they made about us. I do not want us to make it about ourselves."[52]

By the end of the decade, however, difference did tear apart the gay community. Although many white men probably did not even think twice about the race of the clone, the clone's whiteness sent a powerful message to people of color that gay identity was a white identity. Although the historical record does not tell us much about how people of color responded to the macho clone, the proliferation of organizations of gay people of color suggests a breach in the gay community. In the late 1970s, gay Latinos formed an organization known as GALA, which responded directly to the sexism represented by the macho clone in a 1978 pamphlet: "What we would like to emphasize at this point is our concern with the 'Macho Bandwagon' that has been adopted by white gays. We wonder, 'Do you really know what you're talking about?'"[53] Frustrated with white gay men's refusal to deal with their own propagation of sexism and racism, GALA gained national prominence as an organization that took seriously the concerns of Latino gay people who felt isolated from the increasingly white gay movement.[54]

The emergence of the macho icon was not the only reason why people of color began to establish their own organizations and communities. A number of competing, sometimes opposing factors, including the civil rights movement, the black power movement, the counterculture, and the women's liberation movement, gave rise to organizations for people of color. One of the most lucid and compelling connections between sexuality, race, gender, and class can be found in the Combahee River Collective Statement. Written by members of a black feminist lesbian organization active in Boston from 1974 to 1980, the statement described the racism within the feminist movement and the sexism within the black community and called for the creation of both a literal and a textual space for lesbians of color.[55]

That so many gay people of color organized against racism in the gay community and wrote detailed critiques of it is indicative of another response, albeit indirect, to the clone. In the process, the gay community went from being integrated to being segregated.

In addition to what was going on in gay culture, in popular culture, interestingly enough, heterosexual black men took on the mantle of "macho" while heterosexual white men were seen as "sissies." At least, that is how the critic Joe Wlodarz put it in writing about a crop of black exploitation films. Wlodarz perceptively noted that, "as in the writings of Le Roi Jones and Eldridge Cleaver, blaxploitation cinema constantly returns to the signifying power of the black male body in order to establish black male dominance over white men. Gender serves a clear purpose here as whiteness is aligned with weakness and femininity."[56]

In fact, the white macho clone may have been a response to a racialized fear of being perceived as weak and inferior by both heterosexual and homosexual black men. Asserting whiteness as both masculine and muscular in the making of gay male identity responded to the black exploitation films' demeaning treatment of white men as effeminate and inferior. Further, the stark polarities of this possibility may have prevented gay white men from constructing a macho clone that could also be black: to do so would have been to lose their masculine identity, because a black macho clone might appear more masculine and muscular than a white one.[57]

Gender anxieties may have also informed the creation of the clone as well. Throughout the 1970s, many feminists, lesbians, and lesbian feminists stripped their bodies of the signs of traditional femininity—long hair, dresses and skirts, high heel shoes, and jewelry. This effort to deflect the male heterosexual gaze resulted in an image of feminists, lesbians, and lesbian feminists as androgynous. The "dress code," according to one historian, "in some lesbian-feminist communities, for instance, comprised T-shirts, overalls, Levis, hiking boots, no makeup, virtually no dresses or skirts, short hair, and a refusal of leg shaving." As many women changed their appearance in ways that mimicked men's clothing and appearance, gay men were creating the macho clone, which could not possibly be confused with the feminist androgynous type. Whether this differentiation was intentional or subconscious is, of course, impossible to know.[58]

The macho clone also grew out of a larger health and wellness campaign spearheaded by white middle-class men that emphasized nutrition, exercise, and self-help in the late 1970s. Taking its cue from the popular *Our Bodies, Ourselves,* a book on women's health and sexuality written by the Boston Women's Health Collective, self-help books and manuals aimed at white middle-class men began to emerge at the end of the decade. Published in 1979, *Men's Bodies, Men's Selves* became a widely distributed encyclopedia of wellness, including notes on nutrition and diet, exercise, and medical ailments that only related to men, like testicular cancer. Thus, the macho clone emerged within this broader cultural context surrounding the body, health, and wellness and would pave the way, in part, for the fitness craze that developed in the early 1980s.[59]

By the end of the 1970s, many white gay men, especially in major urban centers, no longer understood gay liberation as community and culture and politics, but rather as identity and appearance. After the outward orientation of the early years of gay liberation, they turned their focus inward. Many of them were no longer volunteering for a newspaper, learning about their history, or creating a bookstore for the gay community but spending enormous energy and time instead trying to fit into the mold of the macho clone.

In retrospect, this shift could be interpreted as a sign of the success of gay liberation. Now that recognition had been won in many quarters, many gay people believed that it was okay to spend time perfecting a look because they no longer needed to devote all of their time and energy to fighting for acceptance and equality. In so doing, whiteness, masculinity, and muscularity became the markers of the gay community. As one gay man explained to another about the macho clone's role in creating community, "This scene is a man's world. These guys have nothing to do with 'straights.' They run around with each other—in cliques. These cliques are real tight, sort of like a clan. They hang out together, go out together, and some even work together. And every Saturday night the cliques meet here. That's why I called it a gathering of the tribe."[60]

The many gay men striving to fit the archetype of the macho clone were not all motivated by sexual desire—although it certainly motivated some. The macho clone served less as a symbol of sexual desire or promiscuity and more as a symbol of a new form of gay male identity that captured one meaning of gay liberation. As one gay man noted, "The straight world has told us that if we are not masculine we are homosexual, that to be homosexual means not to be masculine. . . . One of the things we must do is redefine ourselves."[61] In redefining themselves, however, many gay white men may have shattered the notion of gay men as effeminate, but simultaneously submitted to a heterosexism that gay people earlier in the decade had dismissed in their creation of a more feminine aesthetic. The result was an increasingly narrow definition of the gay community that consequently excluded people of color, lesbians, and transgender people. Moreover, in communicating a message to white gay men that masculinity and muscularity mattered more than anything, the macho clone alienated those in the gay white male population who did not subscribe to that ideal.

The history that had led to the macho clone, as well as the debates surrounding it, became lost as the macho clone grew in popularity by the end of the decade. By the early 1980s, the macho clone was omnipresent, and for those who would come out in the 1980s and 1990s, he was a staple of the gay community, his presence seemed almost natural. He was viewed as a timeless part of gay culture that defined the very essence of gay identity. Those who had no memory of a more diverse, less body-conscious identity came to learn the body language spoken by the macho clone.[62]

By the end of the 1970s, the macho clone had erased both the presence of people of color in the gay liberation movement and many white gay men's commitment to combating racism. In 1980, Craig Rodwell began to worry that gay men's commitment to antiracism had begun to wane, and he feared that the Stonewall uprising would be remembered as a political revolt only by white men. His concerns were triggered by the plans to erect a sculpture that memorialized Stonewall. As he explained in a letter to gay local leaders, business owners, and denizens of Greenwich Village:

> The George Segal statue, "Gay Liberation," which has been proposed as a commemorative to the Stonewall Uprising, is an expression of indifference to racism in the Gay community. It perpetuates the false idea that the Gay community and the Gay movement are for white people. The four people depicted in the statue are white; the models are all white; and, contrary to statements from the sponsors, any viewer of this statue will clearly see four white people.... Some of us have been actively opposing this statue; now we need your help.[63]

He asked them to attend a community planning board meeting where the decision would be made about the erection of the sculpture. Arguing that "the only thing that will defeat the statue proposal will be if enough Lesbians and Gay men come to show their opposition," Rodwell ended the letter by summarizing a resolution he wrote with the expectation that his readers would pass along the information to others in the neighborhood: "To demonstrate that Lesbians and Gay men are not indifferent to racism and that the Segal statue is not a proper commemorative monument to the Stonewall Uprising and should not be placed in Christopher Street Park."[64]

Despite Rodwell's robust efforts to persuade the New York gay community of the effects of the macho clone dominating the cultural landscape, the proposal for the statue passed. Segal's statue has stood in Christopher Street Park ever since.

The macho clone was more than just a playful identity that some men donned in order to be attractive, to be accepted, or to be comfortable being themselves. The macho clone also made many gay men forget the history of the 1970s.

CONCLUSION

In hindsight, gay liberation and gay life in the 1970s have come to be defined by sex and, to a lesser extent, politics. In the conventional narrative of that decade, the sexual and political awakening of gay people constituted a revolutionary transformation. When filmmakers, writers, and others chronicle the sex lives of gay men in the 1970s, gay citizens become recognizable to wider audiences who believe that sex defines homosexuality. When historians depict gay people taking to the streets, engaging in sweaty political struggles, carrying posters, and shouting slogans about equality, gay people become recognizable to American audiences because they represent a familiar story of US citizens striving for freedom. Like other oppressed groups over the history of the United States, gay people protested against discrimination and proved their independence, their self-worth, and their place within the republic.

But gay people's lived experiences in the 1970s defy this narrative. They gravitated toward religious institutions that vilified them, and in some instances they created their own churches. Their political efforts took place not only in gay pride marches but also in newspaper offices, in bookstores, and in the homes of intellectuals. They did not just dance to the news of the Stonewall uprising but seized the moment of recognition of their oppression to expose how many of their brothers and sisters were being sent to prison.

Gay people rethought the meaning of homosexuality in the 1970s, and their words, their language, and their ideas were often too sophisticated to be reduced to a catchy slogan on a sign at a pride march. They theorized about ideology, not gender, producing sexuality. They showed that gay people's alleged aberrance did not make them oppressed, but that their oppression made them appear aberrant. They redefined homosexuality by showing the world that gay people had a culture and could not be defined simply by their sexual acts.

By selling novels, scholarly books, and pamphlets and other ephemera, Craig Rodwell demonstrated the viability of a gay literary tradition. By charting gay people's presence throughout history, Jonathan Ned Katz powerfully chronicled gay culture over the course of four centuries. By publishing gay writers writing about gay topics, *The Body Politic* revealed gay people's distinct ideological concerns, social interests, and political attitudes. All of these efforts produced a distinct gay culture and sense of community that connected people based on their sexual orientation. As *The Advocate* explained in the aftermath of the Up Stairs Lounge fire: "Those gay leaders who flew to New Orleans at the first word of the terrible tragedy there June 24 . . . demonstrated that there really is some form of a 'gay community' in this country, as tenuous and vague as it is. There is a bond that links similarly oppressed people, and there is the compassion that springs from that bond."[1]

It was words—words in books, newsletters, newspapers, magazines, advertisements, plays, poems written inside prison cells, and letters written to pen pals—that made that community less "tenuous and vague" over the course of the 1970s and grounded it in a vibrant and emergent gay culture.

In the final stages of completing this book, I often felt like I was wrapping up an intellectual history of the seventies. In their quest to craft a specific gay identity, many gay people turned to various social theories to help them define sexuality. For instance, since democracy had justified their oppression and lack of rights, what could socialism teach them? Throughout the 1970s, gay people searched for alternative political ideologies that could provide them with the tools to critique the power structures that oppressed them. Pamphlets about socialism could be found on the shelves of the Oscar

Wilde Memorial Bookshop. Book reviews and feature articles on socialism filled the pages of gay newspapers, providing the intellectual foundation for thinkers like Jonathan Ned Katz to reimagine history and redefine gay identity. Gay ministers offered sermons that redefined a belief system that had long refused to recognize the plight of gay people.

In reading through the gay press over the course of many years, I came across hundreds of gay people who defined the meaning of gay liberation in the years immediately after it began, yet who have been almost entirely forgotten since then, along with their counter-narrative. These were writers, thinkers, and activists like the poet Paul Mariah, who advocated for prison reform and founded a publishing company that published scores of novice gay poets' writing and other work, and the photographer Gerald Malanga, who worked with Andy Warhol and reviewed books in the gay press. Although Malanga participated in a thriving literary culture in the 1970s and was the subject of a long profile in *Gay Sunshine,* he remains completely unknown, along with Mariah and many others, in gay literary, intellectual, and academic circles today.[2]

In an effort to underscore the literary character of the decade, I chose to begin chapter 6 on gay people in prison with poetry, not politics. I wanted to emphasize that poetry blossomed in one of the most unlikely places in the late twentieth century. In fact, many gay men in the 1970s understood poetry as a crucial part of gay identity and culture. Without romanticizing their predilections, many of them knew of a gay poetry tradition that began with Walt Whitman and Oscar Wilde and had continued with Langston Hughes and Allen Ginsberg. They used poetry and the lives of poets to mark periods of time and generations. When I interviewed a man who lived through the many changes in the Chelsea neighborhood in New York City during the 1970s, he made a nonchalant comment about Oscar Wilde's arrival in America and then pointed down Twentieth Street in the direction of the river, where he said Wilde's boat docked. "She [Wilde] was really something else, honey. Let me tell you." He then described everything from Wilde's coat to his critique of America. He was talking about Oscar Wilde as if he was the neighbor who just moved in next door.[3]

The ways in which periodicals, literature, and history shaped the 1970s have been forgotten. Like the gay community in Berlin that arose in the early twentieth century as homosexuality was being redefined, gay communities and culture proliferated in the seventies in the United States because of the new political, social, intellectual, historical, and religious definitions of homosexuality that flourished then. Gay people had created communities and cultures before the 1970s, but the scope and size of the gay community and its cultural production increased dramatically after the Stonewall uprising. The public dissemination of ideas through the newspapers, the Oscar Wilde Memorial Bookshop, and the countless religious organizations accelerated and intensified the spread of gay culture. The plethora of ideas that a diverse group of writers, thinkers, activists, intellectuals, and leaders discussed and developed in various genres and places redefined homosexuality and advanced the gay liberation movement.

Although gay culture in the 1970s, like so many social movements, defies description through a singular narrative, it is possible to describe its characteristics in general terms. One of my goals in this book has been to shift the focus of the discussion of gay culture from sex to religion, and from intimacy to community. This approach reverses the direction of the usual approach in the study of social movements. The writing of the history of the black civil rights movement, for instance, began with studies of the role of the church and religious communities; the role of sexuality and intimacy in the movement was overlooked at first. New books in the field have now explored the role of sexuality and intimacy in the lives of the black people who shaped the civil rights movement. One exception is the history of women's liberation; over the years those telling this story moved the discussion of feminism from studies of the radical fringes of leftist politics to studies of conservative women.[4]

Likewise, this book may appear to shift the discussion of gay history in order to present a more conservative portrayal of the past. But I hope that my portrait of gay culture in the 1970s is nuanced enough to ward off this critique. For example, the gay religious movement could be read as a history that privileges prayer over pornography, but it should be clear from the history told in these pages that the gay religious communities of the 1970s did not see sex as being at odds with their faith and had a sense of mission that went beyond prayer and worship. Part of the gay religious movement did emphasize these religious activities, the Bible, and the pulpit, but religious gays also confronted antigay antagonists determined to derail the liberation movement, and they refused to back down. Priests and other gay religious leaders often served as spokespersons for the gay community after a crime and talked to the press when hostilities erupted. Rev. Troy Perry demanded that the New Orleans Police and Fire Departments further investigate the Up Stairs Lounge arson attack. Many gay religious groups also served as interlocutors in political organizations and prisons, prefiguring some of the radical prison reform efforts of our own time.[5]

I also hope that, in arguing that sex did not define gay life, this book is not read as a sanitized history of the 1970s. There is little question that sex shaped, informed, and mattered to gay people throughout this decade, but it was not exclusive, as the received narrative has it. Much of what I have described in this book unfolded in the lives of people who were having sex, many of whom saw no contradiction between having sex and participating in the creation of gay culture. Falling into the easy trap of foregrounding sex has the effect of erasing the nuance, the richness, and even the messiness of people's lives. A second-order problem then emerges: writing the history of gay liberation becomes tied to an ideological agenda, in this case one that rationalized the spread of an epidemic by connecting promiscuity to HIV. The problem, to put it more bluntly, lies with the history of the gay community in the 1970s being reduced to a night at the baths.

Today we often see a conflict between the sex in the gay community and the creation of a gay culture. We find it hard to imagine that people were engaged in both, but in fact they were. As one contributor to a Boston newspaper explained, "What could it mean that after we did lay out on Thursday night, the guys would be in Herbe's Ram Rod Room on their knees suckin' dick all night? Was that an informal part of it, something to be ashamed of?"[6]

This gay man did not see the conflict, but we have become accustomed to focusing on it. We see only Herbe's Ram Rod Room, where men met in a dark part of the bar, away from the bartender and the jukebox, to act out the fantasies they read about in erotic short stories or saw on eight-millimeter pornography reels, the fantasies that had been appearing in their dreams since long before they could even legally enter a bar. We do not see that, as this man testifies, even as they got to have sex with other men, some were searching for the meaning of it.

For some gay men during the seventies, sex had one meaning: sex was political, a sign of liberation. The outbreak of an epidemic some years later would offer another meaning. Alarmed by the unknown etiology of the epidemic, doctors, public health officials, and even many gay people returned to the dark part of Herbe's Ram Rod Room, ignoring the jukebox playing music and the bartender pouring drinks. Looking for answers, they looked at the men in those dark corners with no consideration of who they were, where they had been a few hours earlier, or even what had inspired them to drop to their knees. They just reached for a big black marker and wrote in boldface letters PROMISCUOUS SEX on the walls above them. Doctors and public health officials did not really take notice of who was doing the giving and who was doing the receiving in these sexual encounters because, according to the logic of promiscuity as cause, the number of partners rather than the act itself led to the spread of HIV. Years later, public health officials would learn more about the virus and develop a gradation of risk based on sexual activity, but the notion of promiscuity remains part of the calculations about transmission of the virus to this day.

These biosocial realities mattered very little to many historians, filmmakers, and members of the general public, who also rushed to the back of the Ram Rod Room to see the men having sex. Overly interested in covering the walls with their own form of graffiti, they spray-painted the word REVOLUTION on the walls and missed what had happened before the men entered the bar and what they had done when the bar closed. For them, any other aspects of gay liberation seemed like mere embellishment of an otherwise trium-phant if prurient narrative of sexual revolution.

When I imagine the dark corners at the back of the Ram Rod Room, I see the vague outlines of a mass of humans, moving, breath-ing heavily, some grunting. I see the shadowy lives of what I know is a group of men, some huddled in small clusters, some paired off. But of course I can't see the past. Seeing photographs of people from decades ago once made me believe that I could picture the rest of the period. Newspaper clippings that I could touch made me believe that I could grasp the texture of people's lives. Conversations with those who lived during the era made me believe that I could return to another decade with them. But I cannot see the past; I can only try to describe and interpret it. In this book I've tried to describe a moment in the past that for so long could not even be imagined.

I did not write this book because I found myself in a gay com-munity center in Philadelphia as an undergraduate looking at sources that not one nongay academic historian had touched, or would even deign to touch. I did not write it because I took issue with a partic-ular documentary film. I wrote it because I uncovered the lives of people whose experiences, beliefs, and writings left me breathless. Magnanimously and courageously, they volunteered their time, their energy, and their incredible talents to make the world a better place for future generations of gay people.

This book is the longest thank-you note I'll ever write.

ACKNOWLEDGMENTS

This book would not have been possible without the LGBTQ community centers that created archives and libraries to preserve the past. Gay activists, writers, and many others in the community donated the materials they had been saving for years: magazines, newspapers, dog-eared clippings, correspondence, minutes from organizations, playbills, pamphlets, posters, and other ephemera. Then members of the LGBTQ community volunteered their time, energy, and often their own resources to making these records available to the public. If I had relied only on the nation's leading libraries and archives, I would have found only a tiny fraction of the existing material about gay life in the seventies.

Thus, I want to thank all those who donated documents and the many volunteers who cataloged it. I began this project in the William Way LGBT Community Center in Philadelphia and would like to thank Steven Capsuto, the head archivist, who welcomed me first as a volunteer and later as a researcher. His capacious, encyclopedic knowledge of the holdings made me immediately realize the richness of the history of the 1970s. At the Lesbian, Gay, Bisexual, and Transgender Community Center Archives in New York City, Rich Wandel introduced me to binders that indexed the gay press; he then miraculously retrieved extant copies of many short-lived publications. Talking with him about the history of the 1970s also provided me with a useful context in which to read the newspapers, and I am enormously grateful that he created time and space for me to use the archive. Skylar Fein answered many of my research queries about the New Orleans Police and Fire Departments' records on the Up Stairs Lounge fire; he generously led me to his crucial collection of records housed at the Historic New Orleans Collection, Williams Research Center, in New Orleans. Tal Nadan and the staff in the Manuscripts and Archives Division of the New York Public Library provided me with access to important collections and cheerfully welcomed me on Saturdays during the summer of 2012. Loni Shibuyama at ONE Archives at USC spent hours with me tracking down records of gay people of color from the late 1970s. Additionally over the years, countless, often nameless, members of the LGBTQ community created online databases, websites, and social media pages where they posted oral histories, primary sources, and various other records that provided clues about the 1970s. I am indebted to this sprawling historical enterprise that has grown enormously since I first began research for this book over a decade ago.

My next debt is to my agent Brettne Bloom, who helped me think through the narrative structure of the book and taught me the importance of telling a story. At Basic Books, Lara Heimert enthusiastically welcomed the proposal, which meant a great deal to me since she has impeccable taste and a brilliant mind for understanding (and even shaping) new directions in historical scholarship. Before leaving Basic, Tim Bartlett was my editor. From jump, he understood the point of this book and pushed me to strengthen it. His criticisms, analysis, and advice on how to structure the book stayed with me long after he departed from the press. Dan Gerstle picked up where Tim left off. He carefully edited the manuscript, offering astute feedback that sharpened the argument and pruned extraneous paragraphs and sentences. I am very fortunate to have an editor who put a tremendous amount of time and effort into the book and who, most of all, trusted my vision and worked diligently to ensure that the resulting book was accessible to a larger reading public. Melissa Veronesi was an ideal production editor and made the final stages of preparing the book for publication both manageable and enjoyable. Cynthia Buck carefully copyedited the manuscript and polished the prose.

I am very grateful to Warren Smith, James Steakley, Clarence Walker, John D'Emilio, Jerald Moldenhauer, Javier Garmendai, Richard Foster, and, most especially, Jonathan Ned Katz, all of whom shared their stories, insights, and memories of the 1970s.

A number of historians have read drafts of this book and talked me through its major arguments. Since 2006, Nicholas Syrett has discussed this project with me. He read early drafts of the manuscript and as always offered incisive comments, directed me to key books in the field, and helped me think through the broader argument. Christopher Capozzola also read early drafts of the manuscript and over the years discussed with me the evolution of the project. He enthusiastically supported my work on this topic and often asked very smart questions that clarified my thinking and exposed the limitations of a particular argument. During the final stages, he read the entire manuscript and identified important areas to address before the book went into production. Above all, I feel very lucky to have had his support over the years. While in graduate school at Columbia, we may have only passed each other a few times, but he has always understood the bonds that grow out of Fayerweather Hall. As I write these acknowledgments, Timothy Stewart-Winter's much-anticipated monograph on gay history in the second half of the twentieth century is in production. Knowing that he was writing such an important book, I asked him—only having met him once briefly—to read my manuscript. He kindly did and offered valuable comments and suggestions. Allyson Hobbs read parts of the manuscript and offered important formulations on how to shape various parts of the argument; she remains one of my closest friends and my biggest cheerleader. Todd Anten, always my first reader since college, read an early draft and offered his razor-sharp analysis.

Kathleen M. Brown read the manuscript and emailed me her comments after reading each chapter—which turned out to be a rewarding if nail-biting experience. She has been for many years my mentor and friend and her enthusiastic support of this book means the world to me.

When I first decided to work on this project in 2005, I contacted John D'Emilio, the preeminent historian of sexuality, for his opinion on whether the project was even viable. John spent hours talking to me over the phone, read early drafts of the manuscript, and continued to answer my email queries many years later. He actually makes cameo appearances in the book as a historical actor, but his influence on both the history and the historiography are far too great to detail here and worthy of a book of its own.

Over the years I have presented versions of the manuscript at conferences, workshops, and classrooms, where diverse audiences made up of scholars, students, and the general public offered helpful reactions. In 2008 I participated in a plenary with John D'Emilio, Carolyn Dinshaw, Karla Jay, Elizabeth L. Kennedy, and Marc Stein at the Organization of American Historians on Jonathan Ned Katz's scholarship that enriched my understanding of the 1970s and Katz's influence. At the American Historical Association annual meeting in 2013 in New Orleans, Karen Cox encouraged me to continue to search through local archives in New Orleans to uncover newspaper reports about the Up Stairs Lounge fire. Also at that meeting, Melinda Chateauvert provided me with the names of people in New Orleans who knew about the fire. While in New Orleans and then afterward, I was in touch with Misti M. Ates, Glenne McElhinney, and Clayton Delery-Edwards, who helped me track down important sources and provided me with key contacts that enabled me to write chapter 1.

Jen Manion invited me to present the overview of my book in her course on the history of sexuality at Connecticut College in 2011 and later, in 2014, invited me to meet with students at the campus's LGBTQ center to discuss the gay religious movement. Manion's dynamic and smart students proved to be an excellent audience who helped me elucidate my major claims. Also at Connecticut College, I presented a version of the manuscript at an event—jointly sponsored by the Gender and Women Studies Department and the Center for Comparative Studies in Race and Ethnicity and hosted by Mab Segrest and David Canton—that drew an engaged audience. I finished writing a draft of the book at the end of the fall term in 2014 at Connecticut College, where I read parts of it to students in my "Intro to American Studies" course; I am grateful to all my students, whose genuine interest in the topic buoyed my spirits. Special shout-outs to David Garcia Barrera, Sam Hooper, and Cassie Hunter.

Also at Connecticut College, I am grateful to Catherine M. Stock, who wrote many letters of recommendation that supported me and this project and who was always willing to answer questions about the twentieth century. Above all, I am grateful to her and to Lisa Wilson for supporting my decision to work on the 1970s.

I also received travel and research grants from Connecticut College that enabled me to complete this manuscript. Special thanks go to the Research Matters Grants and the R. F. Johnson Faculty Funding. Nancy Lewandowski, Ellen Maloney, and Mary Ellen Deschenes provided often gleeful administrative support.

Since 2006, I have encountered some of the most electrifying and intelligent voices of the next generation in my classes at Connecticut College. They have reminded me of the ways in which history shapes the present and ideas can arouse awareness, responsibility, and emotion. While I cannot name all of them, I want to acknowledge Alex Wood, Kara Meyering, Robbie Tesar, Brian Warner, Mike Coscarelli, Kevin Hartnett, Elizabeth Cooper-Mullin, Christie Clothier, Kate Radlaur, Afua Ferdnance, Jackson Murphy, Caroline Koppelman, Melanie Thibeault, Audrey Schlette, Carter Goffigon, Will Einstein, Jose Garcia, Clayton Witter, Claire Cafritz, and Hannah Feeney.

Since graduate school, Catherine Clinton has been my mentor and friend. She stood by me during the book proposal stage, the many archival trips, and would always, without fail, be willing to listen to whatever quagmire I found myself in while researching and writing this book. In many instances, her brilliant formulations indelibly shaped the content of this book in more ways than I know or even wish to tally.

Many members of my family and friends sustained me during the writing of this book. My parents supported me in immeasurable ways that enabled me to devote the time, energy, and resources to write this book. I am grateful for all that they have done and continue to do for me. Andrea Dalimonte, Sally Anne French, Nick Davilas, Susane Colasanti, Jeanette Mazzocca, Susan O'Donovan, Heather Ann Thompson, Elizabeth Hinton, Monica Gisolfi,

Monique Bedasse, Thavolia Glymph, Jorge Campos, Jaimie Fauth, Dan McLaughlin, Karen O'Neill Mullane, Mike and Yvette Ferrara, Megan Kate Nelson, Freddie LaFemina, and Thea Hunter enthusiastically supported me while I was working on this book and cheered me along.

Sarah Yardeni taught me that actions can be prayers and that negativity can be turned into light.

Brandon Lo Casto teaches me something new every time I talk to him and continues to be one of the most powerful and profound influences on my writing, thinking, and being. He discussed with me key passages in the manuscript and provided me with inspiring messages whenever I thought I had hit a roadblock. He was the first person I let read the completed manuscript because his opinion matters the most.

This book is dedicated to the various communities of friends who, since I came out, have taught me the meaning of a culture to call our own. As they have done in the past, they continue to stand by me.

NOTES

INTRODUCTION

1. *Gay Sex in the 70s,* DVD, directed by Joseph Lovett (San Jose, CA: Wolfe Video, 2005).

2. Journalist Randy Shilts makes a similar argument. See Shilts, *And the Band Played On: Politics, People, and the AIDS Epidemic* (New York: St. Martin's Press, 1987).

3. Richard Berkowitz, "CS People," *Christopher Street,* December 1982. See also Michael Callen and Richard Berkowitz, with Richard Dworkin, "We Know Who We Are: Two Gay Men Declare War on Promiscuity," *New York Native* 50 (November 8–21, 1982); and Richard Berkowitz, "Offense and Defense" (letter to the editor), *Village Voice,* December 28, 1982, both available at http://richardberkowitz.com/2010/06/29/safe-sex-writing-1982-2008 (accessed October 2, 2015). The myriad explanations that circulated within the gay community in the early 1980s regarding the spread of HIV, as incisively uncovered by historian Jennifer Brier, indicate that many within the gay community rejected promiscuity as the cause of HIV. Although Brier shows that many gay activists and writers cogently argued against the narrative of promiscuity as an explanation for the origin of HIV, promiscuity remains a factor today in how many doctors, gay people, and others rationalize HIV transmission. Brier also notes that even those who postulated promiscuity as the cause of HIV did so not simply from a moral or puritanical position but from the position that bathhouses, bars, and pornographic bookstores, by commercializing gay sex, advanced the spread of the virus. Like the rebuttals put forward by gay people in the 1980s against the promiscuity narrative, this position, a key part of the pro-promiscuity narrative, dissolved over time. See Brier, *Infectious Ideas: US Political Responses to the AIDS Crisis* (Chapel Hill: University

of North Carolina Press, 2009). On the biomedical origin of HIV, see Jacques Pepin, *The Origin of AIDS* (Cambridge: Cambridge University Press, 2011).

4. Although some historians have demonstrated the existence of gay communities and culture before the 1970s, many gay people—even those who knew of this history—view the 1970s as a major turning point that gave rise to gay churches, gay newspapers, and other gay political networks and social organizations. On gay culture before the 1970s, see George Chauncey, *Gay New York: Gender, Urban Culture, and the Making of the Gay Male World, 1890–1940* (New York: Basic Books, 1994); John D'Emilio, *Sexual Politics, Sexual Communities: The Making of a Homosexual Minority in the United States, 1940–1970* (Chicago: University of Chicago Press, 1983); Thomas A. Foster, ed., *Long Before Stonewall: Histories of Same-Sex Sexuality in Early America* (New York: New York University Press, 2007); Marcia Gallo, *Different Daughters: A History of the Daughters of Bilitis and the Rise of the Lesbian Rights Movement* (New York: Carroll & Graf Publishers, 2006); Elizabeth Kennedy and Madeline Davis, *Boots of Leather, Slippers of Gold: The History of a Lesbian Community* (New York: Routledge, 1993); Kevin P. Murphy, *Political Manhood: Red Bloods, Mollycoddles, and the Politics of Progressive Era Reform* (New York: Columbia University Press, 2008); Marc Stein, *City of Sisterly and Brotherly Loves: Lesbian and Gay Philadelphia, 1945–1972* (Philadelphia: Temple University Press, 2004); Sharon R. Ullman, *Sex Seen: The Emergence of Modern Sexuality in America* (Berkeley and Los Angeles: University of California Press, 1997).

5. This book focuses on the experience of gay white men and does not by any means purport to chart the diverse experiences of the LGBTQ community. Since my aim was to target the problematic representation of mostly white gay men's sex lives in the 1970s to rationalize the spread of HIV, I began by trying to puncture that portrayal and expose the unreported work of gay men during this period. Along the way, I saw the important work of many lesbians, especially in developing gay religion and the gay press. Yet, as I examined the sources more carefully, it dawned on me that the preponderance of white men throughout the historical record reflected a shift in how the gay community defined itself at the end of the decade. As I explain in the final chapter of the book on the rise of the "macho clone," this new definition excluded much of the LGBTQ community from the mainstream representation of gay identity. Superficially, the book may seem to deal only with white men, but it also tracks how sexism and racism turned gay liberation into a lily-white movement for men only—a development that I challenge throughout the book, particularly in the final chapter.

6. *Gay Sunshine* 1, no. 3 (November 1970).

7. See, for example, *Fag Rag* 5 (Summer 1973); and *The Body Politic*, March 1, 1977.

8. On the gay press before the 1970s, see Martin Meeker, *Contacts Desired: Gay and Lesbian Communications and Community, 1940s–1970s* (Chicago: University of Chicago Press, 2006). On the gay print culture in general, see George Chauncey, *Gay New York: Gender, Urban Culture, and the Making of the Gay Male World, 1890–1940* (New York: Basic Books, 1994); and Marcia M. Gallo, *Different Daughters: A History of the Daughters of Bilitis and the Rise of the Lesbian Rights Movement* (Berkeley, CA: Seal Press, 2006).

9. See, for example, *The Body Politic*, April 1, 1976.

10. *Arizona Gay News,* November 18 and December 9, 1977.

11. *The Body Politic,* January 1, 1975.

12. *The Body Politic,* April 1, 1976.

13. On gay people lamenting the lack of diversity in the movement toward the end of the decade, see *The Body Politic*, June 1, 1978.

14. On sexism within the gay liberation movement, see, for example, *The Body Politic*, January 1972. On early black gay enclaves before Stonewall, see Eric Garber, "A Spectacle in Color: The Lesbian and Gay Subculture of Jazz Age Harlem," in *Hidden from History: Reclaiming the Gay and Lesbian Past,* edited by Martin Duberman, Martha Vicinus, and George Chauncey (New York: New American Library, 1989).

15. Some customers wrote to Rodwell and complained about his bookstore not carrying Kramer's novel. See Brian A. Calia and Charles S. Williams, letter to Craig Rodwell, January 26, 1978; and Craig Rodwell, letter to Brian A. Calia and Charles S. Williams, March 5, 1979; both in box 1, "Professional and Political Correspondence, 1971–1980" folder, Craig Rodwell Papers. Manuscripts and Archives Division, New York Public Library (NYPL), Astor, Lenox, and Tilden Foundations; see also *Fag Rag* 5 (Summer 1973); and *Dignity* 5, no. 4 (April 1974). For more on the public and political reaction to Larry Kramer's writings, see John D'Emilio, *The World Turned: Essays on Gay History, Politics, and Culture* (Durham, NC: Duke University Press, 2002), 64–77.

16. Charley Shively argued throughout *Fag Rag* that various forms of gay sex constituted radical political acts; see *Fag Rag* 5 (Summer 1973).

17. *Fag Rag* 5 (Summer 1973); *Fag Rag* (February–March 1976); *The Body Politic*, April 1 and June 1, 1978; *Dignity* 5, no. 4 (April 1974); Jim Steakley, interview with the author, July 11, 2012.

18. *Gay Sunshine* 10 (February–March 1972).

19. Many gay people in the 1970s viewed democracy and capitalism as flawed concepts and theorized about socialism, Marxism, and other ideologies that could sustain their communities and commitments. See, for example, *The Body Politic*, April 1, 1977; *Fag Rag* 18 (Fall–Winter 1976); *Gay Sunshine* (August 1971); *Gay Sunshine* (August 1972); *Gay Sunshine* (October–November 1972).

20. Gay writers analyzed the meaning of family in the gay press in the 1970s. In an article entitled "Oppression Begins at Home," Brian Waite unpacked the meaning of the nuclear family as a function of capitalism that innately oppresses gay people (*The Body Politic*, July 1, 1972). Heather A. Murray addressed this subject in her study of kinship, *Not in This Family: Gays and the Meaning of Kinship in Postwar North America* (Philadelphia: University of Pennsylvania Press, 2010).

CHAPTER 1: THE LARGEST MASSACRE OF GAY PEOPLE IN AMERICAN HISTORY

1. Roy Reed, "Flash Fire in New Orleans Kills at Least 32 in Bar," *New York Times*, June 25, 1973. On crime in New Orleans in the 1970s, see Philip Aaron Banks, et al., *Plaintiffs-Appellees Cross Appellants*, No. 81-3377. 1983. Print.

2. For a description of the weather that night, see "Investigation Report of Fire," MSS 592, folder 12, Skylar Fein Up Stairs Lounge Fire Collection, Historic New Orleans Collection, Williams Research Center in New Orleans.

3. The eighteenth-century Catholic church in the French Quarter, St. Louis Cathedral, which towers over Jackson Square, had ended services by noon. The former nineteenth-century home of German Lutherans, St. Paul's Church, had also ended services hours earlier. Even the socially minded and community-conscious United Methodist Church, St. Mark's, had closed its doors by early evening.

4. I am drawing on Clayton Delery-Edwards's description of the stairwell; see Delery-Edwards, *The Up Stairs Lounge Arson: Thirty-Two Deaths in a New Orleans Gay Bar, June 24, 1973* (Jefferson, NC: McFarland and Company, 2014), 15–16.

5. Ibid., 17–21.

6. *The Advocate*, August 1, 1973.

7. For accounts of the arson in *The Advocate*: see August 1, 1973; August 15, 1973; November 21, 1973; and December 5, 1973.

8. New Orleans Department of Police, "General Case Report, Det. Charles Schlosser, Det. Sam Gebbia," MSS 592, folder 17, Historic New Orleans Collection, 30.

9. Ibid., 51.

10. Ibid., 27.

11. Ibid., 8. Rusty Quinton's name also appears in accounts as Lindy Quinton.

12. According to the testimony of Richard Soleto, who had been in the Up Stairs Lounge ten to fifteen minutes before the fire, there was one window facing Chartres Street that opened with a clasp and was not barricaded like the other windows. But it was covered with red velvet, which may have obscured it, and the lock may have prevented people from escaping. Some of the men

may have managed to use this window, but in all of the testimonies, accounts, and reports that I have read, only this testimony refers to the window, and it's from someone who was not in the Lounge at the time of the fire. See ibid., 50.

13. Elizabeth Dias, with Jim Downs, "The Horror Upstairs," *Time*, July 1, 2013; Delery-Edwards, *The Up Stairs Lounge Arson*, 49.

14. Scarborough, who sustained serious injuries, was taken to West Jefferson Hospital. "Statement of Michael Wayne Scarborough, WM/27, DOB 1/8/46, Residing 322 Stuart Street, West Monroe, Louisiana, Relative to a Fire Which Occurred at the Up Stairs Lounge About 7:56 PM, Sunday June 24, 1973," MSS 592, folder 15, Skylar Fein Up Stairs Lounge Fire Collection, Historic New Orleans Collection.

15. Delery-Edwards, *The Up Stairs Lounge Arson*, 50, 96.

16. Rev. Troy D. Perry, with Thomas L. P. Swicegood, *Don't Be Afraid Anymore: The Story of Reverend Troy Perry and the Metropolitan Community Churches* (New York: St. Martin's Press, 1990), 83–85.

17. New Orleans Department of Police, "General Case Report," 25.

18. Ibid., 30–31.

19. In his testimony, Joseph Courtney Craighead claims that fifteen to twenty people escaped (ibid., 23). Historian Clayton Delery-Edwards (*The Up Stairs Lounge Arson*, 183, note 6) also estimates that Buddy Rasmussen led twenty people to safety.

20. New Orleans Department of Police, "General Case Report," 22, 30–31.

21. Erik Ose, "Gay Weddings and 32 Funerals: Remembering the Up Stairs Lounge Fire," *Huffington Post*, July 11, 2008. Ose brilliantly uncovered the story of Mitchell's death.

22. "Fire Department Report," MSS 592, folder 17, Skylar Fein Up Stairs Lounge Fire Collection, Historic New Orleans Collection, 30–31.

23. New Orleans Department of Police, "General Case Report," 19, 52–53, 57; Delery-Edwards, *The Up Stairs Lounge Arson*, 45–46.

24. New Orleans Department of Police, "General Case Report," 20.

25. Ibid., 31–33.

26. Reed, "Flash Fire in New Orleans Kills at Least 32 in Bar"; Roy Reed, "Arson Suspected in Deaths of 29 in New Orleans Bar," *New York Times*, June 26, 1973.

27. New Orleans Department of Police, "General Case Report," 12.

28. *The Advocate*, July 18, 1973; New Orleans Department of Police, "General Case Report," 3; *The New Orleans Advocate*, June 10, 2015.

29. New Orleans Department of Police, "General Case Report," 11.

30. The aim of police investigations into fires is to collect information on possible arson and determine who may have committed that crime; the report of the investigation is not the place for commemorating the dead or even

acknowledging their lives beyond the fact that they were victims in the fire. To follow the logic of the surviving record by focusing on the arson plot, however, would be to emphasize the arsonist as the main protagonist in this tragedy and turn those who died into mere victims forming the backdrop of the story. To avoid this framing, I purposely set aside the larger question of who set the fire and instead focused on those who died. Recognizing the Up Stairs Lounge fire as the largest massacre of gay people in US history immediately shifts attention away from the culprit and onto those who died.

31. New Orleans Department of Police, "General Case Report," 7.

32. Ibid., 17.

33. Ibid., 39. To determine the location of Kenneth Harrington's body, I matched the numbers on the police report with those assigned by the fire investigator, which included the locations of the bodies; see New Orleans Fire Department, "Inspection and/or Investigation Report, Fire Prevention Division, New Orleans Fire Department, Fire District: 1st Company: FPD," MSS 592, folder 13, Skylar Fein Up Stairs Lounge Fire Collection, Historic New Orleans Collection.

34. New Orleans Department of Police, "General Case Report," 39.

35. Ibid., 39–40.

36. Ibid., 39–41.

37. Ibid., 50.

38. Delery-Edwards, *The Up Stairs Lounge Arson*, 52–53.

39. Ibid., 73; Johnny Townsend, *Let the Faggots Burn: The Upstairs Lounge Fire* (Booklocker.com, 2011), 302–304.

40. James Massacci Jr., quoted in Alyne A. Pustanio, "The Haunting Tragedy of the Up Stairs Lounge," December 7, 2014, http://www.alynepustanio.com /UPSTAIRSLOUNGE.php (accessed June 21, 2011); see also Delery-Edwards, *The Up Stairs Lounge Arson*, 96–97. Such a story seems sensationalistic, but it may have been true given the dire conditions that the firefighters confronted. According to some accounts, the devastation and carnage were so intense that many of the firefighters had to take breaks because of the gruesome smells of the burned bodies. Thus, it seems very likely that they were either unable to remove Larson's body or lacked the manpower to do so. That being said, I write this note in the wake of Michael Brown's body being left on the street in Ferguson, Missouri, for many hours after a police officer shot the African American teenager. Given that racism may have led to the abandonment of Brown's body, I have to wonder whether homophobia contributed to Reverend Larson's body being left in the window for so long.

41. John LaPlace and Ed Anderson, "29 Killed in Quarter Blaze," *New Orleans Times-Picayune*, June 25, 1973.

42. Ibid.

43. Buddy Rasmussen stated in his report to authorities that he ejected someone from the bar shortly before the fire (New Orleans Department of Police, "General Case Report," 30–31). Michael Scarborough also told authorities that earlier that evening he had been involved in an altercation with a fellow patron who was sitting in the men's room for over two hours. Sensing that he was cruising for sex, Scarborough reported him to another bartender, Hugh Cooley. The man left the men's room and then got into an argument with Scarborough, who "knocked him down." The man got up and yelled, "I'm gonna burn you all out" ("Statement of Michael Wayne Scarborough, WM/27, . . .").

44. George Schwandt, "Holocaust in New Orleans," *The Advocate*, July 18, 1973.

45. See Bruce Hall reporting on the fire for CBS News at "Upstairs Lounge Fire Network News Coverage," June 25, 1973, https://www.youtube.com/watch?t=48&v=cvvRJNQolYM.

46. Schwandt, "Holocaust in New Orleans"; see also Delery-Edwards, *The Up Stairs Lounge Arson*, 71.

47. Delery-Edwards, *The Up Stairs Lounge Arson*, 68.

48. "The Tragedy of the Up Stairs Lounge," The Jimani, http://www.thejimani.com/ourstory/theupstairslounge.html.

49. My analysis here builds on the fire marshal's investigation and the statements of some of the survivors interviewed by the city's arson investigators, who often only faintly recollected others at the Lounge or who knew of them by their first name or, more vaguely, by the street in the French Quarter where they lived. See, for example, "Statement of Mark Allen Guidry," MSS 592, folder 14, Skylar Fein Up Stairs Lounge Fire Collection, Historic New Orleans Collection.

50. GLBTQ, An Encyclopedia of Gay, Lesbian, Bisexual, Transgender and Queer Culture, http://www.glbtq.com/social-sciences/new_orleans,3.html (accessed, January 16, 2015).

51. Perry and Swicegood, *Don't Be Afraid Anymore*, 93.

52. I am drawing on the stories of Buddy Rasmussen and Regina Adams, who left the scene of the fire and only later gave information to the police. Based on the evidence, I believe that the official list of survivors did not include others who had survived but managed to escape without being documented. Throughout the police interrogations, many of the survivors offered conflicting, contradictory, and unclear evidence about the night of the fire: who was there and their affiliation with others in the bar. These problems in the sources lead me to think that there were other survivors, other victims, and other details about the fire that remain unknown. Finally, I should mention that Rasmussen has adamantly refused to talk to the press or to any other

writer or historian about the fire. I understand that his position comes from the distrust held by many gay men throughout the seventies toward dominant power structures, which they suspected of trying to interrogate them to obtain facts about the gay community. Sometimes the story of the past cannot be told. For an example of an interrogation in which the survivor could not name the people in the bar, see "Statement of Michael Wayne Scarborough, WM/ 27, . . ."; on Rasmussen, see Dias and Downs, "The Horror Upstairs."

53. Dias and Downs, "The Horror Upstairs"; Perry and Swicegood, *Don't Be Afraid Anymore*, 96–97.

54. A few years after the fire, when entertainer Anita Bryant's antigay crusade made it to New Orleans, gay people in the Quarter founded the Gertrude Stein Society as a political response to homophobia. Their motivation for forming the group stemmed in part, they said, from the Up Stairs Lounge fire; see Roberts Batson, "New Orleans," GLBTQ, http://www.glbtqarchive.com /ssh/new_orleans_S.pdf.

55. Quoted in James Thomas Sears, *Rebels, Rubyfruit, and Rhinestones: Queering Space in the Stonewall South* (New Brunswick, NJ: Rutgers University Press, 2001), 106.

56. Dias and Downs, "The Horror Upstairs."

57. *The Advocate*, September 26, 1973.

58. *Gay Community Newsletter*, July 5, 1973.

59. As I explain in later chapters, many gay people have turned to the past to help explain the degree of violence and discrimination they have faced. Throughout the 1970s, gay writers, activists, and intellectuals, for example, used the Nazi Holocaust as an analogy, a metaphor, and a symbol to describe gay oppression. In their efforts to both create a "usable past" and trace the existence of gay people throughout history, a number of gay writers have described the burning alive of many gay people during the Salem Witch Trials, a fact that has since faded from both the gay public memory and the historiography on Salem. It is no coincidence that writers in the 1970s evoked the imagery of the Salem Witch Trials burnings in their accounts of the fire at the Up Stairs Lounge. It is also no coincidence that it is Boston writers and journalists who have most often described the burning of gay people at Salem; their proximity to Salem makes me wonder (however romantically) whether a clandestine, potentially subaltern gay memory has persisted over the centuries. For references to Salem in the gay press, see *Fag Rag* 15 (February–March 1976); *Fag Rag* 16–17 (June–July 1976); and Arthur Evans, *Witchcraft and the Gay Counterculture* (Boston: Fag Rag Books, 1978). On witchcraft as a critique of capitalism, see *Fag Rag* 18 (Fall–Winter 1976). On the historiography of Salem, see Carol F. Karlsen, *The Devil in the Shape of a Woman: Witchcraft in Colonial New England* (New York: Norton, 1998); and Mary Beth Norton, *In the Devil's*

Snare: The Salem Witchcraft Crisis of 1692 (New York: Vintage, 2003). See also Erik N. Jensen, "The Pink Triangle and Political Consciousness: Gays, Lesbians, and the Memory of Nazi Persecution," *Journal of the History of Sexuality* 11, no. 1 (2002): 319–349.

60. *Gay Community Newsletter,* July 5, 1973.

61. "25th Anniversary of New Orleans Fire Remembered" (press release), July 3, 1998, http://www.glinn.com/news/obits1.htm.

62. *The Advocate,* November 21, 1973.

63. *The Advocate,* December 5, 1973.

64. *The Advocate,* August 1, 1973.

65. New Orleans Department of Police, "General Case Report."

66. *The Advocate,* February 14, 1973; *The Advocate,* February 28, 1973.

67. *The Advocate,* August 15, 1973.

68. *The Advocate,* August 29, 1974.

69. *Arizona Gay News,* December 30, 1977; *Los Angeles Times,* December 22, 1977; *Los Angeles Times,* December 23, 1977.

70. *The Advocate,* August 1, 1973. For more on gay safe-street patrols, see Christina B. Hanhardt, *Safe Space: Gay Neighborhood History and the Politics of Violence* (Durham, NC: Duke University Press, 2013).

71. *The Advocate,* December 5, 1973; *The Advocate,* February 14, 1974. In 1977 fire struck an MCC church in Phoenix. See *Arizona Gay News,* October 28, 1977.

72. *The Advocate,* February 28, 1973.

73. *The Advocate,* February 14, 1973; *The Advocate,* February 28, 1973; *New York Times,* April 1, 1973.

74. *The Advocate,* February 14, 1973.

75. *The Advocate,* August 15, 1973.

76. *The Advocate,* February 14, 1974.

77. *The Advocate,* October 24, 1973.

78. Ibid.

79. See John Howard, *Men Like That: A Southern Queer History* (Chicago: University of Chicago Press, 1999), 241; see also Dudley Clendinen, *Out for Good: The Struggle to Build a Gay Rights Movement in America* (New York: Simon & Schuster, 2001).

80. Townsend, *Let the Faggots Burn,* foreword; On Fein's exhibitions, see Jonathan Ferrara Gallery, "Skylar Fein," http://www.jonathanferraragallery .com/artists/skylar-fein. When I first discovered references to the Up Stairs Lounge fire in *The Advocate* at the William Way Community Center archive in Philadelphia in 2006, I did not know that Townsend had compiled the interviews. I would only learn about his book years later. Skylar Fein, as I mention in the acknowledgments, was hugely helpful and directed me to crucial

archival sources. In 2014, I pitched the story on the fire to *Time* magazine so that the fortieth anniversary of the fire would be recognized nationally.

CHAPTER 2: THE GAY RELIGIOUS MOVEMENT

1. Rev. Troy L. P. Perry, with Thomas L. P. Swicegood, *Don't Be Afraid Anymore: The Story of Reverend Troy Perry and the Metropolitan Community Churches* (New York: St. Martin's Press, 1990), 47; "MCC State of the Church Report Includes Fire," LGBT Religious Archives Network, http://www.exhibits .lgbtran.org/items/show/110 (accessed August 3, 2015).

2. For more on the women's critique of MCC, see Perry and Swicegood, *Don't Be Afraid Anymore*, 113–119; see also Rev. Elder Freda Smith, interview with Melissa Wilcox, February 24, 2007, Religious Archives Network, http:// www.lgbtran.org/Exhibits/OralHistory/Smith/FSmith.pdf. On the confer- ence, see *The Advocate*, September 26, 1973.

3. *The Advocate*, February 28, 1973; Heather Rachelle White, "Proclaiming Liberation: The Historical Roots of LGBT Religious Organizing, 1946–1976," *Nova Religion: The Journal of Alternative and Emergent Religions* 11, no. 4 (May 2008): 103–105; "Profile: Rev. George Augustine Hyde," Religious Archives Network, October 1, 2015, http://www.lgbtran.org/Profile.aspx?ID=96; and http://www.eucharisticcatholicchurch.org/our-history.

4. Ibid.

5. *The Advocate*, February 28, 1973; Robert Clement, interview with J. Gor- don Melton, August 18, 2007, Religious Archives Network, http://www.lgbtran .org/Interview.aspx?ID=12.

6. "News Release: Homosexuals Meet with Clergy, Washington Area Council on Religion and the Homosexual Formed," May 25, 1965, Barbara Gittings and Kay Tobin Lahusen Papers, Digital Collection, 1962–1972, avail- able at Rainbow History Project, http://rainbowhistory.omeka.net/items /show/4937965; "Profile: Jack Nichols," May 13, 2004, Religious Archives Network, http://www.lgbtran.org/Profile.aspx?ID=74; White, "Proclaiming Liberation," 105–106. For accounts of other episodes in gay religious history, particularly the Council on Religion and the Homosexual in San Francisco, see Nan Alamilla Boyd, *Wide-Open Town: A History of Queer San Francisco to 1965* (Berkeley: University of California Press, 2005).

7. Clement, interview with Melton, August 18, 2007.

8. *New York Times*, May 28, 1971.

9. *The Advocate*, September 21, 1973.

10. "Don't be afraid anymore" became Reverend Perry's rallying cry and the title of his memoir (Perry and Swicegood, *Don't Be Afraid Anymore*). Troy D. Perry and Charles L. Lucas, *The Lord is My Shepherd and He Knows I'm Gay: The Autobiography of the Rev. Troy D. Perry, as told to Charles L. Lucas* (Los Angeles: Nash Publishing, 1972).

11. Louie Crew, *A Book of Revelations: Lesbian and Gay Episcopalians Tell Their Own Coming Out Stories* (Washington, DC: Integrity, 1991), 24.

12. *The Gay Blade* 4, no. 12 (September 1973); Clement, interview with Melton, August 18, 2007.

13. Clement, interview with Melton, August 18, 2007.

14. *New York Times,* April 27, 1975; *The Advocate,* August 4, 1971; *Dignity* 3, no. 9 (November 5); Metropolitan Community Church, "Congregational History," http://www.agcmcc.org/about/congregational-history/ (accessed January 17, 2015); newsletter of the MCC, vol. II, no. 51, June 7, 1970, in box 2, "1970" folder, Craig Rodwell Papers, New York Public Library (NYPL); Todd J. Ormsbee, *The Meaning of Gay: Interaction, Publicity, and Community Among Homosexual Men in 1960s San Francisco* (Lanham, MD: Lexington Books, 2010), 158.

15. *Dignity,* June–July 1974; *The Advocate,* January 16, 1974.

16. White, "Proclaiming Liberation," 114–115; *New York Times,* May 28, 1971; Daniel Sack, "We, Who Once Had Turned Away: Making a Home Through a Mixture of Liturgical Styles in the Metropolitan Community Church," *Anglican and Episcopal History* 65, no. 1 (issue titled "Essays in the History of Anglo-Catholicism in America") (March 1996), 135, 138.

17. White, "Proclaiming Liberation," 106; Robert Clement Papers, NYPL; Clement, interview with Melton, August 18, 2007; Gary Laderman and Luis D. León, *Religion and American Cultures: An Encyclopedia of Traditions, Diversity, and Popular Expressions* (Santa Barbara, CA: ABC-CLIO, 2003), 1049; Ormsbee, *The Meaning of Gay,* 158. On Perry, see *Chicago Tribune,* June 7, 1970. I elaborate on the dynamics of the body culture in chapter 7.

18. *Dignity,* April 1974.

19. *Dignity,* December 5, 1972.

20. *Dignity,* December 1973.

21. *Dignity,* October 5, 1972, 4; "Church Discusses Coalition Possibilities," *Seattle Gay News,* December 7, 1979, 4. Integrity, also organized by gay Episcopalians, continues to this day.

22. Robert Cleath, "Gays Go Radical," *Christianity Today* 15 (1970): 40–41.

23. Clarebel Marstaller to Jeff Keith, May 28, 1974, Holyoke, MA, New England Yearly Meeting of Friends, Jefferson Keith Papers (private collection).

24. Newsletter of the Committee of Concern, August 22, 1974, Minneapolis, MN, Jefferson Keith Papers. On the history of zaps as a tool of political protest, see David Eisenbach, *Gay Power: An American Revolution* (New York: Da Capo Press, 2007). For the Catholic response, see *The Gay Blade* 6, no. 10 (October 1975): 2. For the Unitarian response, see *The Body Politic,* March 1, 1974; *The Body Politic* 1 (1974). On reactions among Episcopalians and other Christians groups, see Integrity, "Frequently Asked Questions: Where Does the Episcopal Church Stand on Gay and Lesbian Issues?" http://www.integrity

usa.org/archive/FAQs/index.htm (accessed January 4, 2015); *The Gay Blade* 6, no. 10 (October 1975): 3; *The Gay Blade* 9, no. 3 (March 1978).

25. *Dignity*, June–July 1975.

26. Father Henry Fehren, "A Christian Response to Homosexuals," *US Catholic* (September 1972).

27. Ibid.

28. "Letters," *Dignity* 3, no. 9 (November 5, 1972): 4.

29. See also Sr. Jeannine Gramick, SSND, "The Myths of Homosexuality," *Dignity*, June–July 1974; *Chicago Tribune*, October 19, 1974.

30. "Yearly Meeting Minutes on Gay Civil Rights," Jefferson Keith Papers; see also *The Advocate*, December 19, 1973; *The Gay Blade* 11 (November 1975).

31. *Chicago Tribune*, October 5, 1974.

32. *Chicago Tribune*, December 27, 1975.

33. *Chicago Tribune*, May 2, 1972.

34. *Chicago Tribune*, May 7, 1977.

35. *Wall Street Journal*, November 7, 1977; *Chicago Tribune*, March 8, 1975; *Chicago Tribune*, May 7, 1977; *New York Times*, October 4, 1977. See also Nancy C. James, *The Developing Schism Within the Episcopal Church, 1960–2010: Social Justice, Ordination of Women, Charismatics, Homosexuality, Extra-Territorial Bishops, Etc.* (Lewiston, NY: Edwin Mellen Press, 2010); "The Split in Episcopal Ranks," *Wall Street Journal*, November 7, 1977; *The Body Politic*, June 1, 1976.

36. For an overview of the Bryant scandal, see Martin B. Duberman, *Left Out: The Politics of Exclusion: Essays, 1964–2002* (Cambridge, MA: South End Press, 2002). Some historians argue that gay people's political campaigns for their rights mobilized the conservative faction in the country to launch its campaign about the sanctity of the family, which was also galvanized, as they rightly point out, by the 1970s debates surrounding abortion and feminism. See, for example, Robert Self, *All in the Family: The Realignment of American Democracy Since the 1960s* (New York: Hill and Wang, 2012). My analysis of the sources, however, shows that the conservative reaction against gay liberation did not stem simply from an aggressive criticism of gay liberation but rather from the gay religious movement's attempt to redefine the meaning of family, church, and community in religious institutions.

37. *Gay St. Louis* (November 1977); see also Randy Shilts, *The Mayor of Castro Street: The Life and Times of Harvey Milk* (New York: St. Martin's Press, 1982), 215–217.

38. In drawing this connection I am by no means blaming gay people for their activism, but rather offering a clearer historical context for the religious right's vehemence toward gay people and underscoring the efficacy of the gay religious movement's efforts. The religious right's loud, pervasive critique of

homosexuality nevertheless drowned out the sounds of the gay religious community and consequently erased its role in initiating the discussion about gay marriage, ordination, and acceptance in the 1970s. Its influence was evident, for example, when gay people launched a massive political campaign to gain the right to marry in the first decade of the twenty-first century and both directly and indirectly drew on the methods, concerns, and rallying cries of the gay religious movement in the 1970s. In her widely reviewed and critically acclaimed book, Jo Becker charts the gay marriage fight for equality without offering a historical context. Her analysis, while smart and engaging, does not acknowledge that 1970s religious activists initiated the gay marriage debate and that the methods used later that led to success drew on this precedent. See Becker, *Forcing the Spring: Inside the Fight for Marriage Equality* (New York: Penguin, 2014). On how the opposition to gay people splintered according to religious beliefs, see *The Body Politic*, July 1, 1977.

39. *The Body Politic*, November 1, 1974.

40. *The Body Politic*, February 1, 1978.

41. *The Body Politic*, November 1, 1974.

42. *The Body Politic*, March 1, 1977.

43. *The Body Politic*, November–December 1974; *Gay Sunshine* 1, no. 2 (October 1970).

44. For more on the complicated place of religion in gay culture, see Moshe Shokeid, *A Gay Synagogue in New York* (Philadelphia: University of Pennsylvania Press, 2003), 16–17.

45. *The Gay Blade* (November 1975); *New York Times*, July 1, 1974.

46. *Fag Rag* 20 (Summer 1977).

47. Ibid.

48. Ibid.; John Mitzel recounts this story and explains Charley Shively's perspective in "John Mitzel Telling Story of Charles Shively Burning the Bible at Boston Pride 1977," http://vimeo.com/56127538 (posted 2013, accessed January 5, 2015).

49. *Fag Rag* 20 (Summer 1977).

50. "John Mitzel Telling Story of Charles Shivley Burning the Bible at Boston Pride 1977."

51. Ibid.

52. See, for example, Eric Foner, *The Story of American Freedom* (New York: Norton, 1999).

53. *Fag Rag* 20 (Summer 1977).

54. *Fag Rag* (June–July 1976): 18–19. For more on Bernier, see "Profile: Rev. Larry Bernier," Religious Archives Network, http://www.lgbtran.org/Profile.aspx?ID=261 (accessed December 23, 2014).

55. *The Body Politic*, January 1, 1975.

CHAPTER 3: THE BIOGRAPHY OF A BOOKSTORE

1. Quoted in Kay Tobin and Randy Wickler, *The Gay Crusaders* (New York: Arno Press, 1975), 69–70. Rodwell inspired gay people around the world to open bookstores; see Ernest Hole, "The Birth of Gay's the Word," *Polari*, January 17, 2012, http://www.polarimagazine.com/features/birth-gays-word.

2. Craig Rodwell to Barbara Love, October 3, 1973, box 6, "Oscar Wilde Memorial Bookshop: Business Correspondence" folder, Craig Rodwell Papers, Manuscripts and Archives Division, New York Public Library (NYPL), Astor, Lenox, and Tilden Foundations.

3. Craig Rodwell, "Oh, Pornography," "Writings by Craig Rodwell" folder, box 1, Craig Rodwell Papers. Rodwell's archives include many essays, like this one, that he wrote and then sent to friends or published in *Queen's Quarterly* or *The New York Hymnal*. Although I have been unable to find a surviving published copy of this essay, that does not mean it was not published.

4. Ibid.

5. "Sex—How Important Is It?" "Writings by Craig Rodwell" folder, box 1, Craig Rodwell Papers.

6. For more on the gay history of Fire Island, see Esther Newton, *Cherry Grove, Fire Island: Sixty Years in America's First Gay and Lesbian Town* (Durham, NC: Duke University Press, 2014).

7. The description of Rodwell's clothing comes from one of the few images of him. A slide features him wearing this shirt and jacket; slides, box 15, Craig Rodwell Papers.

8. Quoted in Tobin and Wickler, *The Gay Crusaders*, 70.

9. "A Bookshop of the Homophile Movement" (mail-order catalog), box 6, "Oscar Wilde Memorial Bookshop" folder, Craig Rodwell Papers; Kevin Bruke, James Jarman, Don Thienpont, and Danny Ventrelli to Craig Rodwell, November 20, 1978, on the St. Matthew Community, 160 Bond St., Brooklyn, NY 11217, box 1, "Professional and Political Correspondence, 1971–1980" folder, Craig Rodwell Papers.

10. In the early 1970s, the famous lesbian political leader Barbara Gittings led an American Library Association task force that reclassified homosexuality from HQ 71.471 ("abnormality and criminality") to HQ 76.5 ("gay liberation"). Gittings and her partner, Kay Tobin, also became consummate allies of Craig Rodwell's, and her experiences in the Oscar Wilde Memorial Bookshop probably had a deep influence on her professional work on the ALA task force. Kay Tobin wrote to Rodwell, extolling the enormous benefits of the bookshop in the creation of gay culture. Kay Tobin Lahusen (and Barbara Gittings) to Craig Rodwell, April 8, 1993, box 1, "Letters of Appreciation 1992–1993" folder, Craig Rodwell Papers. See Barbara Gittings, *Gays in Library Land: The Gay and Lesbian Task Force of the American Library Association: The First Sixteen Years* (Philadelphia: B. Gittings, 1990); and

Norman G. Kester, *Liberating Minds: The Stories and Professional Lives of Gay, Lesbian, and Bisexual Librarians and Their Advocates* (Jefferson, NC: McFarland, 1997).

11. "A Bookshop of the Homophile Movement"; "Sex—How Important Is It?" box 1, "Writings by Craig Rodwell" folder, Craig Rodwell Papers. The description of his register comes from one of the few images of the store; slides, box 15, Craig Rodwell Papers.

12. Tobin and Wickler, *The Gay Crusaders,* 65.

13. John D'Emilio and others have brilliantly documented the development of a gay political movement before the advent of gay liberation in the 1970s, and historians have rightly argued for the existence at various moments in the early twentieth century (and even in the late nineteenth century) of gay enclaves with their own culture. My point here is not to invalidate this history but rather to show that, from Craig Rodwell's perspective, this world was inconspicuous. He may have been aware of this history, but he felt that he needed to establish the bookstore in an effort to promulgate gay culture. To put it another way, there is a difference between what historians know about the past and what people like Craig Rodwell know. Moreover, the changing social climate of the 1960s had compelled Rodwell and others to take political steps to make the gay world more public, and Rodwell, as I mentioned earlier in the chapter, wanted to promote a public vision of homosexuality that had been rejected by the Mattachine Society. On gay and lesbian communities before Stonewall, see John D'Emilio, *Sexual Politics, Sexual Communities,* 2nd ed. (Chicago: University of Chicago Press, 1998); D'Emilio, *The World Turned: Essays on Gay History, Politics, and Culture* (Durham, NC: Duke University Press, 2002), 146–153; Marcia M. Gallo, *Different Daughters: A History of the Daughters of Bilitis and the Rise of the Lesbian Rights Movement* (Berkeley, CA: Seal Press, 2006); George Chauncey, *Gay New York: Gender, Urban Culture, and the Making of the Gay Male World, 1890–1940* (New York: Basic Books, 1994); Marc Stein, *City of Sisterly and Brotherly Loves: Lesbian and Gay Philadelphia, 1945–1972* (Philadelphia: Temple University Press, 2004). On the literary world of gay men long before Stonewall, see Benjamin E. Wise, *William Alexander Percy: The Curious Life of a Mississippi Planter and Sexual Freethinker* (Chapel Hill: University of North Carolina Press, 2012). On the antique shops in midtown Manhattan as gay hangouts in the late 1950s and 1960s, see Javier Garmendai and Richard Foster, interview with Jim Downs, New York City, June 29, 2014.

14. Craig Rodwell to Benjamin C. Willis, Chicago Board of Education, August 14, 1963, box 1, "Professional and Political Correspondence, 1963–1970" folder, Craig Rodwell Papers; Leonard Farbstein, US House of Representatives, to Craig Rodwell, March 23, 1965, ibid.

15. *Life,* June 26, 1964, 66; Craig Rodwell to editor, *Life* magazine, June 26, 1964, box 1, "Professional and Political Correspondence, 1963–1970" folder,

Craig Rodwell Papers. Historian Martin Meeker brilliantly examines the impact of this particular article on a number of other mid- to late-twentieth-century representations of gay people in the media; see Meeker, *Contacts Desired: Gay and Lesbian Communications and Community, 1940s–1970s* (Chicago: University of Chicago Press, 2006).

16. Craig Rodwell to editor, *Life* magazine, June 26, 1964.

17. Craig Rodwell to *New York Times Sunday Magazine,* May 29, 1968, box 2, "1968" folder, Craig Rodwell Papers.

18. Craig Rodwell to editor, *The New York Post,* June 1, 1969, box 2, "1969" folder, Craig Rodwell Papers.

19. Craig Rodwell to "Dear Abby," February 11, 1971, box 2, "1970" folder, Craig Rodwell Papers.

20. Craig Rodwell to Beverly Sills, November 14, 1976, box 2, "1976" folder, Craig Rodwell Papers.

21. *New York Times,* July 19, 1970, box 2, "1970" folder (newspaper clippings), Craig Rodwell Papers.

22. Ibid.; Alfred A. Gross, Executive Director, George W. Henry Foundation, "The American Homophile Movement," an address to clinical training students at Bellevue Hospital, Tuesday, December 5, 1967, box 2, "1967" folder, Craig Rodwell Papers. On Gross, see *New York Times,* June 2, 1987. On the Black Panthers, see "Probe Bomb Threats in Panther Case," *New York Post,* November 27, 1970, box 2, "1970" folder (newspaper clippings), Craig Rodwell Papers.

23. Rita Mae Brown to Craig Rodwell, February 25, 1972, box 1, "Professional and Political Correspondence, 1971–1980" folder, Craig Rodwell Papers. On Tennessee Williams's and Christopher Isherwood's visits to the bookstore, see box 14 (Craig Rodwell photos), Craig Rodwell Papers.

24. At one point, in order to pay the high cost of rent, Craig offered some very light erotica at the bookstore; see *New York Times,* February 3, 2009; Tobin and Wickler, *The Gay Crusaders,* 71.

25. Tobin and Wickler, *The Gay Crusaders,* 71; David Carter, *Stonewall: The Riots That Sparked the Gay Revolution* (New York: St. Martin's Press, 2010), 31–32.

26. Carter, *Stonewall,* 34–35; Randy Shilts, *The Mayor of Castro Street: The Life and Times of Harvey Milk* (New York: St. Martin's Press, 1982), 27–28, 44.

27. Martin Duberman, *Stonewall* (New York: Plume, 1993); Shilts, *The Mayor of Castro Street,* 197–211.

28. "Mattachine Society Stamp" (press release), April 22, 1966, box 2, "1966" folder, Craig Rodwell Papers.

29. Craig Rodwell to Gay Brothers and Gay Sister, February 1972, box 2, "1972" folder, Craig Rodwell Papers, and Kay Tobin Lahusen (and Barbara Gittings) to Craig Rodwell, April 8, 1993. On gay rights demonstrations in

Philadelphia, see Marc Stein's superb study, *City of Sisterly and Brotherly Loves: Lesbian and Gay Philadelphia, 1945–1972* (Philadelphia: Temple University Press, 2004), 291–296.

30. Tobin and Wickler, *The Gay Crusaders*. Kay Tobin and Craig Rodwell would be comrades in the fight for gay liberation for many decades. They participated in early protests together in New York and continued to be political allies even when they were not in the same city. See Kay Tobin Lahusen to Craig Rodwell, December 23, 1970, box 1, "Various Personal Correspondence, 1959–1986" folder, Craig Rodwell Papers. For more context regarding Tobin's request for Rodwell's political help, see *The Body Politic*, September 1980. In Tobin's initial letter to Rodwell, John Francis Hunter was named as the coauthor; Kay Tobin and John Francis Hunter to Craig Rodwell, December 23, 1970, ibid.

31. Mark A. Culhane to Craig Rodwell, June 14, 1972, box 2, "1972" folder, Craig Rodwell Papers.

32. Ibid. In his articles for *Queen's Quarterly* and in his chapter in *The Gay Crusaders,* Rodwell emphasized his commitment to helping young men; see "Draft, February 27, 1971," box 2, "1971" folder, Craig Rodwell Papers; see also Edward Brown to Craig Rodwell, July 14, 1969, box 1, "Professional and Political Correspondence, 1963–1970" folder; and Russell Nile Russell to Craig Rodwell, June 30, 1969, box 2, "1969" folder, both in Craig Rodwell Papers.

33. Culhane to Rodwell, June 14, 1972.

34. Richard Boyle to Craig Rodwell, July 7, 1972, box 1, "Professional and Political Correspondence, 1971–1980" folder, Craig Rodwell Papers.

35. Collin Charles Schwoyer to Craig Rodwell, June 19, 1969, box 1, "Professional and Political Correspondence, 1963–1970" folder, Craig Rodwell Papers.

36. On Rodwell's financial struggle to maintain the Oscar Wilde Memorial Bookshop, see "Venerable Bookstore to Close in Village," *New York Times,* February 4, 2009.

37. Carleton P. Jones III to Craig Rodwell, May 24, 1972, box 1, "Professional and Political Correspondence, 1971–1980" folder, Craig Rodwell Papers. Some gay men disagreed with this stance; they found humanity and personal connections in the porn theaters and bathhouses. This argument is certainly valid for some and, not surprisingly, squares with the way most people remember these places in the 1970s. I am interested in tracking a counternarrative; see, for example, Samuel R. Delany, *Times Square Red, Times Square Blue* (New York: New York University Press, 1999).

38. "Sex—How Important Is It?"; Tobin and Wickler, *The Gay Crusaders,* 71.

39. Craig Rodwell to Istvan Schutz, August 1, 1977, Budapest, Caskterny, Hungary, box 6, "Oscar Wilde Memorial Bookshop: Business Correspondence" folder, Craig Rodwell Papers; Edward Brown to Craig Rodwell, July 14,

1969, box 1, "Professional and Political Correspondence, 1963–1970" folder, Craig Rodwell Papers.

40. Louie to Craig Rodwell, January 22, 1970, box 1, "Various Personal Correspondence, 1959–1986" folder, Craig Rodwell Papers.

41. Anonymous to Terry and Jack, July 30, 1970, box 1, "Anonymous Threatening Letter to 'Jack' of the Oscar Wilde Memorial Bookshop, July–August 1970, Letter from FBI, September 1, 1970" folder, Craig Rodwell Papers.

42. Anonymous to Terry and Jack, July 23, 1970, ibid.

43. John F. Malone to Craig Rodwell, September 1, 1970, ibid. In general, the FBI does not investigate every request it receives.

44. In an interview in the early 1970s, Rodwell said that he worked at the shop exclusively when he first opened it; Tobin and Wickler, *The Gay Crusaders*, 72.

45. For example, the articles including a mention of the word "gay" that are collected in a folder marked "1974" range from a review of a play to articles about a crime, about medicine, about lesbians, and about gay groups' protest against Catholic leaders; see box 2, "1974" folder, Craig Rodwell Papers.

46. *New York Post*, June 27, 1977, box 5, "Homosexuality Clippings" folder, Craig Rodwell Papers; "Village Killer Murdered Six," *New York Post*, April 6, 1979, ibid.; folder on the film *Cruising*, ibid.

47. Thomas B. Morgan, City of New York, Office of the Mayor, to Craig Rodwell, February 3, 1970, box 1, "Professional and Political Correspondence, 1963–1970" folder, Craig Rodwell Papers; David N. Dinkins to Craig Rodwell, April 16, 1993, "Tribute to CR" folder, Craig Rodwell Papers; "Letters of Condolence to Craig's Mother" folder, Craig Rodwell Papers.

48. Tobin and Wickler, *The Gay Crusaders*, 67.

49. I am not arguing that violence between or against gay people was new, but rather that the politics of liberation led to the public establishment of an openly gay institution that became a visible target. Just as arsonists burned down black churches in an attempt to shut down the civil rights movement, the violent attacks against the bookstore and other gay institutions were attempts, I argue, to shut down gay liberation. Further, even though the letter-writer never fulfilled his promise to burn down the Oscar Wilde Memorial Bookshop and murder the employees, his threats should be classified as a form of violence. The historian and the reader know with the privilege of hindsight that these brutal threats did not materialize, but at the time they were being made Craig Rodwell felt endangered; that is why he contacted the police and probably why he kept the threatening letters. On violence among gay people before Stonewall, see Lisa Duggan, *Sapphic Slashers: Sex, Violence, and American Modernity* (Durham, NC: Duke University Press, 2001). On representations of queer violence, see Lynda Hart, *Fatal Women: Lesbian Sexuality and the Mark of Aggression* (London: Routledge, 1994).

50. Tobin and Wickler, *The Gay Crusaders*, 74.

51. Craig Rodwell, Linda Jones, Erica Dattile, and Bruce Gelbert to Captain Rosenthal, Sixth Precinct, West Tenth Street, August 2, 1977, box 2, "1977" folder, Craig Rodwell Papers.

52. Robert Steelman to Craig Rodwell, July 5, 1978, box 2, "1978" folder, Craig Rodwell Papers.

53. Ibid.

54. Craig Rodwell to Robert Steelman, June 20, 1978, ibid. The date on this letter, June 20, predates Steelman's July 5 letter to Rodwell. Steelman must have written a previous letter that did not make it into the manuscript collection or Rodwell mistakenly wrote June instead of July.

55. Tobin and Wickler, *The Gay Crusaders*, 74.

56. Jonathan Ned Katz, interview with Jim Downs, New York City, May 29, 2012.

57. Ibid.

Chapter 4: Gay American History

1. Jonathan Ned Katz, interview with Jim Downs, New York City, May 29, 2012.

2. Simon LeVay, *Queer Science: The Use and Abuse of Research into Homosexuality* (Cambridge, MA: MIT Press, 1997), 29–30.

3. Jonathan Ned Katz, interview with Jim Downs, New York City, May 2006. On the history of Berlin and homosexuality, see Robert Beachy, *Gay Berlin: Birthplace of a Modern Identity* (New York: Knopf, 2014).

4. Jonathan Ned Katz, interview with Jim Downs, New York City, June 23, 2015 and September 12, 2015. Katz talked mostly in our interviews about Hirschfeld's theories and institute transforming the meaning of homosexuality. He did not discuss in great detail the actual culture, everyday activities, and lives of gay people in Berlin during this period. For such a discussion, see Robert Beachy's excellent book, *Gay Berlin*. Katz would later learn more about the world that Beachy describes from his discussions with John Lauritsen, David Thorstad, and James Steakley at the Gay Socialist Action Project meetings, which I describe later in the chapter. While the official publication of the "The Early Homosexual Rights Movement" was in 1973, which is a bit later than the date when Katz first walked into the bookstore, this is his memory of the events recounted during a few interviews. Plus, Katz may have read an unpublished version of the pamphlet at the time in the Oscar Wilde Memorial Bookshop; his informal conversations with the authors who he knew socially also had a profound impact on him—regardless of the actual publication of the pamphlet.

5. Katz, interview with Downs, May 29, 2012.

6. Ibid.

7. "*Life* Visits a Back-yard Movie Set: Jonathan Katz, 13, Films Tom Sawyer," *Life*, June 11, 1951.

8. For a captivating history of Greenwich Village intellectuals in the early twentieth century, see Christine Stansell, *American Moderns: Bohemian New York and the Creation of a New Century* (New York: Metropolitan Books, 2000). Stonewall is often perceived as the start of gay liberation, but historians have demonstrated that the fight for gay liberation began much earlier; some even downplay the significance of Stonewall as a watershed moment in gay American history. See John D'Emilio, *Sexual Politics, Sexual Communities: The Making of a Homosexual Minority in the United States, 1940–1970* (Chicago: University of Chicago Press, 1983); Thomas A. Foster, ed., *Long Before Stonewall: Histories of Same-Sex Sexuality in Early America* (New York: New York University Press, 2007); Marcia Gallo, *Different Daughters: A History of the Daughters of Bilitis and the Rise of the Lesbian Rights Movement* (New York: Carroll & Graf Publishers, 2006); and Elizabeth Kennedy and Madeline Davis, *Boots of Leather, Slippers of Gold: The History of a Lesbian Community* (New York: Routledge, 1993). On the sexual revolution, see David Allyn, *Make Love, Not War: The Sexual Revolution: An Unfettered History* (New York: Routledge, 2001).

9. Katz, interview with Downs, May 29, 2012.

10. Ibid.

11. Ibid.; John D'Emilio, email to Jim Downs, March 2, 2013; see also John D'Emilio, *Making Trouble: Essays on Gay History, Politics, and the University* (New York: Routledge, 1992), xxxii.

12. Katz, interview with Downs, May 16, 2006; D'Emilio, *Making Trouble,* xxxii.

13. Historian Barbara J. Fields makes a similar observation in her brilliant study of racism and ideology; see Karen E. Fields and Barbara Jeanne Fields, *Racecraft: The Soul of Inequality in American Life* (New York: Verso, 2012), 128.

14. Katz, interview with Downs, May 29, 2012. While these ideas were certainly new to Katz and many others in his generation, gay people from earlier epochs, particularly those who formed the radical wing of the Mattachine Society, had reached similar conclusions by employing Marxist ideas to understand social oppression. They had also organized meetings to talk through these conundrums; see D'Emilio, *Sexual Politics, Sexual Communities,* 63–70; see also James T. Sears, *Behind the Mask of the Mattachine: The Hal Call Chronicles and the Early Movement for Homosexual Emancipation* (New York: Routledge, 2006), 151.

15. Katz, interview with Downs, May 2006.

16. Outhistory.org, "Zapping the New York Academy of Medicine, April 6, 1976," http://outhistory.org/oldwiki/Zapping_the_New_York_Academy_of _Medicine,_April_6,_1976 (accessed January 19, 2015).

17. Ibid.

18. Rod Chase, "Notes of a Homosexual," box 2, "1968" folder, Craig Rodwell Papers, NYPL.

19. Katz, interview with Downs, May 29, 2012.

20. "Herbert Aptheker, 87, Dies: Prolific Marxist Historian," *New York Times*, March 20, 2003.

21. William Katz would go on to become a leading historian of African American history, publishing over forty books. The civil rights movement gave birth to a generation of historians whose historical accounts of slavery and emancipation would revise curricula across the country; see Eric Foner, *Who Owns History: Rethinking the Past in a Changing World* (New York: Hill and Wang, 2002); and Jim Downs, ed., *Why We Write: The Politics and Practice of Writing for Social Change* (New York: Routledge, 2006), 27–48.

22. Katz, interview with Downs, May 29, 2012.

23. Katz, interview with Downs, May 16, 2006.

24. Ibid.; Katz, interview with Downs, May 29, 2012. For a link to a radio version of the play, see Pacifica Radio Archives, "Inquest at Christiana: Written and Directed by Jonathan Ned Katz," https://archive.org/details /pra-BB3818.18A.

25. Bernard and Jonathan Katz, *Black Woman: A Fictionalized Biography of Lucy Torry Prince* (New York: Pantheon, 1973). Black historians were writing the history of resistance long before white historians discovered it. See, for example, W.E.B. Du Bois, *Black Reconstruction in America, 1860–1880* (New York: Simon & Schuster, 1935). My point here is to underscore that Katz was among the minority of white scholars who worked on this topic during the 1960s. At the time, the leading white historian to make claims of black resistance was Kenneth M. Stamp; see Stamp, *The Peculiar Institution: Slavery in the Ante-bellum South* (New York: Knopf, 1956).

26. Katz, interview with Downs, May 29, 2012.

27. Ibid.

28. When and how men and women became defined as gay ranks as one of the most central questions in the history of sexuality, and a vast and complex literature has arisen in response to it. The French historian and theorist Michel Foucault argues that the category of "homosexual" or "gay" did not come into use until the late nineteenth century; see Foucault, *The History of Sexuality*, vol. 1, *An Introduction* (1978; reprint, New York: Vintage, 1990). Yet a number of historians have found evidence of earlier communities in which men had sex with men and were intimate with men, challenging Foucault's

claims; see, for example, Richard Godbeer, *Sexual Revolution in Early America* (Baltimore: Johns Hopkins University Press, 2002), and Godbeer, *The Overflowing of Friendship: Love Between Men and the Creation of the American Republic* (Baltimore: Johns Hopkins University Press, 2009). More to the point, historians debate the very language to employ in even discussing this phenomenon; many opt, for example, to define such men as "men who had physical relationships with men" rather than call them "gay," since the term "gay"—as understood in its modern usage—did not come into fashion until the late nineteenth century. I use the term "gay" because many gay men in the 1970s, like Katz, used the term when probing the past. They were just beginning the conversation about the history of sexuality, and Katz himself was identifying the various models used to describe gay people. Further, these debates about the history of sexuality did not gain prominence among scholars until the 1980s and 1990s. For a comprehensive and authoritative overview of gay history before the rise of the term "gay," see Thomas Foster, ed., *Long Before Stonewall: Histories of Same-Sex Sexuality in Early America* (New York: New York University Press, 2007); and Carroll Smith-Rosenberg, *Disorderly Conduct: Visions of Gender in Victorian America* (New York: Knopf, 1985). On the complex intersection of language, history, theory, and identity, see David Halperin, *How to Be Gay* (Cambridge, MA: Harvard University Press, 2012), as well as Jonathan Ned Katz's own contributions to this scholarly debate, *The Invention of Heterosexuality* (New York: Dutton, 1995), and *Gay American History: Lesbians and Gay Men in the USA* (New York: Plume, 1992), 3.

29. Katz's excavation of the gay past was representative of the search for historical antecedents undertaken by other oppressed groups; black civil rights activists and women's liberation groups also surveyed archives to find historical icons for their movements. For analyses of the modern feminists' search for historical antecedents, see Christine Stansell, *The Feminist Promise, 1792 to the Present* (New York: Modern Library, 2010); Nancy A. Hewitt and Suzanne Lebsock, eds., *Visible Women: New Essays on American Activism* (Urbana: University of Illinois Press, 1993); and Nancy A. Hewitt, *Women's Activism and Social Change: Rochester, New York, 1822–1872* (Ithaca, NY: Cornell University Press, 1984). On the black search for historical antecedents, see John Blassingame, *The Slave Community: Plantation Life in the Antebellum South* (New York: Oxford University Press, 1972); and Leon Litwack, *Been in the Storm So Long: The Aftermath of Slavery* (New York: Random House, 1979). On the intersections of race and gender, see Nell Irvin Painter, *Southern History Across the Color Line* (Chapel Hill: University of North Carolina Press, 2002); and Darlene Clark Hine, *Hine Sight: Black Women and the Re-Construction of American History* (Brooklyn, NY: Carlson Publishers, 1994).

30. Jonathan Ned Katz, *Coming Out!*, box 12, "Writings: Coming Out! Typescript" folder, Jonathan Ned Katz Papers, Manuscripts and Archives Division, New York Public Library (NYPL), Astor, Lenox, and Tilden Foundations.

31. Ibid.

32. Ibid.

33. Wayne Dekkar, "His Own Play Brought Out Jonathan Ned Katz," box 13, "Writings—Collateral Papers, *Coming Out!* Reviews" folder, Jonathan Ned Katz Papers.

34. Although RADICALESBIANS wrote this manifesto, Katz cited *The Lavender Menace,* May 1, 1970, as his source. See Katz, *Coming Out!*

35. Many years later, historians Evelyn Brooks Higginbotham and Kathleen M. Brown would demonstrate what Katz was already aware of when he wrote *Coming Out!*—that the term "woman" implicitly meant "white" to colonial and nineteenth-century Americans; see Evelyn Brooks Higginbotham, "African-American Women's History and the Metalanguage of Race," *Signs* 17 (Winter 1992): 251–274; Kathleen M. Brown, *Good Wives, Nasty Wenches, and Anxious Patriarchs: Gender, Race, and Power in Colonial Virginia* (Chapel Hill: University of North Carolina Press, 1996).

36. Katz, *Coming Out!*; see also box 13, "Writings—Collateral Papers, *Coming Out!* Reviews" folder, Jonathan Ned Katz Papers; and *The Advocate,* July 18, 1973. After the publication of *Gay American History,* Katz placed an ad in *The Body Politic,* asking readers to send him "hard-to-find" sources referring to lesbians (*The Body Politic,* October 1, 1977).

37. Katz, *Coming Out!*

38. "Final Speeches from *Coming Out!*," Outhistory.org, http://outhistory.org/exhibits/show/coming-out/speeches (accessed August 10, 2015).

39. *The Advocate,* July 18, 1973.

40. On the history of the play, see "Jonathan Ned Katz Recalls His Play *Coming Out!*," Outhistory.org, http://outhistory.org/exhibits/show/coming-out/coming-out; Thane Hampton, *Gay,* September 4, 1972, and *The Lambda* (newsletter of the Central New Jersey Gay Activists Alliance), November 1972, both in "Reviews of Jonathan Ned Katz's Play *Coming Out!*," http://outhistory.org/exhibits/show/coming-out/reviews (accessed September 27, 2012).

41. Katz, interview with Downs, May 16, 2006; see also "Jonathan Ned Katz Recalls His Play *Coming Out!*"

42. Ian J. Tree in "Reviews of Jonathan Ned Katz's Play *Coming Out!*" *Gay,* July 24, 1972; Katz, interview with Downs, May 16, 2006.

43. "Jonathan Ned Katz Recalls His Play *Coming Out!*"; see also *The Advocate,* July 18, 1973.

44. "Jonathan Ned Katz Recalls His Play *Coming Out!*"

45. Tree, "Reviews of Jonathan Ned Katz's play *Coming Out!*"

46. "Jonathan Ned Katz Recalls His Play *Coming Out!*"; Katz, interview with Downs, May 16, 2006.

47. *The New Republic,* August 11, 1973; Martin Duberman, "The Gay Life: Cartoon vs. Reality?" July 22, 1973, *New York Times.*

48. *Cue,* August 27–September 2, 1973; Al Carmines, "Politics Is Not Art," *New York Times,* July 29, 1973.

49. Katz, interview with Downs, May 16, 2006.

50. Ibid.

51. Katz, interview with Downs, May 29, 2012.

52. *The Body Politic,* March 1, 1977.

53. Katz, interview with Downs, May 16, 2006.

54. David Gibson, "Historian Helps to Reclaim Our Gay Past," *The Body Politic,* September 1976.

55. 1977 flyer, box 6, "Oscar Wilde Memorial Bookshop: Business Correspondence" folder, Craig Rodwell Papers.

CHAPTER 5: THE BODY POLITIC

1. *The Body Politic,* January 1, 1974.

2. Ibid. Throughout the seventies, triangles appeared in newspapers and on book covers, and the pink triangle slowly became a symbol for the gay pride movement. *The Body Politic,* in fact, named its larger publishing company Pink Triangle Press, and groups like Gays Against Moralism used the triangle on their advertisements; see *The Body Politic,* August 1, 1976. In 1987 AIDS activists used the triangle (not inverted) to draw attention to the AIDS crisis by featuring the triangle with the caption, "Silence = Death." For more on that history, see Jason Baumann, "The Silence = Death Poster" (guest post by Avram Finkel), November 22, 2013, New York Public Library, http://www.nypl.org/blog/2013/11/22/silence-equals-death-poster (accessed May 27, 2014). Throughout the 1970s, other gay newspapers reported on the persecution of homosexuals during the Nazis' reign and explained the meaning of the triangle; see, for example, *The Gay Clone,* May 1976.

3. Jim Steakley, Skype interview with Jim Downs, July 11, 2012.

4. Ibid.

5. Ibid.

6. *The Body Politic,* June 1, 1973.

7. *The Body Politic,* January 1, 1974.

8. *The Body Politic,* May 1, 1974.

9. According to historian Peter Novick, the US government's use of the history of the Holocaust as a tool to mobilize American support for Israel during the Yom Kippur War of October 1973 brought the history of the Holocaust into sharp focus; see Novick, *The Holocaust in American Life* (Boston:

Houghton Mifflin, 1999). Historian Hasia Diner challenges Novick's findings, claiming that American Jews were aware of the Holocaust and even raised a great deal of money to support Holocaust survivors in the immediate aftermath of World War II; see Diner, *We Remember with Reverence and Love: American Jews and the Myth of Silence After the Holocaust, 1945–1962* (New York: New York University Press, 2010). Although her argument is cogent, it is important to distinguish between the Holocaust and the persecution of gay people during World War II, which gay historians often introduce as a subject that many readers were not aware of. In fact, the whole point of Steakley's series was that many readers did not know what happened to gay people in concentration camps.

10. Steakley, interview with Downs, July 11, 2012.

11. W. I. Scobie, "Death Camps: Remembering the Victims," *Gay Sunshine* 25 (Summer 1975): 19.

12. The Nazis and the Holocaust continued to be used as both a metaphor and historical antecedent throughout the 1980s. Larry Kramer, for instance, titled his memoir *Reports from the Holocaust: The Making of an AIDS Activist* (New York: St. Martin's Press, 1989). On references to Nazism in the 1970s, see *Arizona Gay News,* January 27, 1978; *The Gay Clone* (May 1976); and *Gay Sunshine* (Summer 1975). Gay newspapers throughout the seventies were chockfull of stories about the gay past, from profiles of Russian writers to accounts of precolonial queer societies in Latin America and Asia to studies of homosexuality in the ancient world. On newspaper treatments of the gay past, see, for example, *Gay Sunshine,* Winter 1975–1976, Spring 1977, and Winter 1977; *Join Hands,* August–September–October 1977 and January–March 1978; *The Body Politic,* May 1, 1974, and March 1, 1978; and *Fag Rag* 15, February–March 1976.

13. Jonathan Ned Katz, interview with Jim Downs, New York City, May 29, 2012.

14. *The Body Politic,* July 1 and November 1, 1977. On the special section on gay history and literature, see, for example, *The Body Politic,* December 1, 1976, which featured an article on Hart Crane; see also *The Body Politic,* June 1, 1976, which included an article on the French novelist George Sand and another on the American poet Amy Lowell. Jerald Moldenhauer, e-mail to Jim Downs, August 27, 2013.

15. "The Gay Press Report," box 5, "The Gay Press Report, 1976" folder, Craig Rodwell Papers, NYPL.

16. Ibid.

17. On the gay press before the 1970s, see Martin Meeker, *Contacts Desired: Gay and Lesbian Communications and Community, 1940s–1970s* (Chicago: University of Chicago Press, 2006). On gay and lesbian communities before

Stonewall, see George Chauncey, *Gay New York: Gender, Urban Culture, and the Making of the Gay Male World, 1890–1940* (New York: Basic Books, 1994); John D'Emilio, *Sexual Politics, Sexual Communities*, 2nd ed. (Chicago: University of Chicago Press, 1998); and Marcia M. Gallo, *Different Daughters: A History of the Daughters of Bilitis and the Rise of the Lesbian Rights Movement* (Berkeley, CA: Seal Press, 2006).

18. John McMillian, *Smoking Typewriters: The Sixties Underground Press and the Rise of Alternative Media in America* (New York: Oxford University Press, 2011),6.

19. For instance, the feminist movement relied on *Ms.* magazine to support the cause; see *Ms.* magazine, "HerStory: 1971–Present," http://www.ms magazine.com/about.asp (accessed May 2, 2014).

20. John Mitzel on *Fag Rag*'s Publishing, https://vimeo.com/56126939 (posted 2013, accessed June 20, 2014). Beginning in the 1970s, lesbian separatism developed both as a way to accentuate women's voices and contributions and as a political strategy to expose the patriarchal forces undergirding society and its institutions, like the press; see Charlotte Bunch, *Passionate Politics: Feminist Theory in Action* (New York: St. Martin's Griffin, 1987); Lillian Faderman, *Odd Girls and Twilight Lovers: A History of Lesbian Life in Twentieth-Century America* (reprint, New York: Columbia University Press, 2012).

21. *Gay Community Newsletter,* June 17, 1973.

22. Ibid. For more on the relationship between gay liberationists and the transgender movement, see Joanne Meyerowitz, *How Sex Changed: A History of Transexuality in the United States* (Cambridge, MA: Harvard University Press, 2004), 235–238; and Susan Stryker, *Transgender History* (Berkeley, CA: Seal Press, 2008), 91–96.

23. "How Do the Laws Oppress Gays? The Why and How of Political Change," *Gay Community Newsletter,* June 17, 1973.

24. Tracy Baim, *Gay Press, Gay Power: The Growth of LGBT Community Newspapers in America* (Chicago: Prairie Avenue Productions, 2012), 338; Rick Bébout, "Beyond," in *Promiscuous Affections: A Life in the Bar, 1969–2000,* January 2000, http://www.rbebout.com/oldbeep/beyond.htm (accessed June 19, 2014).

25. On the press as a collective, see McMillian, *Smoking Typewriters*, 11. On *The Body Politic,* see Bébout, "Beyond."

26. On *The Dallas Voice,* see Baim, *Gay Press, Gay Power,* 307. On *Fag Rag*, see "John Mitzel on *Fag Rag*'s History." On *The Body Politic,* see Bébout, "Beyond."

27. Bébout, "Beyond." For the ads, see *The Body Politic,* December 1, 1975, and February 1, 1978.

28. Historian George Chauncey chronicles the extent to which print culture in New York reported on gay culture and gave clues about its existence; Chauncey, *Gay New York* (New York: Basic Books, 1994), 166–167, 242, 309.

Historian Martin Meeker argued, "Despite all that these gay men knew, their knowledge of the national extent of the gay world likely would have been limited by their own experiences, by what they learned by word of mouth, and by the few items they might have come across in a scattering of books and magazines"; Meeker, *Contacts Desired*, 217–220.

29. *The Body Politic,* September 1, 1976.

30. Ibid.

31. Ibid.

32. *The Body Politic,* November 1, 1974; Bébout, "Beyond."

33. *The Body Politic,* January 1972, as quoted in Bébout, "Beyond."

34. Jerald Moldenhauer, email to Jim Downs, August 27, 2013.

35. "Story of *Fag Rag,* Part 1, with John Mitzel," http://vimeo.com/55809456 (posted 2013; accessed May 28, 2014).

36. Steakley, interview with Downs, July 11, 2012; Moldenhauer, email to Downs, August 27, 2013. The idea that gay people trace their history beyond national borders served as the organizing principle for some of the early work on the history of homosexuality; see Martin Duberman, Martha Vicinus, and George Chauncey Jr., *Hidden from History: Reclaiming the Gay and Lesbian Past* (New York: Dutton, 1989).

37. Moldenhauer, email to Downs, August 27, 2013. I began to see how gay newspapers forged connections and community among disparate gay people across the globe after reading Benedict Anderson, *Imagined Communities: Reflections on the Origin and Spread of Nationalism,* rev. ed. (New York: Verso, 2006). On the history of pan-Africanism, see Tony Martin, *The Pan-African Connection: From Slavery to Garvey and Beyond* (Dover, MA: Majority Press, 1998); and Minkah Makalani, *In the Cause of Freedom: Radical Black Internationalism from Harlem to London, 1917–1939* (Chapel Hill: University of North Carolina Press, 2011). At various moments in the history of women's suffrage and feminism, these activists and groups also sought international solidarity; see Christine Stansell, *The Feminist Promise: 1792 to the Present* (New York: Random House, 2011).

38. For other examples of references to the broader international gay community, see *The Body Politic,* October 1, 1975, January 1 and November 1, 1974, and January 1, 1972.

39. *The Body Politic,* January 1, 1975.

40. Ibid.

41. On India, see *The Body Politic,* November 1, 1977; see also *The Gay Clone,* May Day 1977. On Mishima, see *Gay Sunshine* 31 (Winter 1977). On the Muslim world, see *Gay Sunshine* 32 (Spring 1977). On Africa, see *Gay Sunshine* 33–34 (Summer–Fall 1977). On the West's interpretation of the East, see Edward Said, *Orientalism* (New York: Vintage, 1979); and Catherine A. Lutz and Jane L. Collins, *Reading* National Geographic (Chicago: University of

Chicago Press, 1993). Additionally, Jasbir Puar offers an arresting theoretical critique of the intersections of nationalism, Orientalism, and sexuality and the ways in which the theoretical alignment of these categories, all in the name of a neoliberal gesture to include queer subjects, produce homonationalism; see Puar, *Terrorist Assemblages: Homonationalism in Queer Times* (Durham, NC: Duke University Press, 2007).

42. Gerald Hannon, "Men Loving Boys Loving Men," *The Body Politic*, December/January 1978.

43. "Gerald Hannon: A Chronology of Events," http://www.clga.ca/Material /Records/docs/hannon/ox/chronos.htm (accessed January 14, 2014).

44. Gerry Oxford, interview with Justin Nicholas Hanson, June 29, 2010, as quoted in Justin Nicholas Hanson, "Inside The Body Politic: Examining the Birth of Gay Liberation," honors research thesis (The Ohio State University, 2011), 51.

45. "1977 Has Been the Year of the Children," *The Body Politic*, December 1, 1977.

46. Ibid.

47. *The Body Politic*, December/January 1978.

48. *The Body Politic*, December 1, 1977.

49. Ibid.

50. *The Body Politic* continually reported on the harassment faced by gay teachers and their mobilization efforts; see *The Body Politic*, October 1974, December 1, 1975, June 1, 1976, and May 1, 1977.

51. *Toronto Sun*, December 22, 1977; *Toronto Sun*, December 25, 1977; Michael Graydon, "'Kids, Not Rights, Is Their Craving': Sex Education, Gay Rights, and the Threat of Gay Teachers," *Canadian Review of Sociology/Revue Canadienne de Sociologie* 48, no. 3 (2011): 313–339.

52. Hannon, "Men Loving Boys Loving Men." On gay parenting struggles, see, for example, *The Body Politic*, October 1, 1977, and April 1 and June 1, 1978.

53. "Crisis: In the Midst of Danger: A Chance to Unite," *The Body Politic* (February 1978), "Police Raid Issue."

54. Letters to the editor, ibid.

55. "Crisis: In the Midst of Danger: A Chance to Unite," ibid.

56. *The Body Politic*, February 1, 1978.

57. *The Body Politic*, May 1, 1978.

58. Ibid.; see also *The Body Politic*, March 1, 1978.

59. *Join Hands* 13 (January–March 1978).

60. *Gay Austin* (February 1978).

61. *The Body Politic*, March 1, 1978.

62. *Gay Austin* (February 1978). On the changes in the framing of the case in 1978, see *The Body Politic*, February 1, April 1, June 1, and December 1, 1978.

63. *The Body Politic*, May 1, 1978; Craig Rodwell to a friend, February 5, 1978, newspaper chapter, box 2, "1978" folder, Craig Rodwell Papers.

64. *The Body Politic*, November 10, 1983; Ken Popert, interview with Justin Nicholas Hanson, June 15, 2010, as quoted in Hanson, "Inside The Body Politic," 62.

65. *Regina v. Pink Triangle Press et al.*, No. 4557, Provincial Court, Judicial District of York, Ontario, February 14, 1979, as quoted in Hanson, "Inside The Body Politic," 64.

66. *The Body Politic*, November 1983.

67. *Join Hands* 13 (January–March 1978).

68. *The Body Politic*, April 1, 1978.

69. See *The Body Politic*, March 1, April 1, and May 1, 1978.

70. *The Body Politic*, December 1, 1978. For example, *Gay Sunshine* ran an article on various sexual acts but also illustrated these articles with photos and artwork; see *Gay Sunshine*, October 1970 and November 1970.

CHAPTER 6: "PRISON SOUNDS"

1. Javier Garmendai and Richard Foster, interview with Jim Downs, New York City, June 29, 2014.

2. One of the leading gay prison activists of this period was Mike Riegle. He worked for *Gay Community Newsletter* and made information available about the condition of gay inmates. He also provided gay inmates with books and, later, with health and legal advice. See Mike Riegle Collection, boxes 1 and 2, The History Project, Archives and Records Department, Boston, MA. Regina Kunzel, *Criminal Intimacies: Prison and the Uneven History of Modern American Sexuality* (Chicago: University of Chicago Press, 2008), 206.

3. Various literary critics and historians have charted the development of prison literature as a distinct genre; see H. Bruce Franklin, *Prison Writings in Twentieth-Century America* (New York: Penguin Books, 1998); Judith A. Scheffler, *Wall Tappings: Women's Prison Writings, 200 to the Present*, 2nd ed. (New York: Feminist Press at CUNY, 2002). More recently, the writer Wally Lamb anthologized a volume of writing by prisoners that gained a great deal of notoriety; see *Couldn't Keep It to Myself: Wally Lamb and the Women of York Correctional Institution (Testimonies from Our Imprisoned Sisters)* (New York: Harper Perennial, 2004).

4. *Gay Sunshine* 25 (Summer 1975).

5. For examples within the historiography, see Linda Hirshman, *Victory: The Triumphant Gay Revolution* (reprint, New York: Harper Perennial, 2013); and Eric Marcus, *Making Gay History: The Half-Century Fight for Lesbian and Gay Equal Rights* (New York: Harper Perennial, 2002). This scholarship offers an important record of gay political activism, but what would the historiography look like if political activism, or even the antagonism between gay people

and the state, were not the organizing principle? Doing the research for this book, I certainly saw evidence of political activism and gay people's political battles with the state, but more often I saw countless examples of gay people sidestepping activism and putting more effort into creating gay culture.

6. *Fag Rag* 10, Spring 1973; Tony Sharpe, ed., *W. H. Auden in Context* (Cambridge: Cambridge University Press, 2013); see also Katherine Bucknell, "The Boys in Berlin: Auden's Secret Poems," *New York Times,* November 4, 1990 and Robert Beachy, *Gay Berlin: The Birthplace of a Modern Identity* (New York: Knopf, 2014).

7. *Gay Sunshine* 7 (June–July 1971). The number of gay inmates in prisons cannot be accurately counted. Leaving aside the problems of whether a prisoner would self-identify or be identified as gay, my research showed that prison superintendents did not tally the number of homosexual, lesbian, or transgender inmates. In some prisons, officials segregated gay men in specific floors and units; see, for example, *Fag Rag* 4 (January 1973) and *Cellmate* (April–May 1976). Any count of the number of men even in these places is inconclusive, however, since it remains problematic whether they self-identified as gay. It is certainly reasonable to imagine that a man arrested for sodomy, lewd behavior, or trespassing in an area known to be frequented by gay people would disavow, as part of his defense, any knowledge of or affiliation with gay people.

8. *Join Hands* 5 (August–September 1976).

9. *Gay Sunshine* 8 (August 1971).

10. On Manroot, see James W. Healey, "A Little Madness Helps," *Prairie Schooner* 47, no. 4 (Winter 1973–1974): 339. Other literary critics cite Manroot as part of a larger gay literary tradition that emerged after Stonewall; see, for example, Gregory Woods, *A History of Gay Literature: The Male Tradition* (New Haven, CT: Yale University Press, 1999), 10. Sadly, there is not yet a biography of Paul Mariah, who is a leading figure in American literature. For a sketch of his life, see Stephen Schwartz, "Obituary—Paul Mariah," *The San Francisco Gate,* January 25, 1996. I developed this description of his life and writings by combining various scraps of evidence. *Gay Sunshine* interviewed Mariah while he was in prison, see *Gay Sunshine* 8 (August 1971).

11. Paul Mariah, "The Swimmer Who Never Swam," *Poetry* 116, no. 3 (June 1970): 163; "The Holding Companies' Company," in *Personae Non Grate,* 2nd ed. (San Lorenzo, CA: Shameless Hussy Press, 1973).

12. On Mariah's influence, see Richard Norton, "The Homosexual Literary Tradition: Course Outline and Objectives," *College English* 35, no. 6 (March 1974): 692; and *The San Francisco Gate,* January 25, 1996. For more on Mariah's poems, see Gerard Malanga, "Lingua Franca et Jocundissima," *Poetry* 123, no. 4 (January 1974): 236–241. Gerald Malanga's poetry and photography appeared throughout the gay press; see, for example, *Gay Sunshine* 21 (Spring 1974) and 20 (January–February 1974).

13. *The Body Politic,* December 1, 1978.

14. Ibid.

15. *The Body Politic,* May 1, 1979. On Trifonov's release, see *New York Review of Books,* April 10, 1986; see also Dan Healey, *Homosexual Desire in Revolutionary Russia: The Regulation of Sexual and Gender Dissent* (Chicago: University of Chicago Press, 2001), 247.

16. *Join Hands* 7 (December 1976–January 1977).

17. I am using James C. Scott's term "hidden transcript" as a literal way to theorize the place of poetry within the larger discourse of gay liberation; see Scott, *Domination and the Arts of Resistance: Hidden Transcripts* (New Haven, CT: Yale University Press, 1992).

18. *Join Hands* 7 (December 1976–January 1977).

19. Many gay people were writing and talking about the problem of loneliness, and *Gay Community Newsletter* even advertised a workshop on loneliness; see *Gay Community Newsletter,* July 12, 1973. The literature of the period also highlighted the loneliness felt by many gay men during the 1970s, such as Al Carmines's 1978 musical *The Faggot* and Larry Kramer's widely popular, canonical novel *Faggots,* also published in 1978.

20. *Join Hands* 7 (December 1976–January 1977).

21. *Join Hands* 5 (August–September 1976).

22. *The Body Politic,* December 1, 1977; *Join Hands* 7 (December 1976–January 1977).

23. On the black freedom struggle in prisons, see Dan Berger, *Captive Nation: Black Prison Organizing in the Civil Rights Era* (Chapel Hill: University of North Carolina Press, 2014).

24. *Join Hands* 12 (November–December 1977).

25. Assata Shakur, "Women in Prison: How It Is with Us," *Join Hands* 14 (April–June 1978), originally appeared in *The Black Scholar* (April 1978).

26. Ibid. For a sharp analysis of Assata Shakur, black women, and incarceration, see Joy James, "Framing the Panther: Assata Shakur and Black Female Agency," in *Want to Start a Revolution: Radical Women in the Black Freedom Struggle,* edited by Dayo F. Gore, Jeanne Theoharis, and Komozi Woodard (New York: New York University Press, 2009), 138–160.

27. *Join Hands* 14 (April–June 1978); *New York Times,* February 26, 1989; Angela Davis, "Joan Little: The Dialectics of Rape (1975)," *Ms.* (Spring 2002), http://www.msmagazine.com/spring2002/davis.asp (accessed August 13, 2015); "Black Psychology," *The Black Scholar* 6, no. 10 (July–August 1975): 37–42; Danielle L. McGuire, *At the Dark End of the Street: Black Women, Rape, and Resistance—A New History of the Civil Rights Movement from Rosa Parks to the Rise of Black Power* (New York: Vintage, 2011), 246–278.

28. There was a meeting, for example, of Black Panthers, Young Lords, the Gay Liberation Front, and the women's liberation movement in 1970; see *New*

York Times, July 19, 1970. On the gay liberation movement's formal and documented interactions with the Black Panthers, see *New York Times,* November 28, 1970. Also, Craig Rodwell often clipped, saved, and archived articles about the Panthers; see box 2, "1970" folder, and box 5, "The Gay Press Report, 1976" folder, Craig Rodwell Papers, NYPL.

29. *Gay Sunshine* 24 (Spring 1975). For examples of prisoners writing about lack of community and loneliness in prison, see *Gay Sunshine* 23 (November–December 1974); and "Prison Rape 1970s–90s," B.18, F.10 (box 18), Stephen Donaldson Papers, NYPL.

30. *Fag Rag* 18 (Fall–Winter 1976).

31. *Fag Rag* 19 (Spring 1977).

32. *Gay Sunshine* 23 (November–December 1974). For another example of the section of the classifieds devoted to prisoners, and for the citation to the mailing list quotation, see *Gay Sunshine* 24 (Spring 1975).

33. *The Body Politic,* February 1, 1976; *Gay Sunshine* 10 (January 1972).

34. *Gay Sunshine* 15 (October–November 1972).

35. *Dignity* 5, no. 4 (April 1974). In Boston, Mike Riegle used the *Gay Community Newsletter* to reach out to the incarcerated, and he also visited gay inmates and created outreach programs; for instance, he organized book drives to deliver books to gay inmates. Mike Riegle Collection, boxes 1 and 2, The History Project, http://www.historyproject.org/Downloads/Coll01Mike Riegle.pdf.

36. *Cellmate* (April–May 1976).

37. *In Unity* (December 1975).

38. *The Body Politic,* October 1, 1975.

39. *Cellmate* (April–May 1976).

40. Ibid.; see also *Cellmate* (December 1975).

41. *Cellmate* (January 1976).

42. *Cellmate* (December 1975).

43. *Cellmate* (January 1976).

44. *The Body Politic,* June 1, 1978. Throughout the 1970s, some prisons prohibited gay inmates from receiving gay newspapers in the mail or any other material from a known gay organization; see Margot Karle, "Gay Publications and Prison Censorship," *The Radical Teacher* 16 (1980): 15–17.

45. *Cellmate* (October 1975).

46. *Cellmate* (November 1975).

47. *Cellmate* (November 1975). For more information on this event, see National Council of Churches, "Are There Alternatives to Prison? A Summary Report of the First National Conference on Alternatives to Incarceration, September 19–21, 1975, Boston, Massachusetts," 1976, https://www.ncjrs.gov/App /Publications/abstract.aspx?ID=80087 (accessed September 18, 2014).

48. *Cellmate* (December 1975); *The Gay Christian* (March–April 1974).

49. *Gay Sunshine* 6 (March 1971); On rape, see also *The Advocate* 3, no. 4 (April 1969); *Gay Sunshine* 13 (June 1972); *Join Hands* 2 (February–March 1976) and 13 (January–March 1978).

50. For a radio interview, the activist Stephen Donaldson was once paired with a member of the New York Police Department, who explained that there was no word for "rape" between two men; the only term available was "sodomy," to which the police could add the term "forced" to the charge; Stephen Donaldson radio interview, cassette tape 03498, Stephen Donaldson Papers, Manuscripts and Archives Division, New York Public Library (NYPL), Astor, Lenox, and Tilden Foundations. The legitimacy and language surrounding male rape continued to be discussed as late as 2014; see Nathaniel Penn, "'Son, Men Don't Get Raped,'" *GQ* (September 2014), which explores the increase of same-sex rape in the military.

51. David Eisenbach, *Gay Power: An American Revolution* (New York: Carroll and Graf Press, 2006), 53.

52. Ibid.

53. President Jimmy Carter upgraded his discharge to honorable in 1977; Randy Shilts, *Conduct Unbecoming: Gays and Lesbians in the US Military* (New York: St. Martin's Press, 1993), 14.

54. Captain Clinton Cobb to Mr. A. Washington, Department of Corrections Detention Service, August 24, 1973, "Memorandum, Subject: Statement of Sexual Assault," box 19, Stephen Donaldson Papers; Susan Brownmiller, *Against Our Will: Men, Women, and Rape* (New York: Ballantine Books, 1975), 258–259.

55. Stephen Donaldson, radio interview, cassette tape 03498, Stephen Donaldson Papers.

56. Brownmiller, *Against Our Will*, 258–259.

57. Wayne R. Dynes to Gene, May 16, 1989, "Misc. Outgoing Folder 1960s–90s," B.1, F.24 (box 1), Stephen Donaldson Papers.

58. Donaldson's personal papers include a membership in the Psychedelic Venus Church; see box 18, "Folder Psychedelic Venus Church, 1970," Stephen Donaldson Papers.

59. Susan Brownmiller mentions this argument in her chapter on prison rape; see Brownmiller, *Against Our Will*, 258.

60. G. Gordon Liddy, *Will: The Autobiography of G. Gordon Liddy* (New York: St. Martin's Press, 1996), 433; see also box 19, "White House Protest and Washington DC Jail 1973" folder, Stephen Donaldson Papers; Wayne R. Dynes to Gene, May 16, 1989, Stephen Donaldson Papers; Brownmiller, *Against Our Will*, 258–259.

61. Box 18, Stephen Donaldson Papers.

62. Historian Regina Kunzel, in offering a more nuanced discussion about when and how rape happens in prisons, makes an important and persuasive argument; see Kunzel, *Criminal Intimacy: Prison and the Uneven History of Modern American Sexuality* (Chicago: University of Chicago Press, 2010). Even Susan Brownmiller, in *Against Our Will,* who offers a brilliant critique of rape, seems to imply that male rape was timeless, particularly in her description of Genet's time in prison. In sum, gay liberation and feminism began to make rape visible and historically specific.

63. "What a Letter Can Mean," box 18, folder 10 ("Prison Rape 1970s–90s"), Stephen Donaldson Papers.

64. *Cellmate* (March 1976).

65. For a more elaborate and sophisticated understanding of how gay people, prison superintendents, and the broader culture understood sex between men in prisons, see Kunzel, *Criminal Intimacy.*

Chapter 7: Body Language

1. There were many representations of the "clone" throughout the 1970s. For this particular vignette, I draw heavily on a cartoon depiction in Jim Drew, "Clones," *Gay History*, December 15, 2012, http://gayhistory.wordpress.com/2012/12/15/clones (accessed May 29, 2014). For the authoritative study of the clone, see Martin P. Levine, *Gay Macho: The Life and Death of the Homosexual Clone* (New York: New York University Press, 1998).

2. On contests, see *Arizona Gay News*, September 8, 1978. On "gay Bob," see *Time*, August 14, 1978.

3. George Chauncey, *Gay New York: Gender, Urban Culture, and the Making of the Gay Male World, 1890–1940* (New York: Basic Books, 1994), 87, 192.

4. On gay men's consumption of physique magazines, see Guy Snaith, "Tom's Men: The Masculinization of Homosexuality and the Homosexualization of Masculinity at the End of the Twentieth Century," *Paragraph* 26, nos. 1–2 (March–July 2003): 77–8; and David K. Johnson, "Physique Pioneers: The Politics of 1960s Gay Consumer Culture," *Journal of Social History* 43, no. 4 (Summer 2010): 867–892.

5. For a brilliant analysis of the relationship between gender identity and homosexuality in the early twentieth century, see Chauncey, *Gay New York.*

6. There are few scholarly references to the history of the leather world. As with much of gay history, the history of the gay leather community has been documented by freelance writers, antiquarians, and others interested in the past; see Gay Leather Fetish History, "Gay Leather Bars," http://www.cuirmale.nl/history/leatherbars.htm (accessed November 20, 2014). There is some scholarly work on the leather community after 1969; see, for example, Gayle Rubin, *Deviations: A Gayle Rubin Reader* (Durham, NC: Duke University

Press, 2011); Alex Warner, "'Where Angels Fear to Tread': Feminism, Sex and the Problem of SM, 1969–1993," PhD dissertation, Rutgers University, 2011.

7. For example, in the 1968 play *The Boys in the Band,* which was later made into a movie, the character Hank is masculine and was married to a woman before having a gay relationship with Larry; *The Boys in the Band,* directed by William Friedkin (Cinema Center Films, 1970).

8. For more on Waddell's life, see Tom Waddell, *Gay Olympian: The Life and Death of Dr. Tom Waddell* (New York: Knopf, 1996); Mark Thompson and Randy Shilts, *The Long Road to Freedom:* The Advocate *History of the Gay and Lesbian Movement* (New York: St. Martin's Press, 1995), 136.

9. Christina Hanhardt perceptively charts how many white people throughout the gay liberation movement, beginning in the 1990s and down to the present, have forgotten the critical role played by radical people of color in the making of the movement. Her smart theoretical argument traces the changing understandings of violence, politics, community, and social geography that contributed to this transformation. By contrast, I trace the erasure of diversity within the gay community to the emergence of the macho clone. Our two analyses can stand together, as we both seem engaged in the question of why the movement came to appear whiter over time. See Christina B. Hanhardt, *Safe Space: Gay Neighborhood History and the Politics of Violence* (Durham, NC: Duke University Press, 2013).

10. For a statement about gay activists' understanding that combating racism was a central component of gay liberation, see *Gay Sunshine* 14 (August 1972); Carl Wittman, "A Gay Manifesto by Carl Wittman," in *Gay Flames Pamphlet* 9 (1971), box 2, "1971" folder, Craig Rodwell Papers, NYPL.

11. Michael Bronski, "Gay Liberation," *Znet,* September 1, 1994.

12. *Arizona Gay News,* November 4, 1977.

13. On the split between gay men and lesbians, see Lillian Faderman, *Odd Girls and Twilight Lovers: A History of Lesbian Life in Twentieth-Century America* (New York: Columbia University Press, 1991); Marcia M. Gallo, *Different Daughters: A History of the Daughters of Bilitis and the Rise of the Lesbian Rights Movement* (Berkeley, CA: Seal Press, 2006); Marc Stein, *City of Sisterly and Brotherly Loves: Lesbian and Gay Philadelphia, 1945–1972* (Philadelphia: Temple University Press, 2004).

14. *Gay Sunshine* 1, no. 1 (August–September 1970).

15. *Gay Sunshine* 1, no. 2 (October 1970).

16. *Gay Sunshine* 18 (June–July 1973).

17. *Gay Community Newsletter,* July 12, 1973.

18. "Don't March! It's Part of a Sexist Plot," box 2, "1972" folder, Craig Rodwell Papers. Later in the decade, Rodwell criticized the movement for labeling any literature that remotely dealt with sex and the body as pornography

damaging to women. He added that Radical Effeminists had a "patronizing attitude towards women" and labeled them "phonies." Rodwell subsequently refused to carry Effeminists' publications, claiming "to affirm the idea that not only is Gay good, but Gay Sex is Good." Rodwell did, however, eventually turn to selling various forms of erotica when his business declined. See "Oh, Pornography," box 1, "Writings by Craig Rodwell" folder, Craig Rodwell Papers.

19. "Don't March! It's Part of a Sexist Plot" (newsletter), box 2, "1972" folder, Craig Rodwell Papers.

20. *Gay Sunshine* 14 (August 1972).

21. Historian John D'Emilio also brilliantly examines the relationship between sexism and capitalism; see D'Emilio, "Capitalism and Gay Identity," in *Powers of Desire: The Politics of Sexuality*, edited by Ann Snitow, Christine Stansell, and Sharon Thompson (New York: Monthly Review Press, 1983), 100–113.

22. *The Body Politic*, June 1, 1976.

23. Martin Bauml Duberman, *Male Armor* (New York: Plume, 1975).

24. On *Elagabalus*, see Billy J. Harbin, Kimberley Bell Marra, and Robert A. Schanke, eds., *The Gay and Lesbian Theatrical Legacy: A Biographical Dictionary of Major Figures in American Stage History in the Pre-Stonewall Era* (Ann Arbor: University of Michigan Press, 2007), 144–145.

25. For ads for Duberman's published plays, see *The Body Politic*, December 1, 1975. For reviews of the plays, see *Gay Sunshine* 28 (Spring 1976).

26. *Gay Sunshine* 6 (March 1971).

27. *Gay Sunshine* 8 (August 1971).

28. As Judith Butler perceptively notes, "The body has its invariably public dimension; constituted as a social phenomenon in the public sphere, my body is and is not mine"; see Butler, *Undoing Gender* (New York and London: Routledge, 2004), 21.

29. *Gay Sunshine* 1, no. 1 (August–September 1970); see also *Gay Sunshine* 1, no. 3 (November 1970).

30. *Gay Sunshine* 1, no. 3 (November 1970).

31. While I am making a claim about standard notions of femininity, I am not arguing that gender identity is essential—that it possesses some kind of empirical, objective, or verifiable truth. Rather, I recognize gender as a construction and a performance that exists within particular social and cultural contexts that change over time. Gay men in the 1970s were obviously aware of the cultural scripts governing femininity, and they were playing with them. As I mention earlier in the chapter, they were attempting to forge a particular feminine identity as a way to critique the claims of macho identity and a certain version of masculinity endemic to patriarchal power.

32. See George Chauncey's incisive analysis of the "fairy" in Chauncey, *Gay New York,* 47–64.

33. *Gay Sunshine* 1, no. 3 (November 1970).

34. *Gay Sunshine* 10 (February–March 1972); see also Neal Broverman, "The Gay Clone Everyone Knows," *The Advocate,* October 21, 2013.

35. *The Gay Clone,* May Day 1976, May Day 1977, May 1978, December 1978, and May 1979; *Cruise: The Entertainment to Gay Atlanta,* January 1976, http://outhistory.org/exhibits/show/atlanta-since-stonewall/item/2757 (accessed October 6, 2015); Drew, "Clones." For an example of the ads, see *The Body Politic,* March 1, 1978.

36. For an excellent sociological analysis of the clone, including key hallmarks of this identity, see Levine, *Gay Macho.*

37. *Rolling Stone,* April 19, 1979.

38. Quoted in Alice Echols, *Hot Stuff: Disco and the Remaking of American Culture* (New York: Norton, 2011), 138.

39. Ibid, 136. Historian Alice Echols incisively outlines the criticism of some gay activists that the Village People made gay culture "safe" for straight audiences and presented a sanitized, almost Disney World–like notion of homosexuality to heterosexuals (ibid., 139). I am less interested in gay people's reactions to straight people's understandings of their representation and more interested in the shift in masculinity signaled by the images in the gay community becoming iconic and mainstream.

40. *Arizona Gay News,* April 28, 1977, August 12, 1978, and September 1, 1978.

41. *Arizona Gay News,* August 12, 1977.

42. *The Body Politic,* March 1, 1978; *Arizona Gay News,* January 13, 1978.

43. "Arthur Evans, 1942–2011," http://paganpressbooks.com/jpl/EVANS-OB.HTM (accessed October 26, 2014). Anticipating his death, Evans wrote his own obituary and posted it online before he died on September 11, 2011. Many gay activists, like Evans, understood that libraries and archives historically neglected gay people's history and that their legacies were at risk of being erased. It remains true that much of the history of gay activists and many of their writings are found outside of traditional state and local archives, but these institutions are changing and finally beginning to build gay history collections.

44. "Afraid You're Not Butch Enough?," as quoted in Hidden from the Past: Accessing the GLBT Past, March 5, 2015, https://glbthsarchivesblog.wordpress.com/2012/03/08/dear-funny-blonde-kid/1996_20_garber-zombie-clone (accessed August 14, 2015).

45. Wittman, "A Gay Manifesto by Carl Wittman."

46. Rick Bébout, "Beyond," in *Promiscuous Affections: A Life in the Bar, 1969–2000,* January 2000, http://www.rbebout.com/oldbeep/beyond.htm (accessed June 19, 2014); *The Body Politic,* December 1, 1975, and May 1, 1978.

47. Ibid.

48. Clarence Walker, emails to Jim Downs, November 4 and 12, 2014.

49. *MOM* (November 1979), folder 3, One Archives, University of Southern California (USC).

50. Yolanda Alaniz, "The Personal vs. Political: Third World Conference of Lesbians and Gays," *Freedom Socialist: Voice of Revolutionary Feminism* (Spring 1982). The description of the crowd comes from the program; see "National Third World Lesbian and Gay Conference," folder 3, One Archives, USC. For Lorde's keynote speech, see "National Third World Lesbian and Gay Conference 1979," folder 2, One Archives, USC.

51. Lorde keynote speech, "National Third World Lesbian and Gay Conference 1979."

52. Ibid. On Lorde's impact on analytical discussions of diversity, see, for example, Rachel A. Dudley, "Confronting the Concept of Intersectionality: The Legacy of Audre Lorde and Contemporary Feminist Organizations," *McNair Scholars Journal* 10, no. 1 (2006): article 5; see also Claire Goldberg Moses and Heidi Hartmann, *US Women in Struggle: A Feminist Studies Anthology* (Champaign: University of Illinois Press, 1995), 277–295, 355.

53. GALA, "No One Is Free Until We Are All Free" (pamphlet), 1978, as quoted in Horacio N. Roque Ramírez, "'That's My Place!' Negotiating Racial, Sexual, and Gender Politics in San Francisco's Gay Latino Alliance, 1975–1983," *Journal of the History of Sexuality* 12, no. 2 (2003): 253.

54. On the message received by people of color that the clone was inherently white, I am drawing on Toni Morrison's astute analysis of how readers often assume that "Dick and Jane" from the childhood story are white characters, even though the story assigns no racial markers to the characters. Morrison argues that many readers do not even realize that the characters are racialized because, with whiteness as the default characterization in their imaginations, whiteness has become the norm. Morrison uses the Dick and Jane story in her novel *The Bluest Eye* (reprint, New York: Vintage, 2007) and elaborates on whiteness in her literary analysis *Playing in the Dark: Whiteness and the Literary Imagination* (New York: Vintage, 1993). From the 1990s to the first decade of the twenty-first century, gay men of color directly responded to how whiteness defined the gay community and propagated a particular body type; see, for example, Dwight McBride, *Why I Hate Abercrombie & Fitch: Essays on Race and Sexuality* (New York: New York University Press, 2005).

55. For the classic anthologies that address the intersection of race, gender, and sexuality, see Barbara Smith, *Home Girls: A Black Feminist Anthology* (New Brunswick: Rutgers University Press, 2000), 145–206. Gloria T. Hull, et al., *All the Women Are White, All the Blacks Are Men, But Some of Us Are Brave* (New York: Feminist Press, 1982).

56. Joe Wlodarz, "Beyond the Black Macho: Queer Blaxploitation," *The Velvet Light Trap* 53 (2004): 10–25.

57. I am confident that the white gay world included a few representations of gay macho black men, but I have not uncovered any of these representations in the archives. Martin Levine argues that "black men had some visibility and currency in clone circles, but it was often because of the associations with danger, and a rougher masculinity"; see Levine, *Gay Macho*, 10–11.

58. Yamissette Westerband, "Lesbian Feminism, 1960s and 1970s," Out history.org. http://outhistory.org/oldwiki/Lesbian_Feminism,_1960s_and _1970s (last modified September 16, 2009; accessed November 20, 2014).

59. Sam Julty, *Men's Bodies, Men's Selves* (New York: Dell, 1979); see also Andrew Singleton, "'Men's Bodies, Men's Selves': Men's Health Self-Help Books and the Promotion of Health Care," *International Journal of Men's Health* 2, no. 1 (January 2003): 57–72.

60. Quoted in Levine, *Gay Macho*, 31.

61. Quoted in ibid., 10.

62. For an excellent overview of the persistence of the clone after the 1970s, see Michelangelo Signorile, *Life Outside: The Signorile Report on Gay Men: Sex, Drugs, Muscles, and the Passages of Life* (New York: Harper Perennial, 1998).

63. Craig Rodwell to David, October 11, 1980, box 1, "Professional and Political Correspondence, 1971–1980" folder, Craig Rodwell Papers.

64. Ibid

CONCLUSION

1. *The Advocate*, July 18, 1973.

2. *Gay Sunshine* (February 1974); *Fag Rag* 10 (1973).

3. Richard Foster, interview with Jim Downs, New York City, June 29, 2014.

4. For a brilliant analysis of sexuality during the black civil rights movement whose publication signaled the shift in the historiography, see Danielle L. McGuire, *At the Dark End of the Street: Black Women, Rape, and Resistance—A New History of the Civil Rights Movement from Rosa Parks to the Rise of Black Power* (New York: Vintage, 2011). For an equally brilliant rendering of the impact of sexuality on the life of the civil rights activist Bayard Rustin, see John D'Emilio, *Lost Prophet: The Life and Times of Bayard Rustin* (Chicago: University of Chicago Press, 2004). University of Chicago historian Jane Dailey is currently finishing a much-anticipated study of sexuality during the civil rights era; see also Thaddeus Russell, "The Color of Discipline: Civil Rights and Black Sexuality," *American Quarterly* 60, no. 1 (2008): 101–128; Kwame Holmes, "What's the Tea: Gossip and the Production of Black Gay Social History," *Radical History Review* 122 (2015): 55; Barbara Ransby, *Ella Baker and*

the Black Freedom Movement: A Radical Democratic Vision (Chapel Hill: University of North Carolina Press, 2003). On conservative women's participation in the making of the new right, see Michelle M. Nickerson, *Mothers of Conservatism: Women and the Postwar Right* (Princeton, NJ: Princeton University Press, 2014).

5. *The Body Politic,* July 1, 1977; *The Advocate,* July 18, 1973. I do not argue that gay prison activists in the seventies were pioneers in prison reform—as chapter 6 shows, they had been inspired by the black freedom struggle—but rather that their activism challenges the notion that the gay religious movement was conservative. Their advocacy on behalf of prisoners represented a radical commitment to a reform effort that can be traced to the late 1700s. On early prison reform efforts, see Jen Manion, *Liberty's Prisoners: Carceral Culture in Early America* (Philadelphia: University of Pennsylvania Press, 2015). On current debates about prison abolition, see Angela Y. Davis, *Are Prisons Obsolete?* (New York: Seven Stories Press, 2003). On the critical need to historically situate prisons, see Heather Ann Thompson, "Why Mass Incarceration Matters: Rethinking Crisis, Decline, and Transformation in Postwar American History" (report), *Journal of American History* 97, no. 3 (2010): 703–758.

6. Quoted in Phillip L. Hammack and Bertram J. Cohler, *The Story of Sexual Identity: Narrative Perspectives on the Gay and Lesbian Life Course* (New York: Oxford University Press, 2009), 36.

INDEX

Jim Downs, an associate professor of history at Connecticut College, is currently an Andrew W. Mellon New Directions Fellow at Harvard University. He has written for *Time, Huffington Post,* and the *New York Times,* among other publications. He lives in Cambridge, Massachusetts.